QUR'ANIC
EXEGESES

A HISTORY OF THE METHODOLOGY OF
QUR'ANIC
EXEGESES

RECEP DOĞAN

NEW JERSEY • LONDON • FRANKFURT • CAIRO

TUGHRA
BOOKS

Published by Tughra Books
345 Clifton Ave., Clifton,
NJ, 07011, USA

www.tughrabooks.com

Library of Congress Cataloging-in-Publication Data Available

ISBN: 978-1-59784-380-5

Printed by
Çağlayan A.Ş., Izmir - Turkey

Contents

Chapter 11:
Modern *Tafsīr*

Chapter 12:
Modern *Tafsīr*, Said Nursi, Fethullah Gülen and Their Works

Preface

The Qur'anic text contains universal principles and benefits for all humanity. It is the primary source of knowledge for all Muslims and has been interpreted numerous times by scholars since its revelation. The exegetical approach to the Qur'ān is influenced by the conditions of the time and the needs of the people.

Despite being a single text, just 300 pages long, the rich content of the Qur'ān has afforded multiple types of exegesis, each of them different according to the capacity of the scholar, the conditions of the time and the mentality behind the approach. Other factors influencing the various opinions evident in Qur'ān interpretations are the multiple meanings of words, scholars' aptitude in comprehending the Sunnah and the development of external evidences.

Tafsīr works fall into two categories; tradition-based (*riwāyah*) and reason-based (*dirāyah*). The *riwāyah tafsīr* method interprets the Qur'ān by referencing tradition: first, the Qur'ān itself, then the Sunnah and next the explanations of the Companions (*Saḥābah*) and Successors (*Tabi'in*), thus reflecting as closely as possible the original sources of Islam. The second category, *dirāyah tafsīr*, is reason-based and is also known as *tafsīr bi'l ra'y* (*tafsīr* based on personal opinion). As well as being based on the traditions reported by the Companions and Successors, it also utilizes the use of reason and *ijtihād*. To better understand the Qur'anic verses, this type of exegesis benefits from knowledge of the Arabic language, poetry and other sciences in addition to the narrations.

It is impossible to truly understand and interpret the Qur'ān without an in-depth knowledge and understanding of Arabic philology; the correlative relationship between the two is apparent. In the areas of vocabulary, grammar, rhetoric, and the principles of discourse, the Qur'anic *tafsīr* must comply with the guidelines of Arabic philology. During the Companions' time, rather than providing a commentary on the whole Qur'ān, they concentrated on explaining the words that were vague, unclear, difficult, ambiguous, general or limited. Due to their limited understanding of Arabic, successive generations had a greater need to understand the Qur'anic verses and so applied linguistic methodology in accordance with the rules of Arabic grammar and in addition to the explanations of the Companions. Many books were authored according to this linguistic method.

The time following the death of Prophet Muhammad (pbuh) saw the rapid expansion of the borders of the Islamic world and, as a result, Muslims encountered many new issues and problems. As the primary source of law, it was necessary to turn to the Qur'ān to derive solutions and make new laws. To facilitate this process, interpretation of the verses was required. Interpreting the legal content of the Qur'ān resulted in the juristic exegeses of the Qur'ān and many scholars produced valuable works in this field.

The revelation of the Qur'ān took place over a period of twenty-three years and revelations occurred to address specific issues at specific times resulting in subject matters being spread out across the book, rather than organized into neat categories. The need to group them together encouraged some scholars to produce thematic *tafsīr* to enable an easy comprehension of the text by laymen.

After the first century of *Hijrah*, the appearance of sectarian movements in Islam, such as Mutazalite, Shia and Khārijite, compelled scholars to produce works of *tafsīr*. The absence of a sound Islamic theology led to numerous debates taking place regarding matters of belief, with each group only focusing on verses that supported their philosophy. Deviant sects interpreted the verses without understanding the context and their relationship with other verses. Without *tafsīr* covering the theological facets in the Qur'ān, mainstream *tafsīr* scholars were unable to satisfy the public demand for information. To address this need, they established the sound pillars of Islamic theology based on the Qur'ān and authentic Sunnah, adopting the methodology of Imam Māturidī and Ash'arī in theology and producing new *tafsīr* works.

Islam is not just set of rules or acts to perform, it is a holistic religion which combines both the spirit and body; it meets all the needs of human beings and satisfies their inner and outer dimensions. Sufi masters felt the need to interpret the Qur'ān based on its spiritual dimension. Their aim was to reveal the true essence of humanity by exploring the real nature of existence. Thus, they focused on the inner dynamics of humanity and the cosmos by calling attention to the reality of that which lies beneath and beyond their outer dimension. In their efforts, they produced many Sufi *tafsīr* books.

In the modern age, scholars have tried to interpret the Qur'ān pragmatically and in harmony with modern sciences. Modern exegeses have attempted to answer theoretical questions posed by modernism through the implementation of universal principles to address practical concerns.

In this book, we aim to show the different approaches in Qur'anic exegesis and elaborate each method with examples. I would like to thank Clare Duman for her great efforts spent in editing this book.

Recep Doğan, PhD
17 December 2014
Lecturer Centre for Islamic Sciences & Civilization (CISAC)
Faculty of Arts, Charles Sturt University

CHAPTER 1

Introduction to the History of Qur'anic Exegeses

Introduction

I slamic scholars generally agree that the word 'Qur'ān' is the infinitive form of the verb '*qa-ra-a*' which means 'reading' or 'reciting.' Therefore, its literal meaning is 'a thing recited by adding letters and words to one another.'[1] The verb also has another infinitive form, '*qar'u*,' which means 'to collect'[2] and due to this, some scholars believe that 'Qur'ān' means 'the thing which collects.' A third group holds that, rather than being derived from any existing word, 'Qur'ān' is the proper name given to the book which God sent to His final messenger, Prophet Muhammad (pbuh).

The best description of the Qur'ān is given by God himself:

> Alif. Lam. Mim. This is the (most honored, matchless) Book: there is no doubt about it (its Divine authorship and it being a collection of pure truths). It is guidance for the God-revering, pious who keep their duty to God."[3]

The Qur'ān is the complete collection of revelations conveyed from God to Prophet Muhammad (pbuh) through the angel, Gabriel, over the twenty-three years of his Prophethood. Recorded by scribes on the Prophet's (pbuh) instruction after each revelation, the verses were only compiled into book form after his death. The Qur'ān was transmitted via the most authentic hadith narrations (*mutawātir*) and has been preserved without a single change up until the present day.

The Qur'ān, the holy book of the Islamic faith, is the verbatim Word of God. It has multiple aspects and its recitation is considered a form of worship. The Qur'ān is the oldest form of Arabic literature and represents the best example of it. It is beyond comparison with regards to its style, parables, explanations, scientific content, description of God by His Names, Attributes and Essential Qualities, its guidance, information about the unseen world and many other areas.

---

[1] Rāghib al-Isfahānī, *Mufradaat*, p. 402.

[2] Rāghib, ibid, p. 402.

[3] Qur'ān 2: 1–2.

When compared with other Divinely revealed scriptures, the Qur'ān differs from them all with regards to its time of revelation, its style, language and transmission and its effectiveness on people in satisfying fully both their worldly and spiritual needs.

God empowered His Prophets with miracles that were suitable for their time and the people they were addressing. He gave the miracles of the staff and the hand of light to Moses whilst to Jesus He gave the miracles of healing and bringing the dead back to life. The Qur'ān is the principle miracle of Prophet Muhammad (pbuh) with its eloquence being the most notable of its many attributes.

During the Prophet's (pbuh) time, illiteracy was rife amongst the Arabs and eloquence was highly esteemed. The people of the Arabian Peninsula preserved their tribal pride, history and proverbs in oral poetry. Orators and poets commanded unparalleled respect in society to the point where even wars between tribes started and ended on the words of prominent literary figures. New or meaningful expressions were memorized for their poetic form and articulacy and then handed down to posterity. The most important building in the whole of Arabia, the Ka'ba in Mecca, was adorned with gold inscriptions of the odes of seven poets called the 'Seven Suspended Poems.' The Qur'anic revelation challenged the literary figures of the Arabian Peninsula: "If you doubt what We have sent down on Our servant, produce a *surah* like it,"[4] a challenge which has never been met since then, up until the present day.

The Qur'ān has four main purposes and themes, the overall aim of which is to guide all people to the truth. They are: demonstrating the existence and unity of God, establishing the Prophethood, proving and elucidating the afterlife, its aspects and dimensions, and promulgating the worship of God and the essentials of justice. The Qur'ān is both universal and timeless and addresses all humans, from the layman to the profound sage, simultaneously. The Qur'ān can satisfy every level of human, regardless of education, background or intellectual capacity. It neither ignores nor causes injustice to anyone. It is unique in its ability to address all people equally (being a guidance for all people and the Word of God) regardless of the time or place in which they exist. It is a scripture for all times and for all peoples, both universal and timeless.

As the primary source of the religion of Islam, it is essential that Muslims understand the content of the Qur'ān in order to practice their religion correctly and meaningfully. Expert interpretation and explanation according to the needs

---

[4] Qur'ān 2:23.

of the time is a necessary requirement, as many of the ambiguous expressions cannot be understood by a simple reading. Qur'anic exegesis is essential for Muslims to understand the guidance contained within the Qur'ān to be able to practice the religion effectively and understand the principles pertaining to this world and the afterlife.

The Qur'ān encompasses all the principles necessary for following the path of God but they are not classified according to the different needs of people in the time that they live. Verses were revealed in different literary styles containing information about scientific facts as well as general principles, and explanations are necessary to assist in comprehending these. As a general guide with a limited length, the Qur'ān does not contain detailed solutions for every problem that people will meet until the end of time; it contains main rules, general principles and basic criteria from which can be extracted the solutions to all kinds of problems.

The Qur'ān contains scientific information and principles and has formed the basis of many branches of scientific enquiry. However, its content is not limited to scientific knowledge for there would be no need for a Divine religion as humankind could learn everything through scientific studies. It covers much deeper subjects to do with moral and spiritual issues, which must be understood through expert interpretation. Its guidance in these areas can enable humans to overcome their harmful habits and lead them to a purposeful and moral life.

For the early Muslims, who had a good knowledge of Arabic, there was no alternative book. The rules, stories and style of the Qur'ān held an immense attraction for them and they endeavored to read, understand and practice its teachings in all areas of their lives. The following generations of Muslims, not as familiar with the language and superior eloquent style, required more assistance in understanding the Qur'ān correctly.

The Qur'ān contains various types of verses including *muhkam* (clear, understandable) and *mutashābih* (unclear, ambiguous). *Muhkam* verses are understood from the literal meanings of the words. They assign some actions as *halal* (permissible) or *haram* (forbidden) or define obligatory rulings such as the *salah, Hajj, zakat,* and fasting, etc. *Mutashābih* verses have many possible meanings and need extra evidence to choose one of the meanings over the others. An example is the conjecture letters (*huruf al-muqatta'*) at the beginning of some *surah*, which signify the *mutashābih* verses.

During the life of the Prophet (pbuh), the Muslims accepted *mutashābih* verses as they are but did not struggle to understand their meanings. In addition, the early Islamic scholars did not interpret these verses and referred their knowledge to God. Later scholars however, attempted to study and understand those verses because of their belief that the human intellect cannot be limited. In fact, there was a great need for an accurate interpretation of the Qur'anic verses at that time. It was essential to prevent false interpretations flourishing and to protect the Muslim community from the negative consequences of such interpretations. There is twofold benefit in struggling to understand the meanings of the *mutashābih* verses; first it helps to train the human intellect which works hard to comprehend the real meaning of the verses, (Islam encourages freedom of thought in this sense), and secondly, the foundations of Islam are strengthened as a result of the works produced from this struggle.

Certain deviated Islamic sects made false interpretations of these verses to provide a basis for their views. This forced the early scholars to produce a true *tafsīr* (explanation) of these verses. The unbelievers tried to corrupt Islam by making false interpretations of verses in an attempt to confuse the believers. However, early scholars interpreted the same verses in accordance with the fundamental principles of Islam and the authentic Sunnah and therefore, provided answers for the believers. The efforts that they made were both necessary and accepted. The need for establishing the fundamentals of the Islamic faith based on the Qur'ān produced theological exegeses. This topic will be covered later with examples from this field.

As a book of religion with multi-layered levels of meaning, the Qur'ān contains many words which are used to convey different concepts. The Arabs had knowledge of the literal meanings of these words, but their terminological meanings required explanation. An example of this is the word '*salah*' which literally means 'praying' and 'supplication' but in Qur'anic terminology it is referring to the obligatory daily prayers; '*zakat*' means 'increasing' 'purity' and 'cleaning' but its Islamic meaning is the compulsory charity payment required by rich people; '*Hajj*' means 'purpose' or 'intention' but its Islamic meaning is the pilgrimage to the Ka'ba in Mecca.

The Qur'ān contains some words that have multiple meanings and other multiple words that intend the same meaning. These are called *al-Wujūh wan-Nazāir*. Explanation of these words was necessary to avoid contradictions and to save Muslims from feeling doubtful about the Qur'ān. Additionally, the metaphoric expressions, allegorical explanations, unseen objects, stories and the ambiguous verses, etc. all require expert interpretation. These interpretations gave rise to philological exegeses of the Qur'ān which are looked at in detail later.

The time following the death of Prophet Muhammad (pbuh) saw the rapid expansion of the borders of the Islamic world and, as a result, Muslims encountered many new issues and problems requiring resolution. As the primary source of law, it was necessary to turn to the Qur'ān to derive solutions and make new laws. To be able to do this, interpretation of the verses was required. As previously mentioned, the Qur'ān does not contain detailed rulings for every case for all time, but it does contain the main principles and criteria from which religious rulings can be extracted. Interpretation of the Qur'ān is necessary for Muslim jurists to be able to make *ijtihād* (form legal opinions). Interpreting the legal content of the Qur'ān resulted in the juristic exegeses of the Qur'ān and many scholars produced valuable works in this field. This type of interpretation will be explained with a well-known *tafsīr* book in this field.

The revelation of the Qur'ān took place over a period of twenty-three years and revelations occurred to address specific issues at specific times. Due to this, the subject matters dealt with in the revelations are spread out across the book, rather than organized into neat categories. Therefore, detailed knowledge of the whole of the book, and all subject areas, is necessary to avoid arriving at wrong conclusions by just referencing one part. A proper interpretation of the Qur'ān avoids this issue by explaining the subjects in an orderly way. This need encouraged some scholars to produce thematic *tafsīr* to enable an easy comprehension of the text by laymen.

As the borders of the Islamic world expanded, Muslims encountered new nations, cultures and customs. This enriched Islamic thinking and discussion and led to the development and establishment of many Islamic disciplines. Scholars were named according to the field in which they were expert and, similarly, those who lived the religion on a spiritual level were called 'Sufi.' Whilst not mentioned in the Qur'ān or the Sunnah, the Sufi way of life cannot be refuted. If we look at the example of how the Prophet (pbuh) and his Companions lived, despite winning many battles and achieving the spoils of war their lives remained very humble and spiritual. It is important to remember that Islam is not just set of rules or acts to perform, it is a holistic religion which combines both the spirit and body; it meets all the needs of human beings and satisfies their inner and outer dimensions.

Whilst living in this world, the Prophet (pbuh) focused on the afterlife and, following his example, the Companions did the same, abstaining from comfort and luxury in this life in the hope of enjoying the rewards in the afterlife. The proceeding generations of Muslims began to incline to worldly comforts and

Sufi masters felt the need to interpret the Qur'ān based on its spiritual dimension. Their aim was to reveal the true essence of humanity by exploring the real nature of existence. Thus, they focused on the inner dynamics of humanity and the cosmos by calling attention to the reality of that which lies beneath and beyond their outer dimension. Sufi scholars produced many Sufi *tafsīr* books. This topic is discussed more fully in Chapter 10.

Prophet Muhammad's (pbuh) mission was to explain and practice the teachings contained within the Qur'ān, which is a guide for all humanity for all time. The first person to make *tafsīr*, therefore, was the Prophet (pbuh). Rather than being similar to the later interpretations, his *tafsīr* was the basis for all other interpretations. He was directly responsible for conveying God's message to humankind:

> O Messenger! Convey and make known in the clearest way all that has been sent down to you from your Lord. For, if you do not, you have not conveyed His Message and fulfilled the task of His Messengership. And God will certainly protect you from the people. God will surely not guide the disbelieving people (to attain their goal of harming or defeating you).[5]

As he was chosen by God to convey the Divine message to humankind, it is obvious that Muhammad (pbuh) understood and practiced the revelation best; therefore, when we mention the subject of Qur'anic exegeses, it is he who comes to mind first:

> (We sent them with) clear proofs of the truth and Scriptures. And on you We have sent down the Reminder (the Qur'ān) so that you may make clear to humankind whatever is sent down to them (through you of the truth concerning their present and next life), and that they may reflect[6]

This verse makes it clear that without the Prophet's (pbuh) *tafsīr* it is impossible to comprehend the meaning of some verses such as commanding verses which categorize laws as *wajib*, *mandub* or guidance; the types of prohibitions; rights; penal law and the responsibilities of humans towards each other.[7] These matters cannot be spoken about without referring to the explanations of the Prophet (pbuh).

---

[5]   Qur'ān 5: 67.
[6]   Qur'ān 16: 44.
[7]   Suyūtī, *al-Itqān*, 2/208.

SUMMARY: INTRODUCTION

1. Scholars generally agree that 'Qur'ān' means 'a thing recited by adding letters and words to one another' with some holding that it means 'the thing which collects' and a third group subscribing to the view that 'Qur'ān' is the proper name given to the book which God sent to His final Messenger, Prophet Muhammad (pbuh).

2. The Qur'ān is the complete collection of revelations conveyed from God to Prophet Muhammad (pbuh) through the angel, Gabriel, over the twenty-three years of his Prophethood, and is the holy book of the Islamic faith, the verbatim Word of God with multiple aspects.

3. The Qur'ān is the oldest and best example of Arab literature and is different from all other Divinely revealed scriptures.

4. The Qur'ān is the principle miracle of Prophet Muhammad (pbuh) with its eloquence being the most notable of its many attributes.

5. The Qur'ān has four main purposes and themes, the overall aim of which is to guide all people to the truth. It is both universal and timeless and addresses all humans, from the layman to the profound sage, simultaneously.

6. Qur'anic exegesis is essential for Muslims to understand the guidance contained within the Qur'ān to be able to practice the religion effectively and understand the principles pertaining to this world and the afterlife.

7. As a general guide it contains main rules, general principles and basic criteria from which can be extracted the solutions to all kinds of problems.

8. The Qur'ān contains much scientific information and principles and has formed the basis of many branches of scientific enquiry.

9. The Qur'ān contains various types of verse including *muhkam* (clear, understandable) and *mutashābih* (unclear, ambiguous).

10. During the life of the Prophet (pbuh), the Muslims accepted these verses as they are and did not struggle to understand their meanings.

11. Certain deviated Islamic sects made false interpretations of these verses to provide a basis for their views. This forced the early scholars to produce a true *tafsīr* (explanation) of these verses.

12. As a book of religion with multi-layered levels of meaning, the Qur'ān contains many words which are used to convey different concepts. The Arabs had knowledge of the literal meanings of these words, but their terminological meanings required explanation.

13. The Qur'ān contains some words which have multiple meanings and other multiple words that intend the same meaning. Explanation of these words was necessary to avoid contradictions and to save Muslims from doubt.

14. New problems arising following the rapid expansion of the borders of the Islamic world made it essential to interpret the Qur'ān to derive solutions and make new laws.

15. Detailed knowledge of the whole of the book, and all subject areas, is necessary to avoid coming to wrong conclusions by just referencing one part.

16. Islamic thinking and discussion was enriched with the expansion of the Islamic world and led to the development and establishment of many Islamic disciplines. Scholars were named according to the field in which they were expert.

17. The first person to make *tafsīr* was the Prophet (pbuh) and it was the basis for all other interpretations.

Concepts of the Exegesis; *Tafsīr, Ta'wil* and *Tarjama*

The Qur'ān contains some particular words whose origins, meanings and usage are important to understand such as, *tafsir, ta'wil* and *tarjama*. The word '*tafsir*' is the infinitive form and comes from either the Arabic root '*fa-sa-ra*' or '*sa-fa-ra*.' '*Fasara*,' means 'to explain,' 'to discover,' 'to expose' and 'to uncover,'[8] whilst '*safara*' means 'to uncover something covered,' 'to enlighten' and 'open.'[9] The meaning of both root words is similar, making it possible that the word *tafsir* is derived from one of them. Amin al-Khuli alludes to differences between the words stating that '*safara*' is to discover something material or the outer dimension of things, but '*fasara*' is to discover something immaterial or spiritual.[10]

Ta'wil is the infinitive of the root '*a-wa-la*' which means 'to return,'[11] 'to explain,' 'to discover,' 'to interpret,' 'to translate' and 'the result.'[12] In Islamic terminology, it is giving one out of other possible meanings of the verses[13] or, giving the meaning of the verses according to their context.[14]

---

8 Rāghib al-Isfahānī, *al-Mufradaat*, 380.

9 Ibn Manzūr, *Lisan'ul 'Arab*, 6/369.

10 Amin al-Khuli, *at-Tafsīr Maalimu Hayatihi ve Manhaj al-Yawm*, 5.

11 Ibn Manzūr, ibid, 11/32.

12 Ibn Manzūr, ibid, 11/33.

13 Zarkashī, *al-Burhān*, 2/148.

14 Tabari, *Jami' al-Bayan*, 19/8.

Tafsīr in the Qur'ānic sciences is related to discovering the meanings of the verses. Giving the real explanation is only possible by the author of the words (God), so the true *tafsīr* of the Qur'ān is that which God and His Messenger (pbuh) provided. The Prophet's (pbuh) Companions were hesitant to talk about *tafsīr* because they understood that it is directly related to God and His Messenger (pbuh). In the early days of Islam, the time of the Companions, *tafsīr* was understood to mean the explanations given by God and the Prophet (pbuh). This *tafsīr* was the exact truth with no possibility of mistake.

Ta'wil, on the other hand, implies multiple possible meanings of the verses. This method was preferred by the Companions who used it as a precaution. In *ta'wil*, there is no exact and certain explanation, but there is preference of one among the possible meanings of the verses.

Tarjama means 'to translate something from one language to another,' 'giving a title for a topic,' 'relating one's life story,' 'conveying a message to one who is not within reach,' 'explaining one word in the same language,' 'interpreting and explaining one word from one language to another' and 'directly translating the words from one language to another.'[15] The purpose of *tarjama* is to transfer the meaning of a word, phrase and piece of writing or speech from one language to another without changing or diminishing the meaning from the original. To be able to achieve an exact translation from one language to another, both languages must be equal in: their clear expression; their ability to prove, summarize and explain; their general and specific phrasing; in being able to phrase something without making any exceptions; in being able to phrase something by making exception; and also in the power, exactness, style and eloquence of their phrasing in areas of knowledge and art, etc.

A language is not a static mold merely made up of letters and words, like building blocks. Just as a style of speech or writing gives clues as to a person's character, background, culture and education, so a language holds that information about a nation. It is molded by the nation's history, religion, culture and even landscape. For this reason, it is impossible to meet the above stated conditions to be able exactly to translate a work, word for word, into another language without losing some of its essential meaning. Each language has different specifications, idioms, metaphoric expressions, grammar, phrasing styles, etc. and each language addresses the feelings, logic, reason, emotions and inspirations behind those different styles. A skilled translator may have some level of success in translating

---

[15] Zabīdī, *Tāju'l Arūs*, 8/211; Zarqānī, *Manāhil al-Irfān*, 2/6.

obvious meanings from one language to another, but the subtle undertones, the implications, feelings, logic and inspirations will undoubtedly be missed.

A human being's spirit contains the essential existence of that person. In the same way, the essential existence of a text lies in its meaning. In humans, the bodily features are the externalized form of the spirit and serve as a mirror in which to see into the person's character.[16] A text has the same attribute; the language and styles of the Qur'an give form to its meaning and cannot be separated from it.

The first step to understanding the Qur'an is to understand its language. The miraculous eloquence of the Qur'an gives depth and richness to its meaning. Rich in the arts and creative style, the Qur'an frequently speaks in parables and adopts a figurative, symbolic rhetoric using metaphors and similes used to convey knowledge of all things and to address all levels of understanding and knowledge. Evidentially, it is inconceivable that a complete and true translation of the Qur'an from Arabic into another language can be achieved. The only way to understand the Qur'an accurately is through its interpretation.

SUMMARY: CONCEPTS OF THE EXEGESIS;
TAFSĪR, TA'WIL AND *TARJAMA*

1. *Tafsīr* is discovering the meanings of the verses in the Qur'ān.
2. *Ta'wil* implies multiple possible meanings of the verses.
3. *Tarjama* means to exactly translate something from one language to another.
4. The first step to understanding the Qur'ān is to understand its language.
5. The only way to understand the Qur'ān accurately is through its interpretation.

Conditions for the Interpretation of the Qur'ān

The scholar attempting to interpret the Qur'ān, '*mufassir,*' must meet certain strict preconditions before beginning his work; otherwise, the interpretation is strongly prohibited by the Prophet (pbuh). Making a *tafsīr* of the Qur'ān is a serious responsibility as the Qur'ān is the Word of God so any interpretation is counted as conveying God's intention. People without the necessary qualifications cannot interpret the Qur'ān. The preconditions fall under two categories; the religious

---

[16] Ali Ünal, *The Qur'ān with Annotated Interpretation, Foreword.*

credentials and moral values of the interpreter and his knowledge of the Qur'ānic sciences.

It is imperative that the interpreter of the Qur'ān has impeccable religious credentials. He must have true Islamic belief and strong faith. He must adopt the morality of the Qur'ān and follow the Sunnah of the Prophet (pbuh) strictly. Interpretation of the Qur'ān by someone with false belief results in misinterpretation. Someone who does not strictly follow the Sunnah of the Prophet (pbuh) will not be trusted by the people and will, therefore, be deprived of the blessings of his work. Muslims are not permitted to read the interpretations of corrupt people, as their aim is to damage Islam. Additionally, the interpreter must be pious (*taqwa*), upright (*adālah*) and practice his knowledge. He must abstain from major sins and devote himself to Islam and God. Interpretation of the Qur'ān with the intention of achieving worldly benefits is not permissible. Many people of innovation and deviated sects have interpreted the Qur'ān to support their claims based on their false beliefs, personal whims and misguided purposes. Some of these interpreters posed as pious Muslim believers but aimed to cause harm to Islam by sowing the seeds of doubt in the minds of Muslims.

As well as meeting all the religious and ethical conditions to interpret the Qur'ān, the interpreter must also have a detailed knowledge of the following areas:

a) Arabic philology (grammar, lexicography, words and their meanings, rhetorical studies, etc.)

b) The Science of Eloquence (*Balāghah*)

c) The Sunnah of the Prophet (pbuh)

d) *Fiqh* (Islamic Jurisprudence) and *Uṣūl al-Fiqh* (Methodology of Islamic Jurisprudence)

e) The sciences of the Qur'ān; such as, the occasions behind the revelation of the verses, the abrogating and abrogated verses, *muhkam* and *mutashābih* verses, etc.

f) Science of recitation of the Qur'ān (*Qiraat*)

g) Theology (*Kalām*)

h) The ability to comprehend verses precisely.

i) Abstention from using their own opinion; they must begin their interpretation by using the Qur'ān itself first, then by seeking guidance from the verbal Sunnah, then by referring to the hadith of the Companions and the Successors, and finally by consulting the opinions of other leading scholars.

j) To complete a modern interpretation of the Qur'ān, the interpreter should have a good knowledge of sociology, physiology, astronomy, physics, chemistry, medicine and history, etc. Knowledge in these areas is necessary to make a trusted interpretation of the Qur'ān.

Some scholars hold that even when all the above conditions are met, the exegeses of the Qur'ān cannot be carried out by just one interpreter but should be executed by a group of people who are expert in different fields of science. The Qur'ān contains knowledge of all areas of life at different levels and it is not possible for one scholar to have sufficient knowledge in all these areas.

SUMMARY: CONDITIONS FOR THE INTERPRETATION OF THE QUR'ĀN

1. The *mufassir* must meet certain preconditions before interpreting the Qur'ān.
2. The preconditions fall under two categories; the religious credentials and moral values of the interpreter and his knowledge of the Qur'ānic sciences.
3. It is imperative that the interpreter of the Qur'ān has impeccable religious credentials.
4. The interpreter, as well as meeting all the religious and ethical conditions to interpret the Qur'ān, must also have a detailed knowledge in the many fields mentioned above.
5. Some scholars hold that even with all the above conditions being met, the exegeses of the Qur'ān cannot be carried out by just one interpreter but should be executed by a group of experts in different fields of science.

Primary Sources of *Tafsīr*

1. The Qur'ān

The Qur'ān itself is the first source to be referenced for interpretation. There are facts in the Qur'ān that are mentioned briefly in one place but elaborated in another. Some verses complete the meaning of other verses. Some questions are posed in one part of the book and answered in another part, so there is often no need to look outside the Qur'ān for interpretation. The first and foremost duty of the *mufassir* is to read the Qur'ān in the light of the Qur'ān itself.[17] If the meaning cannot be found within the book, the *mufassir* refers to other sources.

Examples of *tafsīr* of the Qur'ān contained within the Qur'ān:

---

[17] Suyūtī, *al-Itqān*, 2/181–182.

1) The Night of Power.

"We sent it down on a night full of blessings; surely We have ever been warning (humankind since their creation)."[18]

This verse does not clearly state which night is the blessed night in which the Qur'ān was sent down. However, the following verse clarifies this:

"We have surely sent it (the Qur'ān) down in the Night of Destiny and Power"[19]

2) Revelation to Adam.

> Adam received from his Lord words that he perceived to be inspired in him. In return, He accepted his repentance. He is the One Who accepts repentance and returns it with liberal forgiveness and additional reward, the All-Compassionate[20]

In this verse, it is not clear which words Adam received from his Lord, but the Qur'ān explains this in a different verse:

> They said (straightaway): 'Our Lord! We have wronged ourselves, and if You do not forgive us and do not have mercy on us, we will surely be among those who have lost!'[21]

3) Unclear words explained within the verse.

Sometimes unclear words are explained within the same verses. For example:

> And (you are permitted to) eat and drink until you discern the white streak of dawn against the blackness of night; then observe the Fast until night sets in.[22]

The meaning of this verse would be very ambiguous if the Arabic word 'fajr' (dawn) was not mentioned, because the verse literally states that it is permissible to eat and drink until the white thread becomes distinct to you from the black thread. As a result the word 'fajr' removes the ambiguity in this verse.

4) Explanation within the same chapter.

Sometimes the explanatory verse is found within the same *surah* (chapter) as the ambiguous verse. For example:

---

18 Qur'ān, 44: 3.
19 Qur'ān, 97: 1.
20 Qur'ān, 2: 37.
21 Qur'ān, 7: 23.
22 Qur'ān, 2: 187.

In the verse: "Say: 'He, God, the Unique One of Absolute Unity,'"[23] the Arabic word *Aḥād* (Unique One) is explained immediately within the next verse in the same *surah*: "God, the Eternally-Besought-of-All (Himself in no need of anything)."[24]

A further example is the verse: "Lawful for you is the flesh of cattle save what is mentioned to you (herewith)."[25] It is not clear which animals are forbidden to eat but this is explained in the third verse of the same *surah*:

> Unlawful to you (for food) are carrion, and blood, and the flesh of swine, and that (the animal) which is offered in the name of any other than God, and the animal strangled ...[26]

5) Ambiguous verses explained in a different chapter.

Sometimes ambiguous verses are explained in different *surah*. For example: "The Master of the Day of Judgment,"[27] is explained in a different *surah*:

> What enables you to perceive what the Day of Judgment is? Again: What is it that enables you to perceive what the Day of Judgment is? The Day on which no soul has power to do anything in favor of another. The command on that day will be God's (entirely and exclusively).[28]

A further example is the verse: "Eyes comprehend Him not, but He comprehends all eyes."[29] This verse is ambiguous in terms of seeing or comprehending Him. However another verse in a different *surah* removes this ambiguity: "Some faces on that Day will be radiant (with contentment), looking up toward their Lord."[30] This verse makes it clear that believers will see their Lord in Paradise but they still will not comprehend Him.

2. Sunnah

No one knew the Qur'ān better than the Prophet (pbuh), therefore, his explanations are the second most important source of *tafsīr*. Inspired by God with the revelation, Prophet Muhammad (pbuh) fulfilled his mission to deliver and explain

---

23 Qur'ān 112: 1.
24 Qur'ān 112: 2.
25 Qur'ān 5: 1.
26 Qur'ān 5: 3.
27 Qur'ān 1: 4.
28 Qur'ān 82: 17–19.
29 Qur'ān 6: 103.
30 Qur'ān 75: 22–23.

the Qur'ān to all people. As the receiver of the message, he was the only person able to explain it and he was meticulous in ensuring his Companions understood it correctly. Rather than rushing to convey the message, he introduced it gradually, teaching ten verses at a time.[31] This enabled them to memorize the verses, understand them and incorporate the teachings into their lives. When they finished learning ten verses, he would teach them another ten.

As previously mentioned, Prophet Muhammad (pbuh) had a duty to convey God's message to humankind. The Prophets before him also had this same responsibility and they all received the revelation in the language of their nation: "We have sent no Messenger save with the tongue of his people, that he might make (the Message) clear to them."[32] The Qur'ān, despite being revealed in Arabic, is a message for all of humanity until the end of time. Its first addressees were Arabs and God revealed His final revelation in their language. There are many other valid reasons why the last holy book was revealed in Arabic but that discussion is not within the scope of this book.

The Prophet's (pbuh) responsibility was both to convey (tabligh) the Qur'ān and explain (tabyin) any ambiguities. It is a duty of Muslims to read and ponder the Qur'ān so the explanations of the Prophet (pbuh) are of vital importance. The Prophet (pbuh) employed two methods for explaining the content of the Qur'ān. Firstly, he gave explanations of the brief expressions (bayān mujmal) in the Qur'ān, for example; the times of the obligatory prayers (salah), the amount of zakat, the Hajj rituals, etc. Secondly, he was permitted to establish new laws that were not mentioned in the Qur'ān. The following verses are some of those proving his authority to do this:

> He who obeys the Messenger (thereby) obeys God, and he who turns away from him (and his way), (do not be grieved, O Messenger, for) We have not sent you as a keeper and watcher over them (to prevent their misdeeds and be accountable for them)[33]

> Whatever the Messenger gives you accept it willingly, and whatever he forbids you, refrain from it. Keep from disobedience to God in reverence for Him and piety. Surely God is severe in retribution[34]

---

[31] Suat Yildirim, *Peygamberimizin Kur'ani Tefsiri*, 33–34.
[32] Qur'ān 14: 4.
[33] Qur'ān, 4: 80.
[34] Qur'ān, 59: 7.

When God and His Messenger have decreed a matter, it is not for a believing man and a believing woman to have an option insofar as they themselves are concerned. Whoever disobeys God and His Messenger has evidently gone astray.[35]

Muslims are obliged to observe any laws established by the Qur'ān and Sunnah. For example, the Qur'ān conveys God's law forbidding men to marry two sisters simultaneously;[36] the Prophet (pbuh) extended this prohibition so that a man cannot marry a woman and her maternal aunt or paternal aunt together at the same time.[37] Similarly, the Qur'ān prohibits men from marrying their milk mother and milk sister.[38] The Prophet's (pbuh) Sunnah extended this prohibition to the linkage of breast milk between the people including paternal and maternal aunts, the daughter of one's brother (milk brother) and the daughter of one's sister (milk sister).[39]

From the earliest days of Islam, the Prophet's (pbuh) Sunnah has been the second source of *tafsīr* for interpreting the Qur'ān. Hadith books include a section called '*Kitāb at-Tafsīr*' (the Book of Exegeses) which is the *tafsīr* of the Prophet (pbuh). This section is quite small, as the Prophet (pbuh) only made exegeses in response to questions from his Companions. As the Companions accepted the revelations faithfully and without hesitation, they did not ask many questions. However, there are some *tafsīr* examples from the Prophet (pbuh) in the most authentic hadith books.[40] Once the Prophet (pbuh) said; "I do not want to see you sitting in your seats and saying; 'we only follow what we find in the book of God."[41] In this and similar hadiths the Prophet (pbuh) warned Muslims that the Sunnah is binding upon them as the Qur'ān.

SUMMARY: PRIMARY SOURCES OF *TAFSĪR*

The Qur'ān

1. The Qur'ān itself is the first source to be referenced for interpretation.
2. There are facts in the Qur'ān that are mentioned briefly in one area but elaborated in another.

---

[35] Qur'ān, 33: 36.

[36] Qur'ān, 4: 23.

[37] Bukhari, *Saḥīḥ, Nikāḥ*, 27, Muslim, *Saḥīḥ, Nikāḥ*, 37.

[38] Qur'ān, 4: 23.

[39] Bukhari, *Saḥīḥ, Shahada*, 7, Nikāḥ, 20; Muslim, *Saḥīḥ, Rada*, 1,2,9.

[40] Ismail Cerrahoglu, *Tefsir Tarihi*, 1/41–47.

[41] Abū Dāwud, *Sunan*, 2/506; Tirmidhi, *Sunan*, 5/37.

3. Some verses complete the meaning of other verses.

4. Some questions are posed in one part of the book and answered in another part.

Sunnah

5. No one knew the Qur'ān better than the Prophet (pbuh), therefore, his explanations are the second most important source of *tafsīr*.

6. Rather than rushing to convey the message, he introduced it gradually, teaching ten verses at a time.

7. The Prophet (pbuh) employed two methods for explaining the content of the Qur'ān. Firstly, he gave explanations of the brief expressions (*bayān mujmal*) in the Qur'ān.

8. Secondly, he was permitted to establish new laws that were not mentioned in the Qur'ān.

9. Muslims are obliged to observe any laws established by the Qur'ān and Sunnah.

10. From the earliest days of Islam, the Prophet's (pbuh) Sunnah has been the second source of *tafsīr* for interpreting the Qur'ān.

11. Hadith books include a section called '*Kitāb at-Tafsīr*' (the Book of Exegeses) which is the *tafsīr* of the Prophet (pbuh).

Examples from the *Tafsīr* of the Prophet (pbuh)

As was previously mentioned, the primary source of *tafsīr* is the Qur'ān itself. This is the best and most reliable source. Some verses of the Qur'ān mention general rules but then restrict them in other verses; in other verses, rules are mentioned briefly then elucidated in a different section. For this reason, the Prophet (pbuh) himself used the Qur'ān as the primary source of explanation. An example of this is the verse:

> Those who have believed and not obscured their belief with any wrongdoing, they are the ones for whom there is true security, and they are rightly guided[42]

On the revelation of this verse, the Companions felt a great burden and struggled to comprehend its meaning. They asked the Prophet (pbuh): "Is there anyone amongst us who did not do wrong himself?" The Prophet (pbuh) used another verse from the Qur'ān to explain the meaning of 'wrongdoing' (*zulm*) in the verse:

---

[42] Qur'ān, 6: 82.

> When Luqman said to his son by way of advice and instruction: 'My dear son! Do not associate partners with God. Surely associating partners with God is indeed a tremendous wrong.'[43]

The Companions were relieved by this explanation and praised God.[44] The Prophet (pbuh) used the Qur'ān as the primary source to explain this ambiguity and clarify the intended meaning.

The punishment for stealing was established as a general rule by the following verse, but without giving much detail:

> For the thief, male or female: cut off their hands as a recompense for what they have earned, and an exemplary deterrent punishment from God. God is All-Glorious with irresistible might, All-Wise[45]

The Prophet (pbuh) set a limit on this general rule, thereby restricting (takhsis) its scope. He explained: "If one steals a quarter dinar or more, the punishment is applied for him (not for the one who steals less than a quarter dinar)."[46]

In some cases, the tafsīr of the Prophet (pbuh) strengthened the meaning of the revealed verses, rather than bringing new legislation. For example:

> O you who believe! Intoxicants, games of chance, sacrifices to (anything serving the function of) idols (and at places consecrated for offerings to other than God), and (the pagan practice of) divination by arrows (and similar practices) are a loathsome evil of Satan's doing; so turn wholly away from it so that you may prosper (in both worlds).[47]

This verse clearly elucidates the prohibition of intoxicants and the Prophet (pbuh) further strengthened its meaning by saying: "Every intoxicant is haram."[48]

Occasionally, verses appeared to contradict each other. The Prophet (pbuh) clarified the meaning with his explanations (tawḍīḥ al-mushkil). For example:

> Those who hoard up gold and silver and do not spend it in God's cause (to exalt His cause and help the poor and needy): give them (O Messenger) the glad tidings of a painful punishment.[49]

---

43 Qur'ān, 31: 13.
44 Bukhari, Saḥīḥ, Tafsīr, 20.
45 Qur'ān, 5: 38.
46 Abu Dāwud, Sunan, Hudud, 11.
47 Qur'ān, 5: 90.
48 Suyūṭī, al-Durr al-Mansur, 11/314.
49 Qur'ān, 9: 34.

The Muslims understood this verse to mean that any kind of saving or inheritance was prohibited. 'Umar asked the Prophet (pbuh) for clarification about this verse, to which the Prophet (pbuh) replied: "God made *zakat* obligatory upon your extra wealth to cleanse it. However, the inheritance of your wealth has been prescribed when you die."[50] He explained that making money through *halal* (lawful) means and saving it is not *haram* (unlawful). The warning in the verse is for those who store their wealth but do not give its due *zakat*.

Some expressions in the Qur'an are ambiguous due to their brevity. These are later explained by the Sunnah. For example:

> Be ever mindful and protective of the prescribed Prayers, and the middle Prayer, and stand in the presence of God in utmost devotion and obedience.[51]

The reference to 'the middle prayer' in the verse is unclear and ambiguous. The Prophet (pbuh) clarified the meaning of middle prayer as the *'Asr* prayer in a hadith.[52]

In some cases, the Prophet (pbuh) explained the abrogated verses (*bayān al-naskh*) of the Qur'an. *Naskh* is the abrogation of a ruling in a verse by another ruling in a different verse. Rulings were abrogated to lessen the burden on the early Muslims as they adjusted to the new rulings. To understand which rulings in the Qur'an have been abrogated it is essential to know the Sunnah. For example:

"They ask you about the Sacred Month and fighting in it. Say: 'Fighting in it is a grave sin...'"[53]

The ruling in this verse is abrogated by the following verse;

> Nevertheless, fight all together against those who associate partners with God just as they fight against you all together; and know well that God is with the God-revering, pious who keep their duties to Him.[54]

The Prophet's (pbuh) own actions indicated the abrogation of this ruling. In the sacred months of Shawwal and Dhu'l Qa'da he fought against the Hawāzin in Hunayn and against the tribe of Thaqīf in Taif. If fighting during these months was still forbidden, he would not have fought or allowed his Companions to fight.[55]

---

50 Hakim, *Mustadrak*, 11/333.
51 Qur'ān, 2: 238.
52 Tirmidhi, *Sunan, Tafsīr al-Qur'ān*, 3.
53 Qur'ān, 2: 217.
54 Qur'ān, 9: 36.
55 Tabarī, *Jami' al-Bayan*, the interpretation of 2: 217.

The Sunnah and the practice of the Prophet explained the abrogation of the first verse by the second verse.

The Prophet (pbuh) taught his Companions the rulings of Islam by practicing them himself. He introduced the new rulings in this way. For example:

> Once a man came to the Prophet (pbuh) and greeted him saying, 'al-salam alayk' (peace be upon you). The Prophet (pbuh) returned his greeting saying, 'wa alayk wa rahmat Allah' (peace and God's mercy upon you). Than another man came and greeted the Prophet (pbuh) saying, 'as-salam alayk wa rahmatullah' (peace and God's mercy upon you), the Prophet (pbuh) returned his greetings saying, 'wa alayk wa barakat Allah' (peace, God's mercy and His blessings upon you). After that, a third man came and greeted the Prophet (pbuh) saying, 'as-salam alayk wa rahmatullah wa barakatuhu' (peace, God's mercy and His blessings upon you), the Prophet (pbuh) replied to him using the same expression. The third man asked, 'O Messenger of God, may my mother and father be ransomed for you. When you replied to the two previous people, you added extra words to your reply. However, you returned my greeting with the same words. Why did you do this?' Thereupon the Prophet (pbuh) answered; 'You didn't leave me anything more to say (you used all the good and correct words in your greeting an so, I replied with the same words), God says in the Qur'ān; 'When you are greeted with a greeting (of peace and goodwill), answer with one better, or (at least) with the same. Surely God keeps account of all things'[56] I returned your greeting with the same expressions.'" [57]

Occasionally, the Prophet (pbuh) made philological explanations of words in the Qur'ān. When he was asked about the meanings of words, he would answer briefly and in the most beneficial way. He did not burden his Companions with unnecessary details; he gave them the information that was most beneficial for them. At times, he just gave them a synonym of the word, whereas at other times he explained the intended meaning. For example:

"Those who return in repentance to God, and those who worship God, and those who praise God, and those who are 'saihun' ...."[58]

The Companions questioned the Prophet (pbuh) about the meaning of 'saihun' and he explained it as meaning 'people who fast.'[59]

---

[56] Qur'ān 4: 86.

[57] Tabarī, Jami' al-Bayan, the interpretation of 4: 86.

[58] Qur'ān 9: 112.

[59] Hakim, Mustadrak, 11/335.

One aspect of the Prophet's (pbuh) *tafsīr* was to give detailed explanations of ambiguous verses. These explanations served to deepen the faith of the Muslims and helped them to understand the Qur'ān better. He intended to encourage certain behaviors or warn against particular dangers. In some cases, he explained religious concepts by describing past nations. For example:

"Thus, whomever God wills to guide, He expands his breast to Islam"[60]

The Prophet (pbuh) explained this verse in the following way: "When the light of faith enters to the heart of a person, his breast expands and opens." The Companions asked him, "What is the sign of this expansion, is there apparent sign for this?" to which he replied, "Facing towards the eternal life wholeheartedly and denouncing and escaping from the deceiving world and preparing for death before it comes."[61]

The Qur'ān often utilizes parables to explain, remind, encourage, deter, teach and strengthen the faith of the believers. They are an effective means of explaining situations and making them easy to understand. The Prophet (pbuh) sometimes used parables as a form of *tafsīr*. For example:

> God invites to the Abode of Peace (where they will enjoy perfect bliss, peace, and safety,) and He guides whomever He wills to a Straight Path. For those who do good, aware that God is seeing them is the best (of the rewards that God has promised for good deeds), and still more. Neither stain nor ignominy will cover their faces. They are the companions of Paradise; they will abide therein.[62]

The Prophet (pbuh) explained the above verse with the following parable:

> One day the Prophet (pbuh) came to us and said, 'I saw the angel Gabriel in my dream. He was by my head and the angel Michael was by feet. One was telling the other, 'Tell me a parable about this man (the Prophet pbuh),' thereupon the other angel said, 'May your ears hear better and your heart comprehend well, the case of you and the case of your followers is like this parable: A king owned some land and he built a house there. When the house was built he organized a feast there. He sent a messenger to invite people to the feast. Some of the people accepted the invitation and attended the feast, whilst others

---

[60] Qur'ān, 6: 125.
[61] Ibn Kathīr, *Tafsīr*, the interpretation of 6: 125.
[62] Qur'ān, 10: 25–26.

rejected it. The king is God, the land is Islam, the house is Paradise and Muhammad (pbuh) is the Messenger. Whoever heeds his message enters Islam; whoever enters Islam, enters Paradise and benefits from the favors there.'[63]

Sometimes, the Prophet (pbuh) explained the scope of some words in the Qur'ān. For example;

> And (since, unaided, you could not survive in the desert without shelter and food) We caused the cloud (which you plainly saw was assigned for you) to shade you, and sent down upon you manna and quails: Eat of the pure, wholesome things that We have provided for you.[64]

The Arabic word 'manna' means 'favor'[65] but its meaning is not limited to special food bestowed upon the Jews in Moses' time. Rather, its scope is broader and encompasses any favor given without work.[66] The Prophet (pbuh) included the mushroom within the scope of manna[67] and clarified the misunderstanding about the word. He intended to convey that manna did not only apply to the Jews at a specific time, but can be bestowed by God on any people whenever they are in need of such a blessing. He likened the mushroom to manna since it grows by itself without any work of humans.[68]

We can conclude that the Prophet (pbuh) made tafsīr in response to questions about some verses and he volunteered tafsīr for other verses. He was not only responsible for conveying the words of God but also for explaining them in the best possible way. When explaining verses, he always took into account the level of understanding of his addressee and gave explanations accordingly, sufficing their logic, heart and mind. While giving answers, he established the general principles that would be beneficial for all Muslims. The Prophet's (pbuh) tafsīr provides explanations for some of the verses as well as a methodology for correct interpretation of the Qur'ān. The Prophet's (pbuh) Sunnah, as well as the Qur'ān, is not restricted to his lifetime, rather it is a primary source for tafsīr for the whole of time up until Judgment Day.

---

63 Tirmidhi, Sunan, Amthal, 1.
64 Qur'an 2: 57.
65 Ibn Manzūr, Lisān al-Arab, 8/415–423.
66 Ibn Manzūr, Lisān al-Arab, 8/418.
67 Bukhari, Saḥīḥ, 6/22.
68 Aynī, Umda al-Qārī, 8/465–467.

SUMMARY: EXAMPLES FROM THE *TAFSĪR* OF THE PROPHET (PBUH)

1. The Prophet (pbuh) answered questions from the Companions by using another verse from the Qur'ān to remove ambiguity and clarify meaning.
2. The Prophet (pbuh) restricted general rules in the Qur'ān; for example the punishment for theft.
3. The Prophet (pbuh) strengthened the meaning of verses; for example the verse on intoxicants.
4. The Prophet (pbuh) clarified the meaning of verses that seemed to contradict each other; for example the verse about *zakat*.
5. Verses that are ambiguous due to their brevity are sometimes explained by the Sunnah; for example the "middle" prayer.
6. Sometimes the Prophet (pbuh) explained abrogated verses; for example, fighting in the sacred months.
7. The Prophet (pbuh) taught his Companions the rulings of Islam by practicing them himself. He introduced the new rules in this way, practicing them and then teaching others.
8. Occasionally, the Prophet (pbuh) made philological explanations of words in the Qur'ān.
9. One aspect of the Prophet's (pbuh) *tafsīr* was to give detailed explanations of ambiguous verses. These explanations served to deepen the faith of the Muslims and helped them to understand the Qur'ān better.
10. Sometimes he explained religious concepts by describing past nations or by using parables.
11. Sometimes, the Prophet (pbuh) explained the scope of some words in the Qur'ān.
12. The Prophet's (pbuh) Sunnah, as well as the Qur'ān, is not restricted to his time, rather it is a primary source for *tafsīr* for all times.

The Secondary Sources in *Tafsīr*

1. *Tafsīr* by the Companions

During Prophet's (pbuh) life, he served as a source of information for the Companions and explained parts of the Qur'ān that they did not understand. Following his death in 632 C.E. the Companions became the primary authority on the Qur'ān. They had closely observed the events during the life of the Prophet (pbuh) and knew the occasions that had prompted the revelations. This, together with their firm faith, enabled them to understand the Qur'ān better than anyone else. They had learned the Qur'ān, verse by verse, directly from the Prophet (pbuh) and had implemented all its commands into their daily lives.

The Companions varied in their ability to understand the Qur'ān; they were not all at the same level in terms of education and knowledge.[69] Masruq said:

> I sat with the Companions and found some who can feed one person
> with knowledge, some ten people and some one hundred people. I found
> some who can feed the whole earth with knowledge; Abdullah ibn Mas'ud
> is one of them."[70]

The Companions' knowledge of Islam depended on their education, cultural background and the amount of time they spent with the Prophet (pbuh). The most knowledgeable of the Companions delved into *tafsīr* and gave explanations of Qur'anic verses. This included the first four caliphs who were generally highly esteemed in their *tafsīr* authority. This work required extensive knowledge of the Arabic language and of old Arab poetry whose unusual words assisted in comprehending the meaning of some of the foreign words used in the Qur'ān. In addition to these, knowledge of the customs and lifestyle of the old Arabs was beneficial as well as knowledge of the conditions of the 'People of the Book' at that time. Only a few Companions had these qualifications.

When interpreting Qur'anic verses, the Companions first referred to the Qur'ān itself and then the Sunnah to discover whether they had observed anything from the Prophet (pbuh) regarding those verses. If they found the answers in the Qur'ān, they did not say anything on the matter. If neither the Qur'ān nor the Sunnah gave an explanation, they used their own personal opinion to interpret the verses. For example:

> This day I have perfected for you your Religion (with all its rules, com-
> mandments and universality), completed My favor upon you, and have
> been pleased to assign for you Islam as your religion.[71]

Listening to this verse, 'Umar broke down in tears because he understood the time of death for the Prophet (pbuh) was imminent.[72] He believed that if the

---

[69]   Ibn Qutayba, *Kitāb al-Mathāil wal-Jawabāt*, Cairo 1349, p. 8.

[70]   Ibn Sa'd, *Tabaqāt al-Kubra*, Beirut 1957, 2/342–343.

[71]   Qur'ān 5: 3.

[72]   Dhahabī, *al-Tafsīr wal-Mufassirun*, 1/60.

religion was completed, so was the mission of the Prophet (pbuh) and so he would separate from his Companions.

The Companions also referenced other scriptures (*Isra'iliyyat*) in their interpretations, but they were careful to compare the information with the Qur'ān and Sunnah to ensure there were no contradictions before using it. Only if there were no contradictions did they include it in their *tafsīr*, otherwise they omitted this information.

In the main, the Companions' *tafsīr* concerned the occasions behind the revelation of verses. When they used their own opinion for interpreting, it was mostly from a linguistic or religious perspective. They used different methods to explain ambiguous or seemingly contradictory verses. When forming their opinion they utilized their knowledge of Arabic grammar and Arab poetry.

SUMMARY: THE SECONDARY SOURCES IN *TAFSĪR*

Tafsīr by the Companions

1. After the Prophet's (pbuh) death, the Companions became the primary authority on the Qur'an.
2. The most knowledgeable of the Companions delved into *tafsīr* and gave explanations of Qur'anic verses.
3. When interpreting Qur'anic verses, the Companions' first referred to the Qur'ān itself and then the Sunnah to discover whether they had observed anything from the Prophet (pbuh) regarding those verses.
4. If neither the Qur'ān nor the Sunnah gave an explanation, they used their own personal opinion to interpret the verses.
5. The Companions also referenced other scriptures (*Isra'iliyyat*) in their interpretations, but only used them if they did not contradict the Qur'ān and Sunnah.
6. In the main, the Companions' *tafsīr* concerned the occasions behind the revelation of verses.

Examples from the *Tafsīr* of the Companions

The *tafsīr* produced by the Companions was not a comprehensive explanation of the whole Qur'ān. Having lived together with the Prophet (pbuh), they already had a good knowledge of most of it so this was not a necessity for them; they only needed to explain the more difficult parts. The *tafsīr* they produced was expanded by later generations long after the time of the Prophet (pbuh) when ordinary

Muslims struggled with understanding the difficult expressions in the Qur'ān. The Companions who are famous for exegesis are: 'Ali ibn Abū Tālib (d. 661 C.E.), 'Abd Allah ibn 'Abbās (d. 687 C.E.), 'Abd Allah ibn Mas'ud (d. 654 C.E.), 'Ubay ibn Ka'b (d. 650 C.E.), Zayd ibn Thabit (d. 665 C.E.), 'Abd Allah ibn Zubayr (d. 692 C.E.) and Abū Musa al-Ash'arī (d. 664 C.E.). The below are examples of the types of *tafsīr* the Companions produced.

1. The Prophet (pbuh) used to fast on the day of Ashura every year prior to receiving the command of the obligatory Ramadan fast.[73] The following verses legislated the obligatory fast and explained who was exempt from performing it:

> O you who believe! Prescribed for you is the Fast, as it was prescribed for those before you, so that you may deserve God's protection and attain piety. (Fasting is for) a fixed number of days. If any of you is so ill that he cannot fast, or on a journey, he must fast the same number of other days. But for those who can no longer manage to fast, there is redemption (penance) by feeding a person in destitution (for each day missed or giving him the same amount in money).[74]

Muslims jurists have various understandings of the Arabic word 'yutiquna-hu' translated as 'those who can no longer manage to fast.' Ibn 'Abbas understood it to mean someone who is exhausted while fasting and can only observe the fast with extreme difficulty.[75] His interpretation was very old people who can no longer manage to fast. These people are unable to make up the days of the fast that they have missed so they are permitted to pay compensation for each day of Ramadan.

2. "Fleeing from a lion!"[76] The Arabic word 'qaswara' from this verse, translated as 'lion,' caused some disputes among the Companions. Ibn 'Abbas understood it metaphorically and explained it as a harsh noise made by the voice of people.[77] Ibn 'Abbas' explanation fits the context of the verse. The word symbolizes people who escape from listening to the Qur'ān just as animals escape out of fear of wild predators.

3. "Indeed the worst kind of all living creatures in God's sight are the deaf and dumb, who do not reason and understand."[78]

---

[73] Tabarī, *Tafsīr*, 3/419.
[74] Qur'ān 2: 183–184.
[75] Bukhari, *Saḥīḥ*, 6/30; Nasāī, *Sunan*, 4/190–191.
[76] Qur'ān 74: 51.
[77] Ibn Ḥajar, Fatḥ al-Bari, 8/478.
[78] Qur'ān 8: 22.

This verse conveys that for human beings, the worse state is to be deaf and dumb in the face of reality. It is a metaphorical description; they have eyes and ears but do not see or hear the truth; they have tongues but do not confess the truth. Ibn 'Abbās used an example from the tribe Banī Abd al-Dar to make the verse easier to understand.[79] The tribe aided the Quraysh army against the Muslims during the battle of Badr and Ibn 'Abbās used their opposition to Islam in his interpretation to explain the verse.

4. "Spend in God's cause (out of whatever you have) and do not ruin yourselves by your own hands."[80]

> During the Amawi Caliphate, a Muslim army was sent to Istanbul to fight the Byzantine army. The battle became so intense that some of the Muslims soldiers wanted to save their own lives based on the previous verse. They understood the verse to mean that they should not put their lives in danger. However, their misunderstanding of the verse was corrected by one of the Prophet's (pbuh) Companions, Abū Ayyub al-Ansari. He had hosted the Prophet (pbuh) in his house for six months when the Prophet (pbuh) emigrated to Medina. Al-Ansari explained the verse to mean, 'if you do not spend your wealth in the way of God and fight in His way fearlessly you will contribute to your own destruction with your own hands.'[81]

5. "We did not make the vision that We showed you (during the Ascension) but as a trial for humankind to mend their ways, and (in the same way We mentioned) in the Qur'ān the Accursed Tree (the tree in Hell absolutely outside the sphere of God's Mercy)."[82]

> According to ibn 'Abbās, this verse related that the Prophet (pbuh) had seen the Accursed Tree with his own eyes, not just in a dream. The verse is related to the beginning of Surah Isra which describes the Prophet's (pbuh) ascension into the heavens during the journey of *Mi'raj*. The unbelievers mocked the Prophet (pbuh) when he related this journey and some weak believers even renounced Islam because of it. Some scholars hold that this relates to a dream, but this explanation is incorrect as if it were merely a dream, it would not have been such a trial for the people. Therefore, the interpretation of ibn 'Abbās is more appropriate.[83]

---

[79] Tabarī, *Tafsīr*, 9/212.
[80] Qur'ān 2: 195.
[81] Tabarī, *Tafsīr*, the interpretation of 2: 195.
[82] Qur'ān 17: 60.
[83] Tabarī, *Tafsīr*. 9/1–18.

The *tafsīr* of the Companions is the first step in the development of the science of *tafsīr*. This body of work does not contain any theological debate or conflict of ideas as the Companions had a strong and sincere belief and accepted matters unquestioningly. Having been taught directly from the Prophet (pbuh) they were all very close to each other in thought and faith. There is also no interpretation of *fiqh* in their *tafsīr* as they learned the application of those verses directly from the Prophet (pbuh).[84]

The Companions' *tafsīr* undeniably holds an important place in understanding the Qur'ān. After the Prophet (pbuh), they knew the Qur'ān best and their interpretations are more valuable than any personal opinion. If there is an authentic narration from the Companions regarding the interpretation of a verse it is not permissible to accept personal opinion in favor of this. This is the case even if the Companions do not reference the Prophet (pbuh) when explaining the occasions behind the revelation. They learned everything from the Prophet (pbuh) so their words are accepted as his word. They did not make *ijtihād* (use personal opinion) on these topics. As a result, on matters that are not open to interpretation, such as the occasions of revelation, the *tafsīr* and narrations of the Companions are binding.[85] However, scholars vary in opinion on how binding the *tafsīr* of the Companions is when related to matters that are open to interpretation. The majority of scholars (including Abū Ḥanīfa) agree that the *tafsīr* and narrations of the Companions are binding on matters that are not open to interpretation, but their *tafsīr* on other issues is preferable, not binding.[86]

SUMMARY: EXAMPLES FROM THE *TAFSĪR* OF THE COMPANIONS

1. The *tafsīr* produced by the Companions was not a comprehensive explanation of the whole Qur'ān but focused on the more difficult parts.
2. The *tafsīr* they produced was expanded by later generations long after the time of the Prophet (pbuh) when ordinary Muslims struggled with understanding the difficult expressions in the Qur'ān.
3. The *tafsīr* of the Companions is the first step in the development of the science of *tafsīr*.
4. This body of work does not contain any theological debate, conflict of ideas or interpretation of *fiqh* as the Companions had a strong and sincere belief and accepted matters without questioning them.

---

[84] Dhahabī, *Tafsīr*, 1/97–98.
[85] Dhahabī, ibid, 1/95.
[86] Dhahabī, *Tafsīr*, 1/128.

5. The Companions' *tafsīr* undeniably holds an important place in understanding the Qur'ān.

6. If there is an authentic narration from the Companions on a verse it is not permissible to accept personal opinion in favor of this.

2. *Tafsīr* by the Successors (*Tabi'in*)

During the time of the first four caliphs, territorial conquests enabled the expansion of Islam outside the borders of the Arabian Peninsula. From amongst the Companions, rulers and teachers were sent to the new lands to teach Islam. For example, Mu'adh ibn Jabal was sent to Yemen during the time of the Prophet (pbuh) and 'Abd Allah ibn Mas'ud was sent to Iraq during Umar's caliphate. In every major city, the Companions initiated Islamic education and taught the Successors (*tabi'in*) whatever they had learned from the Prophet (pbuh) with regard to Islam and the Qur'ān.

With the rapid spread of Islam, the Muslim community inevitably encountered new problems such as corruption, turmoil and conflict. Different groups and sects emerged and each group tried to support their views using verses from the Qur'ān, sometimes misinterpreting it in order to support their doctrine. There emerged an urgent need to interpret the Qur'ān correctly according to basic Islamic principles in order to prevent conflicts and unite the Muslim community. This attracted many people to the education circles of the Companions; people wanted to learn the truth about Islam and an accurate interpretation of the Qur'ān. Many non-Arab Muslims '*mawāli*' attended these education circles and received their education directly from the Companions in turn becoming outstanding scholars in the field of *tafsīr*. Nāfi,' Ikrimah, Ata ibn Rabah, Sa'id ibn Jubayr and Hasan Basrī are a few of the well-known *tabi'in* in the fields of jurisprudence and exegesis. As non-Arabs, these scholars brought a new perspective to the Islamic sciences and initiated the movements in Islamic thought. This resulted in the establishment of prominent schools in different cities.

The School of Mecca

The Meccan school was established by the profound scholar 'Abd Allah ibn 'Abbās (d. 687 C.E.) with significant contributions from Ā'isha and other Companions in Mecca. 'Abd Allah ibn 'Abbās was named the 'ocean of knowledge' and 'the translator of the Qur'ān' and he can be seen as the founder of *tafsīr* as a science. Ibn Taymiyya said: 'The most famous scholars in the field of *tafsīr* from amongst the *tabi'in* are the students who were educated in the school of Mecca, because 'Abd

Allah ibn 'Abbās educated them.' The most outstanding students of this school were Sa'id ibn Jubayr (d. 714 C.E.), Mujahid ibn Jabr (d. 721 C.E.), Ikrimah (d. 723 C.E.), Ata ibn Abī Rabah (d. 732 C.E.) and Tāwus ibn Kaysan (d. 724 C.E.).

The School of Medina

The school of Medina was particularly important, as Companions of the Prophet (pbuh) inhabited the city for a long time after his death. They taught the Qur'ān and Sunnah to the new Muslims there. This school was established by the profound scholar and Companion 'Ubay ibn Ka'b (d. 650 C.E.). His most notable students were Abū al-Aliya (d. 708 C.E.), Muhammad ibn al-Qurazi (d. 736 C.E.) and Zayd ibn Aslam (d. 753 C.E.).

The School of Kūfa

A leading scholar in the fields of *fiqh* and *tafsīr* was the Companion 'Abd Allah ibn Mas'ud (d. 654 C.E.). An early Muslims and scribe of the Prophet (pbuh) he had spent a lot of time with the Prophet (pbuh) and had often witnessed the explanation of verses directly from him. 'Umar recognized his experience and profound knowledge and sent him to Kūfa to teach Islam. Ibn Mas'ud established his school based on rational principles. He is considered to be the first seed of the development of the *ijtihād* movements and his school was named the 'Iraq Rational School.' His notable students included, Masruq ibn al-Ajda' (d. 683 C.E.), Aswad ibn Yazid (d. 694 C.E.), Murra ibn al-Hamadani (d. 708 C.E.), Amir as-Sha'bi (d. 721 C.E.), Hasan Basrī (d. 728 C.E.), Qatāda ibn Diama (d. 735 C.E.) and Ibrahim an-Nakhāī (d. 726 C.E.).

These schools established a new movement in Islamic thought.[87] Each had its own unique teaching methodology; for example, the schools of Mecca and Medina did not incorporate analogy and personal opinion in their instructions. However, in the school of Kūfa it was a very important process implemented in the solution of difficult or complex problems.

Characteristics of the *Tafsīr* of the *Tabi'in*:

- Their exegesis was applied to the whole Qur'ān and in many cases words and expressions were explained in detail.

- Legal rulings that emerged from the analysis of verses were also included together with historical information.

---

[87] Suyūtī, *al-Itqān*, 11, 242.

- Arabic poetry was utilized to explain the meanings of words used in the Qur'ān. Poetry acted as a dictionary.

- Jewish and Christian sources (*Isra'iliyyat*) were used to explain and add details to stories only mentioned briefly in the Qur'ān.

- *Tafsīr* knowledge was passed orally from master to student in the class setting. No *tafsīr* publication was produced.

SUMMARY: *TAFSĪR* BY THE SUCCESSORS (*TABI'IN*)

1. During the time of the first four caliphs Companions initiated Islamic education in the major Islamic cities and taught the *tabi'in* whatever they had learned from the Prophet (pbuh) with regard to Islam and the Qur'ān.

2. There was an urgent need to interpret the Qur'ān correctly according to basic Islamic principles in order to prevent conflicts and unite the Muslim community.

3. Many non-Arab Muslims '*mawāli*' attended these education circles and received their education directly from the Companions in turn becoming outstanding scholars in the field of *tafsīr*.

4. This resulted in the establishment of prominent schools in different cities, the most notable of which were in Mecca, Medina and Kūfa. These schools established a new Islamic Thought movement.

5. Each had its own unique teaching methodology and their *tafsīr* was applied to the whole Qur'ān. They gave detailed explanations, established legal rulings, and utilized other scriptures and Arabic poetry in their explanations.

6. *Tafsīr* knowledge was passed orally from master to student rather than written as a book.

CHAPTER 2

Riwāyah Tafsīr (Tradition-Based)

Introduction

Qur'anic interpretation is necessary to enable the proper practice of Islam by all Muslims. Muslim scholars have undertaken this essential task according to different methodologies including theological, juristic and thematic, whilst others have utilized an all-encompassing approach. *Tafsīr* works fall into two categories; reason-based (*dirāyah*) and tradition-based (*riwāyah*). *Riwāyah tafsīr* interprets the Qur'ān by referencing tradition: first, the Qur'ān itself, followed by the Sunnah and then the explanations of the Companions (*Saḥābah*) and Successors (*Tabi'in*), thus reflecting as closely as possible the original sources of Islam.

Relying on traditions in interpreting Qur'anic verses, *riwāyah tafsīr* is also known as *naqlī* (relies on reports) and *ma'thūr* (relies on tradition) *tafsīr*. It benefits from the biography of Prophet Muhammad (pbuh) (*Sīrah*), hadiths and history books. This methodology originated from the reports of the Prophet (pbuh), which were memorized and passed on by the Companions and Successors and later compiled into *tafsīr* books. Included in this type of *tafsīr* is the meaning of verses, different Qur'anic readings (*qiraat*), clear and ambiguous verses (*muhkam* and *mutashābih*), the occasions behind the revelation, the abrogating and abrogated verses (*nāsikh-mansūkh*) and information about past nations.

The best and most reliable sources of *tafsīr* are the interpretation of the Qur'ān by the Qur'ān itself, followed by the interpretation of the Qur'ān by the Prophet (pbuh). These cannot be matched or superseded by any other source. These primary sources are followed by the explanations of the Companions who were witness to the revelation and directly taught by the Prophet (pbuh) himself; they were the first Muslims.[88] Sources originating from a report of the Prophet (pbuh), a Companion or a Successor should have a sound basis; there should be a complete chain of narrators (*isnād*) whose narrations are truthful and reliable.[89] The authors of *riwāyah tafsīr* usually included or at least referenced the *isnād* of the narrations. A number of scholars (from both the classical and mod-

---

[88] Von Denffer, *'Ulūm al-Qur'ān*, 124.
[89] Abdullah Saeed, *Interpreting the Qur'ān*, 42.

ern periods) have argued that tradition-based *tafsīr* is the most reliable and preferred method of interpretation. Manna' al-Qattan said:

> What we have to follow and hold onto is the *tafsīr* based on text/tradition. This is because it is the path of true knowledge. It is also the safest way of guarding [oneself] against [attributing] error and deviation to the Book of God.[90]

Other scholars, however, have criticized *riwāyah tafsīr* for specific reasons. Scholars unanimously accept the interpretation of the Qur'ān by the Qur'ān or by authentic Sunnah however, they reject any report that has a problem in its chain of transmission or whose content opposes the Qur'ān and the authentic Sunnah. The reports ascribed to the Companions and Successors contain many conflicts, particularly those transmitted on the authority of Ibn 'Abbas. A lack of investigation into their authenticity resulted in many weak and even forged reports appearing in *riwāyah tafsīr* books. There are three main criticisms of this type of *tafsīr*:[91]

The first criticism is the inclusion of forged hadiths in *riwāyah tafsīr* book. Forgery of hadiths has, for various reasons, been prolific in Islamic history. Some of these false hadiths have found their way *tafsīr* books due to a lack of thoroughness on the part of the authors.

The second criticism is the inclusion of *Isra'iliyyat* (narrations and stories from Jewish and Christian sources) in *riwāyah tafsīr* books, which weakens the validity of the interpretations. In a restricted sense, *Isra'iliyyat* refers to the traditions, reports and religious literature of the Jews, but more commonly it refers to Christian, Zoroastrian and other Near Eastern traditions including folklore. In other words, every non-Muslim contribution used in Muslim exegesis falls under the category *Isra'iliyyat*. The specific usage of the term *Isra'iliyyat* is to denote these different elements, however, the Arabic rule of *taghlib* prescribes that the term is appropriate when material mainly obtained from Jewish sources predominates. *Isra'iliyyat* reports include stories of the Prophets, narratives from creation to the present time and narratives about the specific period from Moses' death to the Israelites' arrival in Palestine.

Isra'iliyyat reports were not utilized frequently by the Companions, however the Successors and later generations increased their reliance on these sources. Many aspects of the Qur'ān can be explained by referring to these sources where there is common ground between the two, however, this material must

---

[90]   Abdullah Saeed, *Interpreting the Qur'ān*, 42.
[91]   Dhahabī, *al-Tafsīr wal-Mufassirun*, 1/156–202.

be used cautiously as it cannot be considered sound according to the standards of hadith science, unless it can be traced back to the Prophet (pbuh) and his Companions.[92]

Ibn Khaldun said:

> The Arabs had no books or scholarship but they wanted to know certain things that human beings are usually curious about, such as the reasons for the existence of things, the beginning of creation, and the secrets of existence. They consulted the earlier People of the Book about it and got their information from them. When the People of the Book became Muslims, they clung to the (information) they possessed, such as information about the beginning of creation and information of the type of forecasts and predictions. The Qur'ān interpreters were not very rigorous in this respect and they filled the Qur'ān commentaries with such material.[93]

Some hold the view that the use of *Isra'iliyyat* sources began during the Companions' time; while others maintain that there were no *Isra'iliyyat* sources during that time.[94] Non-Muslim scholars, however, generally agree that during the first two centuries of Islam Muslims were encouraged to learn about the biblical and extra-biblical Prophets.[95] When the People of the Book converted to Islam, they brought with them their own religious traditions and legends and shared this information with the Muslims, relating to their mention in the Qur'ān, without checking their authenticity first.[96] Ibn Kathīr imposed some limitations on these reports and clarified that *Isra'iliyyat* is quoted for supplementary attestation, not for full support.[97]

The third criticism of *riwāyah tafsīr* is the neglect of reporting the chain of transmission (*isnād*) when ascribing narrations to the Prophet (pbuh) or the Companions. This makes it impossible to verify the original source of these reports. During the Companions' time, they were meticulous in verifying the authenticity of narrations. When they heard any word ascribed to the Prophet (pbuh), they would question the transmitter and only if the report was authentic would they accept it, otherwise it was automatically rejected. However, the time of the Successors was a time of great political and theological conflict. Many hadiths were

---

[92] Von Denffer, *'Ulūm al-Qur'ān*, 133.

[93] Ibn Khaldun, *al-Muqaddima*, Chapter 6, Section 10, Translated by Franz Rosenthal.

[94] Ismail Albayrak, *Re-evaluation The Notion of Isra'iliyyat*, D.E.Ü. İlahiyat Fakültesi Dergisi Sayı XIII-XIV, İzmir 2001, ss. 69–88.

[95] Albayrak, *Re-evaluation The Notion of Isra'iliyyat*, 69–88.

[96] Ahmad Amin, *Fajr al-Islam*, 300.

97 Ibn Kathīr, *Tafsīr al-Qur'ān al-Azīm*, 1/7–8.

transmitted without stating the *isnād* and some groups forged hadith reports to forward their own agenda. Hadith specialists applied strict criteria to forged and weak hadith, but others were not as careful and included them in their books without checking their authenticity.

The most famous books of *riwāyah tafsīr* are:

- Ibn Jarir al-Tabarī (d. 922 C.E.), *'Jami' al-Bayan an Ta'wil al-Qur'ān'*
- Ibn Abī Hātim (d. 939 C.E.), *'Tafsīr al-Qur'ān al-Aẓīm Musnadan an Rasulil- lah wa'l Sahābah wa'l Tabi'in'*
- Abū al-Lays Samarkandī (d. 993 C.E.), *'Tafsīr Abī al-Lays'*
- al-Wāhidī (d. 1075 C.E.), *'al-Wajiz Fi Tafsīr al-Qur'ān al-Aẓīm'*
- al-Baghawī (d. 1122 C.E.), *'Maālim al-Tanzīl'*
- Ibn Atiyya (d. 1151 C.E.), *'al-Muharrar al-Wajiz fi Tafsīr Kitāb al-Aziz'*
- Ibn Kathīr (d. 1372 C.E.), *'Tafsīr al-Qur'ān al-Aẓīm'*
- Jalal al-Din Suyūtī (d. 1505 C.E), *'al-Durr al-Mansur fi'l-Tafsīr bi'l Ma'thūr'*

SUMMARY: INTRODUCTION

1. *Tafsīr* works fall under two categories; reason-based (*dirāyah*) and tradi- tion-based (*riwāyah*).

2. *Riwāyah tafsīr* interprets the Qur'ān by referencing tradition: first the Qur'ān itself, then the Sunnah and then the hadith of the Companions (*Sahābah*) and Successors (*Tabi'in*).

3. *Riwāyah tafsīr's* origin was the reports of the Prophet (pbuh) memorized and passed on by his Companions to the Successors, which were later col- lated and produced as *tafsīr* books.

4. Included in this type of *tafsīr* is the meaning of verses, different Qur'anic readings (*qiraat*), clear and ambiguous verses (*muhkam* and *mutashābih*), the occasions behind the revelation, the abrogating and abrogating vers- es (*nāsikh-mansūkh*) and information about the past nations.

5. The interpretation of the Qur'ān by the Qur'ān itself followed by the inter- pretation of the Qur'ān by the Prophet (pbuh), are the highest and most reliable sources of *tafsīr*.

6. The authors of *riwāyah tafsīr* usually included the *isnād* of the narrations or referenced where it could be found.

7. There are three main criticisms of this type of *tafsīr*: the inclusion of forged hadith, the inclusion of *Isra'iliyyat* and the neglect of including the chain

of transmission (*isnād*) in some of the reports that were ascribed to the Prophet (pbuh) or the Companions.

Tabarī and His Methodology in *Tafsīr*

His Life

Muhammad ibn Jarir at-Tabarī (d. 923 C.E.) was born in 839 C.E. in Amul/ Tabaristan, on the southern coast of the Caspian Sea, present day Iran.[98] He was one of the most important Islamic scholars. Educated at Amul, he was taught by the best scholars of the time memorizing the whole Qur'ān by the age of seven and writing hadith by the age of nine.[99] He completed his education in Ray, Basra, Medina, Baghdad, Syria and Egypt and became an expert in almost every Islamic discipline: exegesis, history, jurisprudence, variant readings of the Qur'ān, tradition, theology, ethics and other areas. He even initiated his own legal school. which later was discontinued. It is reported that he wrote 40 pages a day for a period of 40 years, producing many books in different fields.[100] He is famous for his debates against the Hanbalī School and, notably, he did not accept Ahmad ibn Hanbal as a *mujtahid*, he considered him to be a *muhaddith* (hadith scholar). For this reason he was harshly criticized by Hanbalī followers during his lifetime and after his death.[101]

Tabarī was tall and slim with an eloquent expression.[102] He died on Saturday 26 Shawwal, 923 C.E. and was buried in the yard of his house.[103] Ibn Jawzī said; "the death of Tabarī was concealed from people, because people though that he was of false belief, therefore he was buried during the night."[104]

One point of contest against Tabarī was his view that it permissible to wipe the feet, rather than wash them, during *wudu*.[105] This view earned him the accusation of deviating from Islam. However, this was not true; Tabarī was an objective scholar. The main argument that others used against him was his great love for 'Ali and his descendants,[106] however, this does not justify the accusations against him.

---

[98] Suyūtī, *Tabaqāt al-Mufassirin*, Leiden 1839, s. 31.

[99] Al-Baghdadi, *Tārikh Baghdad*, Egypt 1931, 2/166.

[100] Subkī, *Tabaqāt al-Shāfi'iyya al-Kubra*, 2/135.

[101] Balāzūrī, *Mu'jam al-Buldan*, Egypt 1906, 1/63.

[102] Ibn Jawzī, *al-Muntazam fi Tārikh al-Muluk wa>l-Umam*, Haydarabad 1357, 6/172.

[103] Ibn Hallikān, *Wafayāt al-A>yān*, Cairo 1948, 3/332.

[104] Ibn Jawzī, *al-Muntazam*, 6/172.

[105] Tabarī, *Jāmi' al-Bayān*, Egypt, 10/52–80.

[106] Tabarī, *Tārikh al-Umam wa>l-Muluk*, Cairo, 1939, 2/ 547.

His Teachers and Students

Tabarī was an authority in many Islamic disciplines. He travelled to the centers of knowledge across the Islamic world in order to obtain knowledge. He received hadith lessons from Muhammad ibn Humayd al-Rāzī (d. 862 C.E.). He travelled to Baghdad to learn from Ahmad ibn Hanbal but was unable to reach him whilst he was still alive. In Basra, he learned from San'ani, al-Gazzaz (d. 854 C.E.), Abu'l Esh'as (d. 867 C.E.) and al-Harashi. He went to Kūfa to increase his knowledge and wrote hadith from Hannad ibn Sirri al-Tamimi (d. 857 C.E.), Abu Kurayb Muhammad al-Hamadani (d. 862 C.E.) and Ismail ibn Musa (d. 859 C.E.). He learned Shāfi'ī *fiqh* from Muzani and Mālikī *fiqh* from the students of Ibn Wahb. He also learned different Qur'anic recitations (*qiraat*) from different scholars.[107]

Many scholars benefited from Tabarī's profound knowledge in broad areas, the most well-known of whom were Abū Bakr Muhammad ibn Kāmil, Abdulaziz Muhammad ibn Tabarī, Abu'l Hasan Ahmad ibn Yahya, Abu'l Faraj al-Mu'afi ibn Zakariyya, Ali ibn Abdulaziz al-Dulabi and Muhammad ibn Nasr al-Marwazi.[108]

His Books

A dedicated scholar, Tabarī wrote prolifically across many different fields. He had an extraordinary intellect and profound knowledge. Some of his works are listed below:[109]

- *Tārikh al-Umam wa'l-Muluk*
- *Kitāb Zayl al-Muzayyal*
- *Ikhtilāf al-Fuqaha*
- *Latāif al-Qawl fi Aḥkām Sharai' al-Islam*
- *Tahdhīb al-Āthār*
- *Kitāb Basit al-Qawl fi Ahkan Sharai' al-Islam*
- *Kitāb Adab al-Nufus al-Jayyida*
- *Kitāb al-Qiraat wa Tanzīl al-Qur'ān*
- *Kitāb al-Sharh al-Sunnah*
- *Kitāb Fadāil Abī Bakr and Umar*
- *Kitāb Fadāil Ali ibn Abī Tālib*
- *Kitāb al-Mujiz fi'l Uṣūl*

---

[107] Ibn Nadīm, *al-Fihrist*, al-Matbaat al-Rahmaniyya, Egypt n.d. s. 326.
[108] Baghdadi, *Tārikh Baghdad*, 2/162.
[109] Subkī, *Tabaqāt al-Shāfi'iyya*, 2/136.

His *Tafsīr*

The full title of Tabarī's *tafsīr* is '*Jami' al-Bayan an Ta'wil al-Qur'ān*' which he completed in 883 C.E. Preserved in handwriting in different libraries up until the 19th century, it was later published as 30 volumes in Egypt. Many scholars benefited from the knowledge in this *tafsīr* and acknowledged its value.[110] Tabarī's work is of great value and has no equal in comprehensive usage and referencing. Previous *tafsīr* works that had been written then lost over time are preserved through his work. '*Jami' al-Bayan*' is one of the most famous *tafsīr* books ever written and is perhaps the most voluminous work in existence today. It belongs to the class of *tafsīr bi al-riwāyah* and is based on the reports from the Prophet (pbuh), the Companions and the Successors, noting and evaluating the various chains of transmission. However, some of the reports it contains are not sound and these are not clearly indicated, and it also includes some *Isra'iliyyat*.

Features of '*Jami' al-Bayan*':

- The primary source to interpret the Qur'anic verses is the Qur'ān itself.
- Narrations from the Prophet (pbuh), the Companions and the Successors are referenced when giving explanations.
- Old Arabic poems are utilized when explaining some words.
- Philological analysis is used, particularly in cases where no narration exists about a certain verse.
- *Isra'iliyyat* reports (some of which are intellectually problematic) are used and related from Wahb ibn Munabbih.
- The concept of the existence of foreign words in the Qur'ān is rejected. Rather, he accepts that some foreign words were incorporated into the Arabic language prior to the Qur'anic revelation and, since they are coherent with Arabic grammar, it is erroneous to class them as 'foreign.'
- Theological matters are discussed with the Sunni position being adopted against the Mutazalite doctrines.
- Islamic law topics are discussed; different opinions are narrated then analyzed and preference is given to one over the others.
- The seven modes of Qur'anic revelation (*Ahruf Sab'a*) are discussed and the different readings of words in the Qur'ān are explained.
- Interpretation of verses is carried out by first referencing the Qur'ān, then the Sunnah and then the reports of the Companions. Some of the sources

---

[110] Suyūtī, *Tabaqāt al-Mufassirīn*, s. 31.

for the *tafsīr* were Ibn 'Abbās, Ibn Mas'ud, Mujāhid, Said ibn Jubayr, Ikrimah, Qatāda, Farrā and Abd al-Razzaq ibn Hammam.

- Arab linguists' views were utilized such as those of Kisaī, Farrā and Ahfash.
- The books of *qiraat* and jurisprudence were referenced and utilized.

Tabarī's methodology involved checking the Qur'ān and Sunnah first for an explanation and then interpreting the verse accordingly. Following this, he would relate the opinions of the Companions and the Successors, first summarizing their different views and then preferring one over the others. This methodology is unique to Tabarī *tafsīr* and distinguishes his work when compared with other written *riwāyah tafsīr*. Only when Tabarī could not find any reports to explain the verses would he resort to philological explanations.

Tabarī refrained from making *tafsīr* based on mere opinion and even allocated a chapter of his book to discussing this matter[111] determining that it is not possible to give personal opinion without supporting it from the Sunnah.[112] He generally referenced the full chain of transmitters when mentioning reports but has been noted for occasionally using reports without giving the *isnād*. He was knowledgeable in *uṣūl* hadith and the process of evaluating hadith. Tabarī usually provided his own opinion when he accepted or rejected the views of others and did not accept views that contradicted the consensus of the scholars. For example, he rejected the opinion that God cannot be seen, as there are authentic reports in the Sunnah regarding this subject and Sunni scholars have consensus on this matter.[113]

Tabarī's *tafsīr*, with its reports from the Prophet (pbuh), Companions and Successors, resembles an encyclopedia and stands out amongst the works of other scholars. It can also be considered a source for Arab philology, history, Islamic jurisprudence, Arabic grammar, *qiraat* and poetry. His book preserves many different views and enables us to understand the intellectual level of his time; it is a priceless work for anyone who wants to delve into the field of *tafsīr* and its history.

SUMMARY: TABARĪ AND HIS METHODOLOGY IN *TAFSĪR*

1. Tabarī (d. 923 C.E.) was one of the most important Islamic scholars.
2. He completed his education in Ray, Basra, Medina, Baghdad, Syria and Egypt and became an expert in almost every Islamic discipline.

---

[111] Tabarī, *Tafsīr*, 1/78.
[112] Tabarī, ibid, 1/77–79.
[113] Tabarī, *Tafsīr*, 12/20.

3. He is famous for his debates against the Hanbalī School.

4. Tabarī was an objective scholar and arguments against him are unjust.

5. He was taught by the best Islamic scholars of his time, and many scholars in turn benefited from his extensive knowledge.

6. Tabarī wrote prolifically across many different fields. He completed his *tafsīr*; 'Jami' al-Bayan an Ta'wil al-Qur'ān' in 883 C.E. It is of great value and has no equal in comprehensive usage and referencing.

7. Previous *tafsīr* works that had been written then lost over time are preserved through his work.

8. His work belongs to the class of *tafsīr bi al-riwāyah* and is based on the reports from the Prophet (pbuh), the Companions and the Successors, noting and evaluating the various chains of transmission.

9. Tabarī first checked the Qur'ān and Sunnah for an explanation and interpreted the verse according to these. Then he related the opinions of the Companions and the Successors, first summarizing their different views and them preferring one of them.

10. Tabarī refrained from making *tafsīr* based on mere opinion.

11. He was knowledgeable in *uṣūl* hadith and the process of evaluating hadith.

12. Tabarī usually provided his own opinion when he accepted or rejected the views of others and did not accept views that contradicted the consensus of the scholars.

13. Tabarī's *tafsīr*, with its reports from the Prophet (pbuh), Companions and Successors, resembles an encyclopedia and stands out amongst the works of other scholars.

SURAH FATIHA (THE OPENING)

سُورة الفَاتِحَة

مكِّيّة وآياتها سَبْع

﴿٣﴾ اَلرَّحْمٰنِ الرَّحِيمِ ﴿٢﴾ اَلْحَمْدُ لله رَبِّ الْعَالَمِينَ ﴿١﴾ بِسْمِ الله الرَّحْمٰنِ الرَّحِيمِ

﴿٦﴾ اهْدِنَا الصِّرَاطَ الْمُسْتَقِيمَ ﴿٥﴾ اِيَّاكَ نَعْبُدُ وَاِيَّاكَ نَسْتَعِينُ ﴿٤﴾ مَالِك يَوْمِ الدِّينِ

﴿٧﴾ صِرَاطَ الَّذِينَ اَنْعَمْتَ عَلَيْهِمْ غَيْرِ الْمَغْضُوبِ عَلَيْهِمْ وَلَا الضَّالِّينَ

Surah Fatiha (The Opening)

1. In the Name of God, the All-Merciful, the All-Compassionate
2. All praise and gratitude (whoever gives them to whomever for whatever reason and in whatever way from the first day of creation until eternity) are for God, the Lord of the worlds,
3. The All-Merciful, the All-Compassionate,
4. The Master of the Day of Judgment.
5. You alone do We worship and from You alone do we seek help.
6. Guide us to the Straight Path,
7. The Path of those whom You have favored, not of those who have incurred (Your) wrath (punishment and condemnation), nor of those who are astray.

Tafsīr

First Verse: بِسْمِ اللهِ الرَّحْمَنِ الرَّحِيمِ *In the Name of God, the All-Merciful, the All-Compassionate*

The explanation of "بِسْمِ": Abu Ja'far said:

> God Who is exalted and has holy names taught good manner to His Messenger Muhammad (pbuh) by putting His beautiful names before all His actions. He introduced Himself to the Prophet (pbuh) with these names before anything else. Therefore, it is Sunnah (right path) to all humanity and the right way to follow by starting the conversations and writings with them (names of God) first...[114]

Humankind is obliged to begin every action, whether verbal or practical, by invoking the Name of God. *Basmala* does not contain a verb commanding this but the meaning is implicit in the word itself. When one begins reading the Qur'ān with "*bism Allah al-Rahman al-Rahim*" he understands that he must begin the recitation with *basmala* because God has commanded it. Similarly, he utters *basmala* before any action; standing, sitting, etc. because he understands this is the implied command. Mentioning the *isnād* of the narration, Ibn Abbas reports:

> The first thing which Jibril (as) brought to Muhammad (pbuh) was the command; O Muhammad! say 'أَسْتَعِيذُ بِالسَّمِيعِ الْعَلِيمِ مِنَ الشَّيْطَانِ الرَّجِيمِ' (I seek refuge in Who hears and knows from expelled Satan) and then 'بِسْمِ اللهِ الرَّحْمَنِ الرَّحِيمِ' (In the Name of God, the All-Merciful, the All-Compassionate). After that Jibril

---

[114] Tabarī, *Jami' al-Bayan an Ta'wil al-Qur'ān*, Interpretation of 1:1.

(as) told him to utter 'bism Allah,' mention the name of your Lord when you sit and stand up.[115]

Tabarī explains that just as the infinitive forms of words can sometimes be used as a verb, the *basmala* can be understood to contain a hidden command to utter it before every action. Supporting his view with linguistic arguments and examples from Arabic poetry he shows that many infinitive word forms in the Arabic language are used as verbs; therefore, *basmala* can be understood in the same way when the infinitive form is used. When a person intends to recite the Qur'ān, he starts with بِسْمِ اللهِ الرّحْمَنِ الرّحِيمِ and this means: I begin with the Name of God.

Before slaughtering an animal, a Muslim must recite the *basmala*. Tabarī's opinion is that if one utters "باللهِ" (with God) whilst slaughtering an animal, it is not the same as saying "بِسمِ اللهِ" (in the Name of God)[116] because this is not the Sunnah of this action. It is obvious that an Arabic speaker would not understand the two to mean the same. Through this example we can see how Tabarī discussed issues of jurisprudence and indicated his preference from amongst the various views.

Abū Sa'id reported:

> The Messenger of God said; "The mother of Jesus gave her son to the scholars to teach him. The teacher asked Jesus, 'write بِسمِ (with name)' and Jesus said, 'what is بِسمِ?' The teacher replied, 'I do not know.' This time Jesus said, '(Each letter in بِسمِ indicates certain meaning) 'baa' is for favors of God, 'sin' is for praising Him and 'mim' is for His kingdom.[117]

Tabarī's analysis of the authenticity of reports is demonstrated through his criticism of the above hadith, which he claimed had a weakness in its chain of transmission. He checked the authenticity and intended meanings of reports, before giving his own opinion.

The explanation of "اللهِ": Tabarī starts his analysis by relating from the early reports: Abū Ja'far said, "This is the Name of God and its meaning is the One which makes all creation His servant and He is worshipped by everything."[118] Ibn Abbas reports, "God is the One who has sovereignty over everything and therefore He is worshipped."[119] Having referenced these reports, Tabarī confirms them and

---

[115] Tabarī, ibid.

[116] Abandoning *basmala* when slaughtering an animal is not permissible.

[117] Tabarī, ibid.

[118] Tabarī, ibid.

[119] Tabarī, ibid.

supports his view linguistically, holding that being God is equal to be being the One who is worshipped. He cites the following verse as evidence; "وَيَذَرَكَ وَءَالِهَتَكَ" (forsake you and your deities?).[120] Ibn Abbas interpreted the word "ءَالِهَتَكَ" (deities) in this verse to mean 'worship' and Mujahid (a pupil of Ibn Abbas) reported the same view.[121] Tabarī holds that the root word for "اللّٰه" is "الإلٰه" (God) and it became "اللّٰه" after the reduction of 'hamza' (the Arabic letter 'a') and by combining the two 'lam' together.

The explanations of "الرَّحْمٰنِ الرَّحِيمِ" (the All-Merciful, the All-Compassionate): Tabarī explains that both words are derived from the same root "رحم" (mercy); *Rahmān* is in the form of 'fu'lan' and *Rahīm* is in the form of 'fa'īl.' This is typical of name formation in Arabic. The derivation of both attributes from the same root, which means mercy, raises the question of why it is repeated. Despite being derived from the same root, their meaning isn't exactly the same. In Arabic, there are many ways to produce names and attributes from verbs, however, despite being derived from the same root, the meanings are not the same. Tabarī gives a linguistic explanation and then supports this with reports on the interpretation of *Rahmān* and *Rahīm*, some of which are mentioned below.[122]

Reports convey that the mercy in *Rahmān* encompasses all creatures, but in *Rahīm* it only covers believers. Abū Sa'id al-Khudri relates from the Prophet (pbuh): "Isa ibn Maryam (Jesus, son of Mary) said, '*Rahmān* indicates God's mercy in this world and the next one, but *Rahīm* indicates His mercy only in the afterlife." These reports clarify the difference between these two Attributes; the mercy in *Rahmān* is general and covers everything, but the mercy in *Rahīm* is limited and only covers certain creatures. God may reward the believers with the mercy of *Rahīm* in this world by guiding them to the truth; belief in God and His Messengers, righteous deeds and the afterlife; only they are admitted to Paradise. Mercy (*Rahman*) is an attribute of God that is bestowed upon everything without exclusivity. The whole of humanity, including the unbelievers, are blessed with this mercy in the form of the rain, which brings forth vegetation, health, the intellect, and much more. Everyone, believer and unbeliever, is the recipient of this mercy in this world, however, only believers can benefit from the mercy in *Rahīm* in this world and the afterlife. Linguistically, *Rahmān* is an attribute which is exclu-

---

[120] Qur'ān 7: 127.

[121] Tabarī, ibid.

[122] Tabarī, *Jami' al-Bayan an Ta'wil al-Qur'ān*, Interpretation of Fatiha 1:1.

sive to God; no one can be named with it or share it. However, it is permissible to call some of God's creatures 'Rahīm.'[123]

Tabarī mentions that some scholars hold the view that the pagan Arabs in Muhammad's (pbuh) time did not know the meaning of Rahmān, but he rejects this argument saying that the people denied it even though they knew its meaning. He argues that knowledge of something doesn't automatically necessitate belief in it; denying something is not always related with ignorance. In fact, the Jews in Muhammad's (pbuh) time knew him as they knew their own children but most of them did not believe in him:

> Those who were given the Book (before) know him (the Messenger with all his distinguishing attributes) as they know their own sons; yet those who ruin their own selves (by concealing this truth, being overcome by their lusts and worldly interests)—they do not believe.[124]

Tabarī explains that a principle characteristic of the Arabic language is that a name is given before its associated attributes. This can also be seen here, as God's private name "Allah" is used before His Attributes, 'Rahmān and 'Rahīm.' God mentioned His private name first to prepare the listeners for praising, exalting and glorifying Him.

Along with other sources, Tabarī utilized Arabic grammar to understand the Qur'ān. He always referred to the Qur'ān first as the primary source. For example, he brings the following verse as evidence to support the view that 'Allah' and Rahman can be used interchangeably; "Say: 'Call upon Him as Allah (God) or call upon Him as ar-Rahman (the All-Merciful). By whichever Name you call upon Him, to Him'"[125]

Second Verse: الْحَمْدُ لِلَّهِ رَبِّ الْعَالَمِينَ *All praise and gratitude are for God, the Lord of the worlds,*

Tabarī explains that the beginning of the second verse, الْحَمْدُ لِلَّهِ (All praise and gratitude are for God) refers to sincere thankfulness to God exclusively. Everything in the universe is created with His mercy and sustained with His favors, therefore only He deserves thankfulness. He has provided innumerable bounties and has given humankind the capacity to fulfill His commands. Praising and thanking God symbolizes the continuity of His favors in the next world. The people

---

[123] Rahīm is used as an attribute for the Prophet Muhammad in the Qur'ān: 9:128.
[124] Qur'ān 6: 20.
[125] Qur'ān 17: 110.

who obey His rules and fulfill their duties will be granted eternal happiness in Paradise.

Tabarī relates reports from the early scholars to support his explanation. Ibn Abbas reported; "The expression all praise and gratitude for God "الحمد لله" is thankfulness to God for His favors, guidance and other things." Hakam ibn Umayr (the Companion) relates from the Prophet (pbuh); "When you say 'All praise and gratitude are for God, the Lord of the worlds' you thank God and for this, He will increase His favors." In another report, the Prophet (pbuh) said; "There is nothing more beloved to God than praising Him, for this reason He praised Himself with "الحَمْدُ لله" (All praise and gratitude are for God)."[126]

Tabarī holds that *hamd* (praise) and *shukr* (thanks) can be used interchangeably. The use of *hamd* with the preposition 'al' (the) conveys the meaning that all forms of praise and gratitude are for God. If *hamd* was used without 'al' it would have a different meaning. By praising Himself with the best form of expression, God taught humankind how to honor Him in the best way because He deserves all kinds of praise with His perfect Attributes. The clear expression "all praise and gratitude are for God" negates the need to include a separate command to praise God. This is a characteristic of Arabic; if the intended meaning is made clear by the context, the number of words used can be reduced. For instance, the command 'utter' is omitted from "all praise and gratitude is for God" but the context makes it clear that the command is implicit in the phrase. Using poems from Arabic literature to support his argument, Tabarī proves the permissibility of omitting some words if they can be understood from the context.

رَبّ (the Lord); the Arabic word 'Rabb' (the Lord) has different meanings:

- A master who is obeyed.

- To correct and improve something to its full capacity.

- To train.

Used as a Name of God, this word conveys the meanings: 'Our Lord who is exalted and glorified,' 'the Master and Sovereign to whom there is nothing equal or similar,' 'the One who provides, trains, sustains and maintains the welfare of His servants' and 'the Owner who creates and commands all.' Tabarī demonstrated his expertise in the Arabic language by using linguistic explanations to elucidate the terminological meaning of 'Rabb.'

The word, "العَالَمِين" (the worlds), is the plural of 'عالم' which means 'a world' and may indicate the different worlds among God's creatures. Each world is spe-

---

[126] Please refer to Tabarī *Tafsīr* for referencing of all these reports.

cific to a different species; humans, *jinn* (metaphysical creatures), animals, etc. and each has been created by God. Tabarī relates from Ibn Abbas who said; "All praise and gratitude are for God, He created everything in the heavens and earth, whether they are known or unknown." With this explanation, he interpreted 'the worlds' as meaning all created things. In another report, Ibn Abbas interpreted it to mean humankind and *jinn*. Sa'id ibn Jubayr said; "It is the children of Adam and also it is every nation in the human and *jinn* species."

Third Verse: الرّحمَنِ الرّحيم *The All-Merciful, the All-Compassionate*

The explanation for this is under the first verse, in *basmala*. In Tabarī's opinion, *basmala* is not a verse of Surah Fatiha. Its inclusion as a verse would mean it is repeated within the *surah*, which doesn't happen in such close succession anywhere else in the Qur'ān. Using logical arguments, Tabarī refutes the view that *basmala* is a verse of Surah Fatiha, indicating that he uses some reason-based (*dirāyah*) methods in his *tafsīr* and therefore demonstrating its uniqueness.

Fourth Verse: مَلك يَوْم الدّين *The Master of the Day of Judgment*

Tabarī begins by mentioning the different readings for "مَلَك يَوْم الدّين" (The Master of the Day of Judgment) and then indicates his preference. [127] Some recite it as *maliki* (مَلك), others recite it as *māliki* (مالك) and others recite it as *mālika* (مالك). Linguists are unanimous in agreeing that that *malik* (مَلك) is derived from *milk* (المِلْك) which means 'sovereignty,' and *mālik* (مالك) is derived from *mulk* (المُلْك) which means 'ownership.' These various readings add depth and richness to the meaning of such verses. If the verse is recited as *maliki* (مَلك) the meaning is; 'the kingdom, sovereignty and power will belong to God alone on Judgment Day.' The world harbors dictators and tyrants who battle for power and sovereignty. When they meet with their Lord on Judgment Day, they will certainly understand their nature as humble servants and where the real power lies. They will realize that only God is glorified, exalted and has exclusive power. This reality is expressed in another verse:

> The Day when they will come forth (from death), with nothing of them being hidden from God. Whose is the absolute Sovereignty on that Day? It is God's, the One, the All-Overwhelming (with absolute sway over all that exist).[128]

This verse informs God's servants, particularly those in positions of power and authority, that they will be humbled and humiliated in front of Him on

---

[127] Please refer to this book for more information about various readings on the Qur'ān.
[128] Qur'ān 40: 16.

Judgment Day; He alone has the ultimate power and decides the destiny of His servants.

If the verse is recited as *māliki* (مالك) the meaning can be explained by the report of Ibn Abbas; "On Judgment Day, in the presence of God, no one will own anything the way they owned something in this world." He then recited the following verses; "No one will speak except him whom the All-Merciful allows, and he will speak the truth"[129] and "On that Day, all will follow the summoning voice straightforwardly without any deviation, and all voices will be humbled before the All-Merciful, and you will hear nothing but a hushed murmur."[130]

Having presented the readings and their explanations, Tabarī's prefers the first over the others, explaining that it encompasses the second reading in its meaning.[131] Sovereignty includes ownership and if God is alone in sovereignty and kingdom it is naturally understood that He is also the Owner of everything and nothing can share this ownership with Him. The second reading is narrower in scope as ownership does not encompass kingdom and sovereignty. Indicating this type of preference is not usually included in *riwāyah tafsīr*.

God is always the Lord of the worlds and nothing is associated with His Lordship. However, as this world is a trial for God's servants, not everyone will understand this, only those who use their intellect to discover the truth. However, the truth will be presented to everyone in the afterlife, which indicates the end of the trial. There will be no need to use the intellect to understand the truth, as its presentation will be clear and unarguable. It is wrong to assume that God is only Lord on Judgment Day. His Lordship is veiled in this world and is only discoverable by use of the intellect. But, he creates, trains, maintains and sustains everything in this world. Humankind must use their free will to understand the nature of God and appreciate His favors. Success in this trial results in rewards in the afterlife, whereas denial results in punishment. Tabarī used logical arguments to refute wrong assumptions and this makes his *tafsīr* an exceptional example of *riwāyah tafsīr*.

If the word *mālik* (مالك) is recited with an 'a' sound for the last letter '*kaf*' (ك) it is grammatically understood that there is a hidden 'O.' This reading is related to the next verse and conveys the meaning, 'O the Master of the Day of Judgment! You alone do We worship and from You alone do we seek help.' Giving a linguistic interpretation, Tabarī then uses examples from Arabic poetry to sup-

---

[129] Qur'ān 78: 38.
[130] Qur'ān 20: 108.
[131] Tabarī, *Tafsīr*, Chapter Fatiha, Interpretation of 1: 4.

port his arguments. He explains that in Arabic, after mentioning a person in the third person, the narrator can then refer to him in the first person as if present, thus changing the course of the speech. It is also possible to then change back to the third person. In the third verse, God is referred to in the third person, then in the fourth verse He is referred to in the first person. This grammatical feature is also present in the following verse; "When *you* are in the ship, and the ships run with their voyagers with a fair breeze, and *they* rejoice in it."[132]

يَوْم الدِّين *Judgment Day*;

Tabarī explained 'al-dīn' (الدِّين) to mean accounting for the deeds of the servants and rewarding or punishing them accordingly.[133] He brought evidence from Arabic poetry to support his explanation and, additionally, he used two other verses to explain the meaning; "No indeed! But (being deluded) they deny *the Last Judgment* (in the other world)."[134] In this verse, al-dīn is used to mean seeing the consequences of the deeds. In the second verse; "How is it you will not be called for accounting"[135] the derivation of 'dīn' (madinin) is again used to mean seeing the consequences of the actions. Following this explanation, Tabarī presents some of the early scholars' interpretations of 'the Master of Judgment Day,' a few of which are mentioned below.[136]

Ibn Abbas' holds that the Day of Judgment is when all creatures will be called to account for their deeds; the consequences of their actions will be revealed and they will be rewarded or punished accordingly. However, God has the absolute authority to forgive His servants and creatures according to His will as only He has sovereignty over them. Ibn Mas'ud, Anas ibn Malik and some other Companions agree with this interpretation. Qatāda and Ibn Jurayj made similar interpretations and explain this verse to mean a day on which God will treat His servants according to their deeds.

Fifth Verse: إِيَّاكَ نَعْبُدُ وإِيَّاكَ نَسْتَعِينُ *You alone do we worship and from You alone do we seek help*

Tabarī interprets this verse to mean; 'O God! we revere You, we humbly bow before You and we confess our weakness and dependence upon You. O Lord! We only recognize your Lordship not the others.'[137] Ibn Abbas reported:

---

[132] Qur'ān 10: 22.

[133] Tabarī, *Tafsīr*, Chapter Fatiha, Interpretation of 1: 4.

[134] Qur'ān 82: 9.

[135] Qur'ān 56: 86.

[136] Please refer to Tabarī's *Tafsīr* for the full version of these reports.

[137] Tabarī, *Tafsīr*, Chapter Fatiha, Interpretation of 1: 5.

> Jibril told Muhammad to say 'You alone do we worship, You alone do we believe, fear and hope O our Lord!' Servanthood can be actualized only with humbleness before God.[138]

'From You alone do we seek help' is interpreted as; we only seek help from You for our servanthood, to be obedient and for all matters. Idol worshippers seek help from their idols but we only seek help from You. We are sincere in our belief that You are the source of help for all matters. Ibn Abbas understood the meaning of this verse to be seeking help from God to worship Him properly and for all other matters.[139] Clearly, the duty of proper worship is only achievable with help from God. Servanthood is necessary as long as humankind exists, but there is no guarantee that one will being able to fulfill the demands of servanthood without deviating from that which God has commanded. Thus, seeking help from God to fulfill the obligations of servanthood is necessary for the servants. The Mutazalite view is that it is necessary for God to help His servants if He commands or prohibits something for them. Tabarī rejects this and takes the Sunni position in this discussion; if help had already been granted, the verse would be meaningless. He holds that this verse clearly encourages believers to seek help from God alone; this shows that His help is not preordained for everyone, rather He commands his servants to seek His help for their servanthood. This exemplifies Tabarī's occasional delving into theological debates in his *tafsīr* where he takes the Sunni position against the other sects.

Sixth Verse: اهْدِنَا الصِّرَاطَ الْمُسْتَقِيمَ *Guide us to the Straight Path*

Tabarī interprets this verse to mean; guide us to the straight path and do not let us stray from it. In other words, help us to live according to what You have commanded and don't let us deviate from this correct way of life for as long as we live.[140]

Ibn Abbas reports; Gabriel told Muhammad (pbuh) to say 'guide us to the straight path and inspire us with it.'[141] Inspiration in this context means to help one to remain on the straight path forever. To ask for God's guidance to the straight path is to seek His help in performing one's duties and abstaining from what is prohibited. The meaning of this verse is similar to the previous verse; both encourage servants to petition God for help in their worship. Humans are not aware of whether they will deviate from the straight path in the future therefore, they are

---

[138] Tabarī, ibid.
[139] Tabarī, ibid.
[140] Tabarī, *Tafsīr*, Chapter Fatiha, the interpretation of 1: 6.
[141] Tabarī, ibid.

encouraged to continually seek God's help in this regard. Tabarī relates different ent views on the interpretation of this verse and follows these with his preference, refuting the others with logical arguments.

Islamic scholars understand 'straight path' to mean a clear way without any crookedness or ambiguity; the path which God has ordained and is content with. To be on this path is to be in the favor of God, but remaining on it requires God's help as only He can ensure this. The straight path is that of the Prophets, trustworthy people and martyrs and God bestows His favors upon them. God guided them to accept Islam, believe in Muhammad (pbuh) and enact his Sunnah. Ali reports; the Prophet (pbuh) said; 'the straight path is the book of God.'[142] Jabir ibn Abdullah, Ibn Mas'ud, Anas ibn Mālik and many other Companions interpreted the straight path to mean Islam. Abu al-'Āliyah explained it as the way of the Prophet (pbuh), Abū Bakr and Umar.

Seventh Verse: صِرَاطَ الَّذِينَ أَنْعَمْتَ عَلَيْهِمْ غَيْرِ الْمَغْضُوبِ عَلَيْهِم وَلاَ الضَّآلِّينَ *The Path of those whom You have favored, not of those who have incurred (Your) wrath (punishment and condemnation), nor of those who are astray.*

This verse elaborates on the previous verse giving more detail about the straight path. Tabarī explained it further by referencing another verse:

> Whoever obeys God and the Messenger (pbuh) (as they must be obeyed), then those are (and in the Hereafter will be, in Paradise) in the company of those whom God has favored (with the perfect guidance)—the Prophets, and the truthful ones (loyal to God's cause and truthful in whatever they do and say), and the witnesses (those who see the hidden Divine truths and testify thereto with their lives), and the righteous ones (in all their deeds and sayings and dedicated to setting everything right). How excellent they are for companions![143]

Tabarī said; God commanded the Prophet (pbuh) and his Companions to request His guidance to the straight path, which is described in the seventh verse. Ibn Abbas held that the path of those upon whom God bestows favors is the path of the believers whom God has favored with obedience and proper worship; they obey God and worship Him alone. Some scholars interpreted these people as believers, some as Prophets and others as Muslims.[144] Tabarī holds that obedience and worship are only achieved as favors from God.

---

[142] Tabarī, ibid.

[143] Qur'ān 4: 69.

[144] See Tabarī *Tafsīr* for detailed information about these reports.

غَيْرِ الْمَغْضُوبِ عَلَيْهِمْ *(not of those who have incurred (Your) wrath (punishment and condemnation)*

Tabarī analyzed this section according to the rules of Arabic grammar and explained that the people on the straight path are saved from punishment and condemnation. God has guided these people to the straight path, therefore they do not deviate or incur His wrath. It would be problematic to assume that people were on the straight path for a certain period of time and earned God's favors but then deviated and thus incurred His wrath. In this case, people cannot be considered to be on the straight path. God, Who has knowledge of all things and for Whom there is no past and future, knows that these people will deviate later and therefore would not introduce them as being those on the straight path. Referencing expert linguists from Basra and Kūfa, Tabarī discusses their reading styles, explaining how the different readings affect the meaning of the verse and refuting them if such a reading is not proper for the context of the verse. Following this he indicates his preference and gives its grammatical explanation.

The following verse explains the people who incurred God's wrath:

> Shall I tell you of a case, the worst of all for recompense with God? Those whom God has cursed (excluded from His mercy), and whom He has utterly condemned, and some of whom He turned into apes, and swine, and servants of false powers (who institute patterns of rule in defiance of God)— they are worse situated and further astray from the right, even way.[145]

This verse clarifies that those who disobey God having received his favors will be punished. It is a warning to the believers not to make the same mistake. Ibn Abī Hātim reports; "The Prophet (pbuh) said, 'those who have incurred (Your) wrath (punishment and condemnation) are the Jews (who lived in certain place in certain time).'"[146]

Scholars dispute the meaning of 'wrath' and is ascription to God with some opining that it merely means punishment in the same manner as those who have wrath against God. They present the following verse to support their view; "So finally when they incurred Our condemnation, We took retribution on them, and We caused them to drown all together."[147]

وَلَا الضَّالِّينَ *(nor of those who are astray);*

---

[145] Qur'ān 5: 60.

[146] Tabarī, *Tafsīr*, see the interpretation of 1: 7. Tabarī mentions many more reports they all are in the same meaning, refer to the book to see them all.

[147] Qur'ān 43: 55.

Tabarī refutes the argument of linguists who reduce the word (لا) 'nor' in this verse, supporting his view with evidence from Arabic poetry, which disproves their claim. He makes a long linguistic explanation after which he outlines his own opinion and rejects the others, explaining وَلَا الضَّالِّينَ (nor of those who are astray) with another verse:

> O People of the Book! Do not go beyond the bounds in your religion, (straying towards) other than the truth, and do not follow the lusts and fancies of a people who went astray before, and led many others astray, and they strayed (as again others do now) from the right, even way.[148]

In many reports the Prophet (pbuh) explained these people to be Christians who lived at a certain time.[149] Ibn Abbas said; "God let them deviate into sectarian movements. He inspired us to His true religion that is there is no God but God and He does not have any partner."[150]

All those who stray from the straight path are labeled 'deviated' (ضال) in Arabic. God refers to Christians in this way as they strayed from the straight path having received clear guidance to it. God described each group with their attributes to warn believers against making the same mistakes. Tabarī explains guidance and deviation theologically elucidating that nothing happens without the permission and creation of God; the good deeds of his servants make him content as opposed to their bad deeds, but still He creates both. If servants use their free will for bad deeds, God creates them as those who will be unhappy. Since He is the Guide and the One who causes deviation, He creates the consequences for all actions. The following verse exemplifies this concept in the Qur'ān:

> Do you ever consider him who has taken his lusts for his deity, and whom God has (consequently) led astray though he has knowledge (of guidance and straying), and sealed his hearing and his heart, and put a cover on his sight? Who, then, can guide him after God (has led him astray)? Will you not then reflect and be mindful?[151]

Tabarī holds that the Qur'ān is the most comprehensive Divine book that supersedes all previous revelations. Moreover, it contains meanings and aspects that are exclusive to the Qur'ān. The glorious Qur'ān challenged the Arab poets to invent a chapter similar to it but they were unable to fulfill the challenge. There are many

---

[148] Qur'ān 5: 77.

[149] See all the reports in Tabarī *Tafsīr*, Chapter Fatiha, the interpretation of 1:7.

[150] Tabarī, ibid.

[151] Qur'ān 45: 23.

miracles in the Qur'ān and it is the biggest and most important miracle of Prophet Muhammad (pbuh). Tabarī explains why the Qur'ān is superior to all previous scriptures and finishes this chapter a report regarding its importance:

The Prophet reported from his Lord:

> God, the Glorious and Exalted, said, 'I have divided the prayer between Myself and my servant equally and My servant shall be granted what he asked for.' Therefore, when the servant says, 'all praises and thanks are due to God, the Lord of the universe,' God says, 'My servant has praised Me.' When he says, 'the Most Beneficent, the Most Merciful,' God says, 'My servant has extolled Me.' When he says, 'Master of the Day of Judgment,' God says, 'My servant has glorified Me.' When he says, 'You Alone we worship and Your aid alone do we seek' God says, 'this is between Me and My servant and My servant shall have what he requested.' When he says, 'guide us to the Straight Path, the Path of those whom You have favored, not of those who have incurred Your wrath, neither of those who have gone astray,' God says, 'this is for My servant and My servant shall have what he asked for.'[152]

Verses 1–4 of Surah Fatiha belong to God. In them, the servant addresses God in the third person, praising Him; they serve as a ladder to rise to His Presence and thereby the servant attains the dignity of addressing Him in the second person in verses 5–7. At this point, the servant addresses a petition to the One praised with His most comprehensive Attributes in the preceding verses. According to the report mentioned above, verse 4 belongs to both God and the servant, whereas the final verses (5–7), where the servant prays to God for his most pressing need (i.e. right guidance), belong to the servant.

Summary: Chapter Fatiha and Its *Tafsīr*

First Verse

1. When a reciter begins reading the Qur'ān with "*bism Allah al-Rahman al-Rahim*" he understands that he must begin the recitation with *basmala* because it has been commanded by God. Similarly, he utters *basmala* before any action; standing, sitting, etc.

2. Tabarī explains that sometimes the infinitive forms of words convey the meaning of the verb; He supports his view with both linguistic arguments and examples from Arab poetry.

---

[152] Muslim, *Saḥīḥ*, Salah, 38.

3. Tabarī critically analyzed reports before accepting them. He checked the authenticity and intended meaning of the report, then gave his own opinion.

4. Tabarī holds that the root word for "الله" is "الإله" (God) and it became "الله" after the reduction of 'hamza' (the Arabic letter 'a') and by combining the two 'lam' together.

5. After the linguistic explanation, Tabarī cites some reports for the interpretation of *Rahmān* and *Rahīm*.

6. Some scholars claim that the pagan Arab's in Muhammad's (pbuh) time did not know the meaning of *Rahmān*. Tabarī rejects this argument. He supports his view by arguing that knowledge of something does not necessarily mean believing it.

7. Tabarī utilized Arabic grammar, along with other sources, to understand the Qur'ān. He always referred to the Qur'ān first as the primary source.

Second Verse

8. The beginning of the second verse, الحَمْدُ لله (All praise and gratitude are for God) refers to sincere thankfulness to God exclusively.

9. Tabarī holds that *hamd* (praise) and *shukr* (thanks) can be used interchangeably. In Arabic, if the intended meaning is made clear by the context, the number of words used can be reduced.

10. Tabarī benefited from linguistic explanations to elucidate the terminological meaning of '*Rabb*' showing his expertise in the Arabic language.

11. The word, "العَالَمِين" (the worlds), is the plural of 'عالم' which means a world and may indicate the different worlds among God's creatures. With this explanation he interpreted 'the worlds' as meaning all created things.

Third Verse

12. Tabarī holds the opinion that *basmala* is not one of the verses of Fatiha because if it was, it would have been repeated twice in the *surah* and no verses are repeated twice in close succession in the Qur'ān. He used logical arguments to refute the conflicting view that *basmala* is a verse of Fatiha.

Fourth Verse

13. There are different readings for "مَلِك يَوْم الدِّين" (The Master of the Day of Judgment). Tabarī mentions all of the different readings and prefers one over the others.

14. Tabarī's opinion is that the first reading is the preferred one because it encompasses the second reading in its meaning. Indicating this type of preference is not usually something that is included in *riwāyah tafsīr*.

15. In his *tafsīr*, Tabarī used logical arguments to refute wrong assumptions and this makes his *tafsīr* an exceptional example of *riwāyah tafsīr*.

16. If the word *mālik* (مالك) is recited with an '*a*' sound for the last letter '*kaf*' (ك) it is grammatically understood that there is a hidden '*O*.' Tabarī explains this linguistically and uses examples from Arabic poetry as evidence for his arguments.

17. Tabarī explained '*dīn*' (الدِّين) to mean accounting for the deeds of the servants and rewarding or punishing them accordingly. He brought evidence from Arabic poetry to support his explanation and additionally, he used two other verses to explain the meaning.

Fifth Verse

18. Tabarī's interpretation of this verse is; 'O God! we revere You, we humbly bow before You and we confess our weakness and dependence upon You. O Lord! We only recognize your Lordship not the others.'

19. Tabarī rejects the Mutazalite view of this verse and takes the Sunni position in this discussion.

20. This shows an example of Tabarī's occasional delving into theological debates in his *tafsīr* where he takes the Sunni position against the other sects.

Sixth Verse

21. Tabarī interpreted this verse to mean, guide us to the straight path and don't let us stray from it.

22. Tabarī relates different views on the interpretation of this verse and follows these with his preference, refuting the others with logical arguments.

Seventh Verse

23. Tabarī said; God commanded the Prophet (pbuh) and his Companions to petition Him for guidance to the straight path.

24. Tabarī holds that obedience and worship are only achieved as favors from God.

25. Tabarī analyzed this section using Arabic grammar rules and explained that the people on the straight path are saved from punishment and condemnation.

26. Tabarī mentions the views of expert linguists from Basra and Kūfa and discusses their reading styles explaining how the different readings affect the meaning of the verse and refuting them if such a reading is not proper for the context of the verse.

27. He prefers the true reading and its grammatical explanation at the end.

28. Tabarī refutes the argument of linguists who reduce the word (ﻻ) 'nor' in this verse. He supports his view with evidence from Arabic poetry and proves the wrongness of their claim.

29. After a long linguistic discussion he outlines his own opinion and rejects the others.

30. Tabarī holds that the Qur'ān is the most comprehensive Divine book that supersedes all previous revelations.

CHAPTER 3

Riwāyah Tafsīr, Ibn Kathīr and His Tafsīr

Introduction

As was outlined in Chapter 2, the source for *riwāyah tafsīr* is tradition reports. When a report is a narration of the Prophet (pbuh), Companions or Successors, it should have a sound basis; the *isnād* should be reliable and complete.[153] The Prophet (pbuh) explained words and verses in the Qur'ān when his Companions asked him. The explanation of the Qur'ān by the Qur'ān itself and the explanation of the Qur'ān by the Prophet (pbuh) are the two highest sources of *tafsīr* and cannot be equaled or superseded by other sources. In his explanations of the Qur'ān, the Prophet (pbuh) used other verses or his Sunnah. For the *mufassir* these sources are the most important when approaching *tafsīr*. Following these are the reports of the Companions, the witnesses to the revelation and students of the Prophet (pbuh). They were the first Muslims and learned everything directly from the Prophet (pbuh) himself.[154]

Riwāyah tafsīr contains information about the meaning of the verses, the various readings of the Qur'ān (*qiraat*), verses with a clear meaning (*muhkam*) and verses with an ambiguous meaning (*mutashābih*), the occasions behind the revelation, the abrogated and abrogating verses (*nāsikh-mansūkh*), and past nations and the news about them. *Riwāyah tafsīr* utilizes the biography of Prophet Muhammad (pbuh) (*sīrah*), hadith and history books to acquire the information. It was initiated as the reports from the Prophet (pbuh) to the Companions and was passed on orally to the Successors. Later, scholars collated the reports into *tafsīr* books.

This chapter introduces the methodology and *riwāyah tafsīr* of prominent scholar, Ibn Kathīr followed by his interpretation of verses from Surah Fīl (The Elephant).

SUMMARY: INTRODUCTION

1. The source for *riwāyah tafsīr* is tradition reports.
2. The *isnād* of the reports should be reliable and complete.

---

[153] Abdullah Saeed, *Interpreting the Qur'ān*, 42.
[154] Von Denffer, *'Ulūm al-Qur'ān*, 124.

3. The explanation of the Qur'ān by the Qur'ān itself and the explanation of the Qur'ān by the Prophet (pbuh) are the two highest sources of *tafsīr* and cannot be equaled or superseded by other sources.

4. *Riwāyah tafsīr* contains information about the meaning of the verses, the various readings of the Qur'ān (*qiraat*), verses with a clear meaning (*muhkam*) and verses with an ambiguous meaning (*mutashābih*), the occasions behind the revelation, the abrogated and abrogating verses (*nāsikh-mansūkh*), and past nations and the news about them.

Ibn Kathīr and His Methodology in *Tafsīr*

His Life and Education

'Imad ad-Din Abū al-Fidā Ibn Kathīr was born to an imam in a village near Damascus in 1301 C.E.[155] Losing his father at a young age, Ibn Kathīr was educated by his older brother and together they moved to Damascus when he was still a child.[156] He was later educated in *Fiqh* (Islamic Jurisprudence) by Burhān al-Din al-Fazarī (d. 1329 C.E.) and Kamal al-Din ibn Qādi (d. 1326 C.E.).[157] He also learned from the scholars Ibn Asakir (d. 1323 C.E.), Āmidī (d. 1325 C.E.) and Ibn Taymiyya (d. 1328 C.E.).[158]

Ibn Kathīr wrote books on *fiqh,* hadith, history and *tafsīr* which became well-known during his lifetime and were read by many. He continued to attend the classes of Hafiz Mizzī (d. 1341 C.E.) and married his daughter. He was granted *ijāzah* (special permission to be qualified to teach Islamic disciplines) by famous scholars such as Qarafi and Dabbūsī and lectured on different Islamic fields at prominent schools.[159] During his career he taught many students some of whom, such as Ibn Ḥajar (d. 1448 C.E.), went on to become famous scholars.

Ibn Kathīr has been labelled the second Tabari due to his extensive knowledge and works across a broad range of Islamic disciplines. Many famous scholars are indebted to his profound knowledge; for example, Dhahabī said; "He is an imam, jurist, *muhaddith* (hadith scholar) and *mufassir*."[160] Ibn Ḥajar said; "He produced many good works and people benefitted from his books."[161] Ibn Kathīr

---

[155] Zarqānī, *Manāhil al-Irfān*, 1/498.
[156] Manna al-Kattān, *Mabāhith Fi Ulūm al-Qur'ān*, 386.
[157] Abdullah Mahmud Shahada, *Tārikh al-Qur'ān wa'l-Tafsīr*, 177.
[158] Zaylāī, *Tazkirat'ul Huffāz*, pp. 57–59.
[159] Suyūtī, *Tabaqāt al-Mufassirīn*, 1/110–112.
[160] Dhahabī, *al-Tafsīr wa>l-Mufassirūn*, I/242–247.
[161] Ibn Ḥajar, *al-Durar al-Kamina*, 1/399–400.

followed the Ash'arī School in theology and the Shāfi'ī School in Islamic juris-prudence (*fiqh*). Some scholars criticized his friendship with Ibn Taymiyya but it was without foundation. Ibn Kathīr died in 1373 C.E. and was laid to rest next to Ibn Taymiyya's grave in Damascus.[162]

His Books

Some of Ibn Kathīr's works which were read by many scholars are:

- *Al-Bidāya wan-Nihāya*—a history book containing information about gener-al human history, starting with Prophet Adam up until his own lifetime.
- *Al-Ijtihād Fi Talab al-Jihad*—a book about the importance of juristic opin-ion in Islamic law.
- *Fadāil al-Qur'ān* and *Jam'ihi*—a book detailing the virtues of the Qur'ān and its compilation.
- *Ahādīth al-Tawḥīd and wa'l Rad ala-Shirk*—a book about the unity of God and the rejection of associating partners with God.
- *Al-Bā'ith al-Hasis Sharh Ikhtisār Ulūm al-Hadith* - a book about hadith meth-odology which is a summary of Ibn Salah's book.
- *Al-Takmil Fi Ma'rifah al-Thiqāt wa'l-Duafa wa'l-Majahid*—a book about the people who relate hadith.
- *Tabaqāt al-Shāfi'iyya*—a book about scholars in the Shāfi'ī school.
- *Manāqib al-Imam Shāfi'ī*—a book containing the stories of Imam Shāfi'ī.
- *Adillah al-Tanqīh Fi Fiqh al-Shāfi'iyya* –a book containing the methodology of Shāfi'ī *Fiqh*.

His Methodology in *Tafsīr*

To be able to understand more about the *tafsīr* of Ibn Kathīr, chapter 105 (The Elephant) of the Qur'ān is used below to demonstrate the general characteris-tics of his work. His book '*Tafsīr al-Qur'ān al-Aẓīm*' is one of the more famous *riwāyah tafsīr* works, perhaps second only to Tabarī, and has been published in four and five volumes. It focuses on the soundness of the reports, rejects all for-eign influences such as *Isra'iliyyat*, and it discusses the *sanad* of various reports often in detail making it one of the more valuable books of *tafsīr*. He was extreme-ly careful when using both Christian and Jewish scriptures for the interpreta-tion of some Qur'anic verses.

Some of the features of Ibn Kathīr's *tafsīr* are:

---

[162] Suyūtī, *Tabaqāt al-Mufassirīn*, 1/110–112.

- He use the Qur'ān first and then the Sunnah as his primary sources for interpretation; checking other verses for an explanation first and then the Sunnah if he could not find the answer. If unsuccessful here, he would check the reports of the Companions. He prioritized the importance of *isnād* (the chain of narrators) and always mentioned it when reporting from the Prophet (pbuh) or the Companions. In short, Ibn Kathīr interpreted the Qur'ān in the light of the Qur'ān first, then the Sunnah and after that in the light of the early scholars.
- He categorized the verses into groups and explained them together.
- He utilized hadith methodology, particularly for authenticating reports.
- He was very careful checking the authenticity of reports and would make preferences when considering different opinions, giving priority to the strongest.
- Despite it being a *riwāyah tafsīr*, he sometimes used logical arguments to explain verses.
- He did not accept foreign influences (*Isra'iliyyat*) on the interpretation of the Qur'ān.
- He considered the variant readings of the Qur'ān and explained the meaning of each.
- He narrated selectively and discerningly from previous scholars including Tabarī, Ibn Abī Hātim and Ibn Atiyya.
- He indicated his preference from amongst the different interpretations.
- When interpreting verses he related to legal rules and delved into juristic debates. He mentioned the views of *mujtahids*. He gave their arguments and made preferences between them.
- He included a minimum of philological explanations in his work.
- The end of his work is devoted to a section on the virtues of the Qur'ān.

SUMMARY: IBN KATHĪR AND HIS METHODOLOGY IN *TAFSĪR*

1. Ibn Kathīr was born near Damascus in 1301 C.E.
2. He was educated by his older brother and later by renowned scholars of his time.
3. Ibn Kathīr wrote books on *fiqh*, hadith, history and *tafsīr*.
4. He was granted *ijāzah* by famous scholars and lectured on different Islamic fields at famous schools.

5. Ibn Kathīr has been labelled the second Tabarī due to his extensive knowledge and works across a broad range of Islamic disciplines.

6. Ibn Kathīr followed the Ash'arī School in theology and the Shāfi'ī School in Islamic jurisprudence (*fiqh*).

7. The *tafsīr* of Ibn Kathīr focuses on the soundness of the reports, rejects all foreign influences such as *Isra'iliyyat*, and discusses the *sanad* of various reports often in detail making it one of the more valuable books of *tafsīr*.

SURAH FĪL (ELEPHANT)

بِسْمِ اللهِ الرَّحْمٰنِ الرَّحِيمِ

اَلَمْ تَرَ كَيْفَ فَعَلَ رَبُّكَ بِاَصْحَابِ الْفِيلِ ﴿١﴾ اَلَمْ يَجْعَلْ كَيْدَهُمْ فِى تَضْلِيلٍ ﴿٢﴾

وَاَرْسَلَ عَلَيْهِمْ طَيْرًا اَبَابِيلَ ﴿٣﴾ تَرْمِيهِمْ بِحِجَارَةٍ مِنْ سِجِّيلٍ ﴿٤﴾

فَجَعَلَهُمْ كَعَصْفٍ مَاْكُولٍ ﴿٥﴾

Surah al-Fīl (The Elephant)

In the Name of God, the All-Merciful, the All-Compassionate

1. Have you considered how your Lord dealt with the people of the Elephant?
2. Did He not bring their evil scheme to nothing?
3. He sent down upon them flocks of birds (unknown in the land),
4. Shooting them with bullet-like stones of baked clay (an emblem of the punishment due to them),
5. And so He rendered them like a field of grain devoured and trampled.

Tafsīr

Surah Al Fīl (105) was revealed in Mecca and describes God's favor to the Quraysh in preventing the people of the elephant from destroying the Ka'ba.[163] The *surah* is named after the word *al-Fīl* (the elephant) which is mentioned in its first verse. The people of the elephant are the Abyssinians whose army included a number of elephants. In 571 C.E., fifty days before the birth of Prophet Muhammad (pbuh), the Abyssinians, led by Abraha, attacked Mecca with the intention of destroying

---

[163] The interpretation of Surah Fīl is quoted directly from Ibn Kathīr, *Tafsīr*, 105: 1–5.

the Ka'ba. The verse gives the detail of the attack and the subsequent consequences. God turned their plot against them, humbled them and eventually destroyed them all.

In an attempt to attract the Arab pilgrims to his own city San'a (in Yemen), Abraha erected a great temple. The Meccans were not strong enough to defend their city and the Ka'ba against Abraha's powerful army, but God informed their most powerful tribe, the Quraysh, through Divine Providence, that he would protect it. He promised to honor the Ka'ba by sending an illiterate Messenger, Muhammad (pbuh), as the final Prophet.

The story of the people of the elephant is briefly summarized in Surah Buruj (the Constellations), the story of People of the Ditch, in Ibn Kathīr's book. Dhu Nuas was the last king of Himyar (Yemen). A polytheist, he ordered the killing of the Christians, numbering around twenty thousand. Only one escaped death; Daws Dhu Tha'laban escaped and fled to Damascus, seeking protection from the Christian emperor, Caesar. Caesar wrote to the Negus, the king of Abyssinia (present day Ethiopia), who was closer than him to Yemen. On receiving Caesar's letter, the Negus dispatched two governors, Aryat and Abraha, along with a great army to Yemen to seek out the king. The great army searched and looted the city and drowned the king when they found him, liberating the Abyssinians from their tyrant ruler. However, they had severe disputes amongst themselves, fighting each other continually until the two leaders suggested a duel to settle the matter; "There is no need to fight, instead let us settle this with a duel, and the one left standing will be the ruler of Yemen." Both Abraha and Aryat accepted the terms and a duel was held. A water channel at the appointed place kept both from fleeing during the battle. In the battle, Aryat struck Abraha with his sword, splitting his nose and mouth and slashing his face. Seeing this, Abraha's guard intervened, killing Aryat. Abraha returned to Yemen wounded and on recovering, became the commander of the Abyssinian army. Hearing of what had passed, the Negus sent a letter holding Abraha accountable for the events and threatening him with cutting off his forelock and confiscating his land. Abraha sent an envoy with gifts to the Negus along with a sack of soil from the land and a piece of hair cut from his forelock. He asked the king to walk upon the soil and accept the hair to fulfill his oath. The gifts appeased the Negus who subsequently forgave Abraha.[164]

The explanation that Ibn Kathīr gave about the background of Abraha served to make the verses easier for the readers to understand. It wasn't clear who Abra-

---

[164] Ibn Kathīr, *Tafsīr*, 105: 1–5.

ha was or how he came to command a large Abyssinian army. This information enabled them to see the bigger picture and understand Surah Fīl better. This demonstrates that Ibn Kathīr not only reported stories but also gave them purpose. On occasion, he criticized such stories and indicated his preferences from among the different reports. The life story for Abraha continues as follows in his *tafsīr* book:

Informing the Negus that he would build him an unrivalled church in Yemen, Abraha set about the construction of a huge church in San'a. Beautifully crafted and decorated on all sides with precious stones, it was named Al-Qullays by the Arabs due to its size and astonishing beauty. Abraha's intention was that the Arabs should make their pilgrimage to his magnificent church, rather than to the Ka'ba, but some of the Arab tribes, including the Quraysh, became very offended by this and rejected the offer. One member of the Quraysh tribe travelled to the church and, entering it during the night, relieved himself then escaped unseen. On seeing such a grave insult, the custodians of the church reported it to Abraha who swore he would raze the Ka'ba down to the ground.[165] In the meantime, the Quraysh further insulted the church. Muqātil ibn Sulayman reports:

> A group of young men from the Quraysh entered the church and lit a fire on a windy day. The church was burned and collapsed to the ground. This offense infuriated Abraha more. He assembled a huge and powerful army so that none could stop him from accomplishing his goal. There was a huge elephant the like of which had never been seen before. This elephant was called Mahmud and it was sent to Abraha from the Negus, specifically for this military expedition. They aimed to use this elephant to demolish the Ka`ba. When the Arabs heard this, they felt hopeless against such an army. However, it was an obligation for them to defend the Sacred House and fight whoever intended to harm it. For this purpose, Dhu Nafr, the greatest chief from Yemen wanted to fight against Abraha. He announced that he was assembling an army of Arabs to defend the Sacred House. The people responded to him and joined his army. But Abraha defeated them easily on the first occasion, because God's Will was different. He wanted to protect the Ka'ba Himself, to honor and venerate it. The army continued on its way. It was confronted by other Arab tribes, but again Abraha defeated them and captured their leader (Nufayl ibn Habib). At the beginning, Abraha wanted to kill him, but he thought he could use him as guide to the Ka'ba. When they approached Taīf, the people of Thaqīf went to Abraha and appeased him for their idol called Al-Lāt. Abraha accepted their plea and treated them generously. In return, they gave him a man named Abū Righal as a guide. When they reached a place known as

---

[165] Ibn Kathīr, ibid.

Al-Mughammas near Mecca, they camped there. Abraha sent his troops to check the area. They captured some camels and other grazing animals of the Meccans including about two hundred camels of 'Abd al-Muttalib. After that, Abraha sent an envoy to Mecca. He asked that the leader of the Quraysh be brought to him. Abraha also asked the envoy to inform the people that he would not fight against the Quraysh unless they tried to prevent him from destroying the Ka'ba. The envoy went to the city and related the message to 'Abd al-Muttalib. Thereupon 'Abd al-Muttalib said; "By God! We have no desire to fight him, nor do we have any power to do so. This is the Sacred House of God, and the house of His confidant Abraham. If God wishes to prevent Abraha from destroying it, it is His House and His Sacred Place He can do as He wishes. However if He lets him destroy it, by God, we have no means to defend." Upon hearing this, the envoy told him that he could come with him to meet Abraha in person. 'Abd al-Muttalib accepted the offer and went with him. When Abraha saw him, he was impressed by him because 'Abd al-Muttalib was tall and handsome. Thus, he descended from his seat and sat with him on a carpet on the ground. Then he asked his translator to ask if he needs anything. 'Abd al-Muttalib replied to him; "I want my camels to be returned." Abraha was surprised with this answer and said; "I was impressed when I saw you first, but now I don't feel the same after you have spoken to me. You are asking me for your camels instead of the Sacred House which is the foundation of yours and your forefathers' religion. I have come to destroy it, but you do not speak to me about it." Upon this 'Abd al-Muttalib said; "Verily, I am the owner of the camels. As for the House, it has its Owner and He will defend it." Abraha answered in arrogance; "Nothing can stop me." 'Abd al-Muttalib said; "Do whatever you can do."[166]

Another report describes that the Tihama tribe offered Abraha a third of their wealth in return for leaving the Ka'ba unscathed, but Abraha refused their offer. Nevertheless, he returned 'Abd al-Mutallib's camels upon which 'Abd al-Muttalib returned to Mecca and ordered the residents to leave the city advising them to shelter on the mountains to be protected against the army. He then went to the Ka'ba and locked its doors, imploring God to give them victory over Abraha, supplicating; "The most important thing for anyone is the defense of his property. O my Lord! Defend Your House. They cannot defeat Your army, rather they will lose the war tomorrow." 'Abd al-Muttalib then left the Ka'ba, and joined the Meccans at the top of the mountains.[167]

---

[166] Ibn Kathīr, ibid.
[167] Ibn Kathīr, ibid.

One of the characteristics of Ibn Kathīr's *tafsīr* was to highlight the most important aspect of the story, giving a lesson to the readers. On occasion, he criticized the reports to prevent people getting a false impression whilst at other times he gave the full report to show the full picture and make the verse easier to understand. Additionally, he indicated his preference when more than one report was available. The story continues:

The following day, Abraha prepared his army to enter the sacred city and requested the elephant (Mahmud) be ready. As the army was ready to march, Nufayl ibn Habib approached the elephant, whispering into its ear; "Kneel down Mahmud! Do not go to Mecca, turn around and return to your land, because you are in the holy land of God." He then quickly left the area and escaped to the mountains. To everyone's surprise, the elephant knelt down and would not rise even when beaten. Abraha's men tried everything, treating the animal cruelly, beating it with axes and stabbing it with hooks to break its will, but nothing worked; the elephant remained kneeling. However, when they turned it towards the direction of Yemen, it stood and walked quickly. Each time they tried to turn it towards Mecca, it knelt down and would only walk in any direction other than towards Mecca. They tried to move it towards the Ka'ba several times without any success.

Whilst they were trying to persuade the elephant to march on the Ka'ba, God sent flocks of sea birds to attack Abraha and his army. Each bird carried three stones the size of chickpeas and lentils; one in each claw and one in its beak. It can be understood from the word *ababil*, translated here as birds, that this was a species unknown in the Hijaz. The birds dropped the stones on the army killing the soldiers whenever they were hit with them. The scene was one of panic and fear. The army fled asking for Nufayl to direct them home. However, Nufayl was on top of the mountain with the Quraysh observing the punishment they incurred. Even Nufayl satirized their situation saying that it was impossible for the army to flee from the One True God as He was their Pursuer; they were defeated.

Ibn Isḥāq reported that Nufayl said these lines of poetry at the time:

Didn't you live with continued support
We favored you all with a revolving eye in the morning (i.e., a guide along the way).
If you saw, but you did not see it at the side of the rock covered mountain that
which we saw. Then you will excuse me and praise my affair, and do not
grieve over what is lost between us.
I praised God when I saw the birds, and I feared that the stones might be

thrown down upon us. So all the people are asking about the whereabouts of Nufayl, as if I have some debt that I owe the Abyssinians.[168]

It is reported from Ata' ibn Yasar and others that not all the army was killed immediately in that hour of retribution; rather some of them were broken down gradually, limb by limb, whilst trying to escape. This was the case for Abraha who was broken down limb by limb until he eventually died in the land of Khath'am.[169]

Ibn Isḥāq said that as they left Mecca they were struck down and destroyed along every path and at every water spring. Abraha's body was battered and beaten with stones, his men carried him but he fell apart piece by piece until finally, on arrival in San'a, he was just like a baby chick. He did not die until his heart fell out of his chest.[170]

Ibn Isḥāq reports that when God sent Muhammad (pbuh) as His final Messenger he reminded the Quraysh of the favors He had bestowed upon them, including how He saved them from the Abyssinian attack. This victory had enabled them to remain in Mecca safely for a period of time.[171] The event became so famous in Arabian history that the year of its occurrence was named the Year of the Elephant.

The Arabs were honored with the sending of the final Prophet (pbuh) but they were unaware of this blessing. To remind them of His favor, God revealed two chapters of the Qur'ān specifically addressed to them:

Al-Fīl (The Elephant)

1. Have you considered how your Lord dealt with the people of the Elephant?
2. Did He not bring their evil scheme to nothing?
3. He sent down upon them flocks of birds (unknown in the land),
4. Shooting them with bullet-like stones of baked clay (an emblem of the punishment due to them),
5. And so He rendered them like a field of grain devoured and trampled.

Al-Quraysh

1. (At least) for (God's constant) favor of concord and security to the Quraysh,
2. Their concord and security in their winter and summer journeys,
3. Let them worship the Lord of this House (the Ka'ba),
4. Who has provided them with food against hunger, and made them safe from fear.

---

[168] Ibn Kathīr, *Tafsīr*, Surah Fīl.
[169] Ibn Kathīr, ibid.
[170] Ibn Kathīr, ibid.
[171] Ibn Kathīr, ibid.

These two chapters explain that if the Quraysh accepted the message of the Prophet (pbuh) which was sent by God, then they would continue to receive His favors.

Ibn Hishām said that *abābīl* (أَبَابِيل), which is translated as 'flocks,' is plural and that Arabs did not use its singular form. *Sijjīl* (سِجِّيل) which is translated as 'baked clay' is explained by Abū 'Ubayda as 'something solid.' Some commentators have pointed out that this word is two Persian words joined together by the Arabs to make one word; *Sanj* means stones and *Jil* means clay. The rocks are composed of these two. *'Asf* (عَصْف) is the leaves of the crops that are scattered. Ḥammad ibn Salama reports; the expression *tayran abābīl* (طَيْراً أَبَابِيلَ) is 'birds in groups.' Ibn Abbas said that *abābīl* means (groups) 'one follows another.' Hasan Basrī and Qatāda translated it as 'many.' Mujāhid interpreted *abābīl* as 'various and successive groups' and Ibn Zayd interpreted it as 'different, coming upon them from everywhere.' The famous linguist Kisai said that the singular of *abābīl* is *Ibil*. [172]

Ibn Kathīr did not analyze the words of this *surah* himself but related the opinions of early scholars. This is a main characteristic of typical *riwāyah tafsīr*. Ibn Kathīr did not engage in reason-based arguments, rather he mentioned the views of the early scholars and interpreted the verses in light of these. On occasion, he benefited from the reports in Tabarī's *tafsīr*. For example, the following report is quoted from there:

وَأَرْسَلَ عَلَيْهِمْ طَيْراً أَبَابِيلَ *He sent down upon them flocks of birds*: This verse explains that the birds came upon the army in sections just as camels march in sections in their herds. Ibn Abbas said that the birds had beaks similar to those of predatory birds and paws like a dog. Ikrimah commented that the expression *tayran abābīl* means they were green birds that came from the sea with heads like predatory animals. Ubayd ibn 'Umar said they were black birds like sea birds and had stones in their beaks and claws. Ibn Kathīr examined all these reports and found them all authentic according to hadith criteria.

Ubayd Ibn 'Umar reports:

> When God wanted to destroy the People of the Elephant, he sent birds upon them from the direction of the sea. Each bird was carrying three small stones; two stones with its feet and one stone in its beak. They gathered in a straight line over their heads and shrieked very loudly and threw what was in their claws and beaks. Every stone that fell upon the head

---

[172] Please refer to Ibn Kathīr, *Tafsīr*, Surah Fīl, for all these reports.

of any man came out of his back. Whenever a stone hit its target it came out from the other side of the body. Additionally, God sent a mighty wind to increase the speed of the stones resulting in the destruction of the army.[173]

فَجَعَلَهُمْ كَعَصْفٍ مَّأْكُولٍ *And so He rendered them like a field of grain devoured and trampled*:

Said ibn Jubayr understood this (كَعَصْفٍ مَّأْكُولٍ) to mean straw and the leaves of wheat. Makhul and Hasan Basrī interpreted it as the fodder that is given to animals. Ibn 'Abbas said; '*asf* (عَصْف) is the shell of the grain, just like the covering of wheat. Ibn Zayd explained it as the leaves of vegetation that becomes dung when defecated by the animals.

Based on the previous reports, Ibn Kathīr arrived at the following conclusion; God destroyed them and repelled them in their enmity. They could not achieve their aim, rather God destroyed them all. Only one wounded person survived to return to his native land and report what had happened; his body was split open, exposing his heart. He relayed the events to the people, and then died. Ibn Kathīr continued to give the full history of the Abyssinians to enable people to under-stand the whole picture. In this way, readers could connect both the past and pres-ent and make sense of the verses.

To demonstrate how God protects the holy city of Mecca, Ibn Kathīr mentioned the following report:

> When the Messenger (pbuh) of God approached the mountain pass that would lead him to the Quraysh on the Day of Al-Hudaybiya, his she-cam-el knelt down. Then the people attempted to make her get up but she refused. So, the people said; "Qaswa is stubborn." The Prophet (pbuh) rejected this statement saying; "Qaswa has not become stubborn, for this is not her character. Rather, she has been stopped by He Who pre-vented the Elephant of Abraha. I swear by He in Whose Hand is my soul, they (the Quraysh) will not ask me for any matter of the treaty in which the sacred things of God are honored except that I will agree with them on it." Then he beckoned the she-camel to rise and she stood up.[174]

It is reported that on the day of the conquest of Mecca, the Prophet (pbuh) said:

---

[173] Ibn Kathīr, *Tafsīr*, The interpretation of Surah Fīl.
[174] Bukhari, *Saḥīḥ, Shurut* (Conditions), 891.

Verily, God prevented the Elephant from entering Mecca but He gave temporary permission to His Messenger (pbuh) to enter it. Now its sacredness has returned just as it was sacred yesterday. So, let those who are present inform those who are absent.[175]

This is the end of the *tafsīr* of Surah Fīl, and all praise and thanks are due to God.

Ibn Kathīr concluded the interpretation of Surah Fīl with these reports from the Prophet (pbuh). He brought our attention to the sacredness of Mecca. Even the Prophet (pbuh) only had temporary permission to invade the city. By including reports such as these, Ibn Kathīr demonstrated his careful selection criteria. His main aim was to make the verses more comprehensible in the light of the most authentic reports and extract the most accurate lessons from them. In this regard, his book is one of the most reliable works of *riwāyah tafsīr*.

SUMMARY: SURAH AL-FĪL *TAFSĪR*

1. The *surah* was revealed in Mecca and describes God's favor to the Quraysh in preventing the people of the elephant from destroying the Ka'ba.

2. The *surah* is named after the word *al-Fīl* (the elephant) which is mentioned in its first verse.

3. In 571 C.E., fifty days before the birth of Prophet Muhammad (pbuh), the Abyssinians, led by Abraha, attacked Mecca with the intention of destroying the Ka'ba. God turned their plot against them, humbled them and eventually destroyed them all.

4. Ibn Kathīr explained the background of Abraha to make the verses easier for the readers to understand. This information enabled them to see the bigger picture and understand Surah Fīl better.

5. Ibn Kathīr not only reported stories but also gave them purpose.

6. On occasion he criticized such stories and indicated his preferences from among the different reports.

7. One of the characteristics of Ibn Kathīr's *tafsīr* was to highlight the most important aspect of the story, giving a lecture or lesson to the readers.

8. Additionally, he indicated his preference when more than one report was available.

9. The Arabs were honored with the sending of the final Prophet (pbuh) but they were unaware of this blessing. To remind them of His favor, God

---

[175] Bukhari, ibid.

revealed two chapters of the Qur'ān specifically addressed to them: Al-Fīl (The Elephant) and Al-Quraysh.

10. Ibn Kathīr did not analyze the words of this *surah* himself but related the opinions of early scholars.

11. Based on the previous reports, Ibn Kathīr arrived at the following conclusion; God destroyed them and repelled them in their enmity. They could not achieve their aim, rather God destroyed them all.

12. Ibn Kathīr concluded the interpretation of Surah Fīl with reports from the Prophet (pbuh) bringing attention to the sacredness of Mecca.

CHAPTER 4

Dirāyah Tafsīr
(Reason-Based Exegesis)

Introduction

The second category of *tafsīr* is reason-based *tafsīr* known as *dirāyah tafsīr* or *tafsīr bi'l ra'y* (*tafsīr* based on personal opinion). This type of *tafsīr* is not based only on the traditions reported by the Companions and Successors; it is also based on the use of reason and *ijtihād*. To better understand the Qur'anic verses, this type of exegesis utilizes knowledge of the Arabic language, poetry and other sciences in addition to the narrations.[176] The *mufassir* uses grammar, speaking styles, meanings of words and their usage in the context to shed light on Qur'anic verses. He also investigates Arab poetry, the occasions behind the revelation, the knowledge of abrogating and abrogated verses and other sciences that are necessary in interpreting the Qur'ān.[177] In *dirāyah tafsīr*, the scholars first apply to the traditions of the Prophet (pbuh) and Companions for the meaning of the verses. If unsuccessful here, they examine the verse and form their own opinion. In doing this they examine the nuances of phrasing in the language, the various linguistic connotations implied by the words and other factors.[178] The narrations of the Prophet (pbuh) and Companions are not ignored in these works; they are supplemented by the personal opinions of the *mufassir*.

The need for this form of reason-based (*dirāyah*) exegesis emerged at a time when the expansion of the Muslim world resulted in the confrontation of new issues and challenges. The conversion of non-Arabs to Islam brought a mixture of different cultures, attitudes and ideas, causing many new problems. Finding the solution to these problems required examining the Qur'ān from many different angles. Linguists interrogated it from a linguistic stance, theologs from a theological position, jurists from a legal point of view and Sufis enquired into its spiritual dimension. Each scholar approached the Qur'ān according to his own needs and perspective, resulting in many different types of exegesis. As a group, these works are known generally as *dirāyah tafsīr*.

---

[176] Ismail Cerrahoglu, *Tefsir Usulu*, 230.
[177] Dhahabī, *al-Tafsīr wa'l-Mufassirūn*, 1/255.
[178] Zarqānī, *Manāhil al-Irfān*, 1/517.

Following the many disputes witnessed by the first two centuries of Islam, the debate on the methodology of the two types of *tafsīr* (reason-based and tradition-based) emerged. Its subject was more to do with *fiqh* issues than the actual interpretation of the Qur'ān, as *fiqh* had emerged as a discipline a lot earlier. For example, Abū Ḥanīfa occasionally made juristic opinion (*istiḥsān*) and left the *qiyās* (analogy) in the favor of public benefit.

As the source of solutions to problems until the end of time, it is necessary for the Qur'ān to be continuously interpreted for its exegesis is necessary for the Muslim world. The practice of interpretation however, must be carried out with the utmost care, as interpreting the revelation is equivalent to speaking on behalf of God. The Prophet (pbuh) himself warned his community against interpreting the Qur'ān based on their own opinions without being qualified to make *tafsīr*.[179] Scholars have classified *dirāyah tafsīr* into two categories; praiseworthy and blameworthy. The first type is based on opinion that is in agreement with the sources of *tafsīr*, the rules of religion and the Arabic language. The second type is produced without proper knowledge in these areas; it is based on mere opinion and is rejected.[180] Only a scholar who fulfils strict criteria is qualified to embark on an interpretation of the Qur'ān; those who do not are considered as committing a grave sin. For *dirāyah tafsīr* to be accepted, it must meet the following conditions:[181]

- Firstly, the verse must be interpreted in the light of the Qur'ān and then in the light of the authentic Sunnah.
- It is not permissible to use weak or forged reports; authentic reports should be explained in the light of the Sunnah.
- The *mufassir* should take into consideration the interpretation of the Companions.
- The *mufassir* should avoid giving his personal opinion when the words of the verses do not support this.
- The *mufassir* should not stray from the literal meaning of the verse and should accept the interpretation that is not in conflict with the principles of Islam.
- The *mufassir* should have an intrinsic knowledge of the Arabic language and the principles of Islam and should utilize these in his interpretation.

---

[179] Tirmidhi, *Sunan, Tafsīr al-Qur'ān*, 1.
[180] Suyūṭī, *al-Tafsīr wa'l-Mufassirūn*, 1/255–256.
[181] Dhahabī, *al-Tafsīr wa'l-Mufassirūn*, 1/274–275.

- He should refrain from sectarian perspectives and from misinterpretation.
- He should abstain from interpreting such verses whose true meaning is only known by God.
- He should avoid inserting his own whims, personal desires and caprices into the interpretation.

It is clear that to interpret the Qur'ān the *mufassir* should be suitably qualified. The first chapter of this book details the sciences, criteria, principles and methods required of a *mufassir*. In general they are the knowledge of Arabic, eloquence (*balāghah*), the various readings (*qiraat*), the sciences of the Qur'ān (*muhkam-mutashābih, nāsikh-mansūkh, mutlaq-muqayyad*, etc.), the sciences of hadith[182] and, additionally, modern sciences such as sociology, phycology, astronomy, physics, chemistry, medicine, etc.

Since the beginning of Islam, the topic of the permissibility of *dirāyah tafsīr* has been a source of dispute. One group of scholars accepts it whilst the other rejects it. There were some scholars who abstained from conducting this type of interpretation and wanted to prevent others from doing so as well. However, the supporting group argued that a scholar with the necessary qualifications is permitted to use personal opinion in the interpretation of the Qur'ān. Below are the main arguments used against *dirāyah tafsīr*:

- Making *tafsīr* based on personal opinion is to speak about religious matters without sufficient knowledge and is forbidden by God: "My Lord has made unlawful ... that you speak against God the things about which you have no sure knowledge."[183] The counter argument to this is that to seek knowledge and use logical arguments to gain this knowledge is not prohibited; in the absence of definite evidence, Islamic law permits one to act upon speculative (*zannī*) evidence. The four imams of the legal schools accepted and made *ijtihād* based on speculative evidence. Before he sent Mu'adh ibn Jabal to Yemen, the Prophet (pbuh) asked him how he would judge if he encountered a problem. Thereupon he answered that he would resort to the Qur'ān first, the Sunnah second and then his personal opinion last. The Prophet (pbuh) approved his methodology and even praised him as being guided to the right path (Sunnah).[184]

---

[182] Suyūtī, *al-Itqān*, 231.
[183] Qur'ān 7: 33.
[184] Abū Dāwud, *Sunan, Kitāb al-Aqdiya*, 3585.

- In informing us that the Prophet (pbuh) has the authority to explain the Qur'ān, God implicitly informed us that anyone else was prohibited from such an act:

> (We sent them with) clear proofs of the truth and Scriptures. And on you We have sent down the Reminder (the Qur'ān) so that you may make clear to humankind whatever is sent down to them (through you of the truth concerning their present and next life), and that they may reflect.[185]

The counter argument to this is that the verse does not mean that the Prophet (pbuh) has the exclusive permission to explain the Qur'ān. There are many verses which the Prophet (pbuh) made no comment about, therefore it is the duty of Muslim scholars to explain them; this is indicated by the ending of the verse; 'they may reflect' meaning that Muslims must try to understand it.

- Some hadith clearly prohibit Muslims from interpreting the Qur'ān based on their own personal opinion, for example; "whoever interprets the Qur'ān based on his/her personal opinion better prepare his seat in Hell"[186] and "whoever speaks about the Qur'ān without evidence is wrong even if he tells the truth."[187] According to some scholars, these hadiths prove that it is not permissible to make *tafsīr* based on personal opinion. The counter argument is that the Prophet (pbuh) strictly forbade interpreting the Qur'ān without being suitably qualified, however, once one is qualified it is not forbidden,[188] It is in fact a duty upon Muslims to understand it according to their time and conditions, for the Qur'ān is the eternal speech of God.

- Many reports clearly demonstrate the Companions and early scholars, out of fear, were reluctant to interpret the Qur'ān.[189] This is partially true; some Companions did refrain from making *tafsīr* but there are many examples of others interpreting the Qur'ān. For example, Abū Bakr interpreted some verses disclaiming; "If the interpretation is true it is from God, if not it is from me and Satan."[190] Additionally, the Prophet (pbuh) himself supplicat-

---

[185] Qur'ān 16: 44.

[186] Tirmidhi, *Sunan, Tafsīr al-Qur'ān*, 1.

[187] Tirmidhi, ibid.

[188] Dhahabī, *al-Tafsīr wa'l-Mufassirūn*, 1/258–259.

[189] Baghawī, *Meālim al-Tanzīl*, 1/35; Dhahabī, *al-Tafsīr wa'l-Mufassirīn*, 1/260.

[190] Baghawī, *Meālim al-Tanzīl*, 1/403.

ed God to endow Ibn Abbas with knowledge to interpret the Qur'ān.[191] We can see from these evidences that it is permissible to make *dirāyah tafsīr* if the necessary qualifications have been achieved.

The most famous *dirāyah tafsīr* are;

- Fakhr al-Dīn al-Rāzī (d. 1209 C.E.), *Mafātih ul-Ghayb (Tafsīr al-Kabīr).*
- Qādi Baydāwī (d. 1288 C.E.), *Anwar al-Tanzīl wa Asrār al-Ta'wil.*
- Nasafī (d. 1310 C.E.), *Madārik al-Tanzīl wa'l-Haqāiq al-Ta'wil.*
- Hāzin (d. 1340 C.E.), *Lubab al-Ta'wil fi Ma'an al-Tanzīl.*
- Abu Hayyan (d. 1344 C.E.), *Bahr al-Muhīt.*

INTRODUCTION: *DIRĀYAH TAFSĪR* (REASON-BASED *TAFSĪR*)

1. *Dirāyah tafsīr* is based on the traditions reported by the Companions and Successors and on the use of reason and *ijtihād*.
2. It utilizes knowledge of the Arabic language, poetry and other sciences in addition to the narrations.
3. Scholars first apply to the traditions of the Prophet (pbuh) and Companions for the meaning of the verses. If unsuccessful here, they examine the verses and form their own opinion.
4. This need for reason-based exegesis emerged when the expanding Muslim world began to confront new issues and challenges and interpretation of the Qur'ān was required to find solutions.
5. Different scholars from different disciplines interpreted the Qur'ān from many different angles and collectively these works are known as *dirāyah tafsīr*.
6. Following the many disputes witnessed by the first two centuries of Islam, the debate on the methodology of the two types of *tafsīr* (reason-based and tradition-based) emerged.
7. Scholars have classified *dirāyah tafsīr* into two categories; praiseworthy and blameworthy.
8. For *dirāyah tafsīr* to be accepted, it must meet strict conditions.
9. Since the beginning of Islam, the topic of the permissibility of *dirāyah tafsīr* has been a source of dispute. The following are the main arguments used against *dirāyah tafsīr* each of which can be countered:
   a) Making *tafsīr* based on personal opinion is to speak about religious matters without sufficient knowledge and is forbidden by God.

---

[191] Dhahabī, *al-Tafsīr wa'l-Mufassirīn*, I/262–263.

b) In informing us that the Prophet (pbuh) has the authority to explain the Qur'ān, God implicitly informed us that anyone else was prohibited from such an act.

c) Some hadith clearly prohibit Muslims from interpreting the Qur'ān based on their own personal opinion.

d) Many reports clearly demonstrate the Companions and early scholars, out of fear, were reluctant to interpret the Qur'ān.

Fakhr al-Dīn Rāzī and His *Tafsīr*

His Life and Education

Muhammad ibn 'Amr al-Husain ibn Ali al-Qureshi al-Taymi al-Tabaristani, (d. 1209 C.E.) was born in Ray in 1149 C.E. A profound scholar, he was famous in the areas of theology, philosophy, grammar, science, logic, commentary, maths, astronomy and physics. His profound knowledge earned him the title of Fakhr al-Din al-Rāzī (the praised of the religion). He produced works in every field and was a source of inspiration for many scholars.

Rāzī was first educated by his father, Diya al-Din, an expert in *Kalām*. To complete his education, he travelled to many cities renowned for their centers of knowledge. In Kharizm (in central Asia) he debated with Mutazalite[192] scholars, opposing their doctrines and defending the Sunni position, eventually being driven out of the city. He went to Bukhara, Samarkand, Gazna and the cities of India. He was always treated with respect, but in Bukhara the opposing group stirred people against him and he was forced to leave the city.

His extraordinary intellect enabled him to learn many different sciences in a short time and produce works in each field. For him the most honorable science was *Kalām* because it introduces God to humankind with His Names, Attributes and Essential Qualities. The influence of his father imbued in him a great passion for *Kalām* and he memorized many books in this field. He was well versed in the history of religious sects and was able to distinguish between false and accurate information in this area. Although he knew Ghazali well and appreciated his knowledge, he occasionally criticized him. Rāzī learned Islamic philosophy and used it when necessary.

---

[192] It is an Islamic school of theology based on reason and rational thought that flourished in the cities of Basra and Baghdad during the 8th–10th centuries.

Rāzī began his scholarly career in poverty but when he died at 63 he was at the height of his fame having authored more than 100 books and gained prestige for his scholarship and debating skills. He often presented moderate approaches before refuting the opposing views. He died in 1210 C.E. on the first day of Eid al-Fitr (at the end of Ramadan). It is reported that he was poisoned by a follower of the Karramiyya[193]sect.[194]

His *Tafsīr*

Rāzī's book '*Tafsīr al-Kabīr*' or '*Mafātih al-Ghayb*' is one of the most comprehensive in the field of reason-based (*dirāyah*) *tafsīr* and covers many areas including some beyond the scope of *tafsīr*. This was criticized by some scholars who remarked that his *tafsīr* included everything along with the interpretation of the Qur'ān.[195] However, he was very influential on the following generations and we can observe that just as Tabarī's *tafsīr* was the peak of the *riwāyah* (narration-based) *tafsīr*, Rāzī's *tafsīr* was the best example of a *dirāyah* (reason-based) *tafsīr*. Although it is a reason-based *tafsīr*, Rāzī also included many narrations in his work. This is indicative of the time and vibrant educational environment when scholars engaged in many sciences including *tafsīr, uṣūl, fiqh*, hadith, *Kalām*, philosophy and logic. Rāzī utilized all these sciences in his interpretations of the verses, following the methodology of both *Kalām* and philosophy however, he later confessed that the wisdom extracted from the Qur'ān itself is above anything else.[196]

Rāzī often debated against materialist and naturalist scholars, challenging them on every possible occasion. He worked to bring attention to the wisdom contained in the Qur'ān and encouraged people in this regard. At the beginning of his work, when he interpreted Surah Fatiha, he explained his methodology, and then followed it for the rest of his *tafsīr*. He approaches each chapter of the Qur'ān as if it is a separate book, interpreting it in detail. He also mentions his debates and travels and occasionally dates the chapters when the interpretation is completed. This led to confusion amongst scholars, some of whom claimed he

---

[193] Karrāmiyya is a sect that takes its name from a man named Muhammad ibn Karrām al-Sijistānī. An ascetic given to a life of abstinence; his ideology is that of God being a body, which will be visible in the hereafter, and that the Qur'ān is uncreated.

[194] For more information about his life, education and books please refer to; Subkī, *Tabaqāt Shāfi'iyya*, 8/81–96; Ibn Hallikān, *Wafayāt al-A'yān*, 3/381–385; Suyūtī, *Tabaqāt al-Mufassirīn*, 39; Dhahabī, *Mizan al-I'tidal*, 2/324; Ibn Ḥajar, *Lisān al-Mizan*, 4/426–429.

[195] Ibn Hallikān, *Wafayāt al-A'yān*, 3/381–385.

[196] Ibn Kathīr, *al-Bidāya wa'l-Nihāya*, 13/55.

did not complete the work alone.[197] This view, however, is not sound. Rāzī's motivation for his work was to defend the Qur'ān using logic against the attacks aimed at it.[198] During his lifetime, there was much political and social upheaval and this led him to write his *tafsīr*. In his opinion the Ash'arī sect is better than the Mutazalite and this feature is the general tone of his book.

Some of the characteristics of his *tafsīr* are:

Each *surah* is approached as a separate book containing many chapters. His interpretations reflect this containing many divisions and subdivisions. Different matters are discussed in each chapter and each contains prefaces, evidences, wisdom, legal rules and views. His *tafsīr* covers legal issues, logical arguments, linguistic details and theological matters, thus readers move from one discipline to another. At times, Rāzī digresses completely from exegesis and falls into discussion of deep topics, particularly in the field of *Kalām*. However, he extracted his theological views from the Qur'ān and always used methodical and logical arguments. His view was critical of the Mutazalite and other non-Sunni schools of thought but was always based on reasoned arguments.

Rāzī often discussed moral issues and extracted lessons from the stories of pious people mentioned in the Qur'ān to bring peoples' focus to its main purpose. His methodology was to explain the different views and their arguments before critically analyzing them. Then he would make his preference amongst them and giving the reason for this, supported by evidence. He emphasized important concepts, mentioning them several times in different places in his work. He also gave the opinions of previous exegetes in order to inform the readers about their views.[199]

When interpreting a verse, Rāzī investigated the Qur'ān first to see whether it held the explanation in another verse; he mentioned the benefits of this approach in *tafsīr*.[200] He used logical arguments without hesitation by relying on the principles of *uṣūl*, believing that using reason and authentic reports (the Qur'ān and authentic Sunnah) is not contradictory because both come from the same source. He provided many examples and arguments to support his claim.

It is essential for *mufassir* to have a profound knowledge of the interpretations of the Companions and Successors and Rāzī was no different; he applied the same method in his *tafsīr* greatly emphasizing their opinions, particularly relat-

---

[197] Dhahabī, *al-Tafsīr wa'l-Mufassirīn*, 1/292–296.

[198] Rāzī, *Tafsīr al-Kabīr*, 13/46–56.

[199] Rāzī, *Tafsīr*, 7/6–8.

[200] Rāzī, ibid, 14/117.

ing to the literal meaning of words, the occasions behind the revelations, and the various readings and their rules. He preferred the interpretations of Ibn 'Abbas above all others and related from him the original meanings of words, the stories, the occasions behind certain verses and matters on various readings.[201] Where two reports from Ibn 'Abbas contradicted each other, he would reconcile them or prefer one of them. If, however, the report was against logic or historical fact, he criticized and rejected it.[202] Rāzī was critical of the use of *Isra'iliyyat* sources claiming they were unreliable due to the weakness in their authenticity and he rejected all the *Isra'iliyyat* reports ascribed to Ibn 'Abbas.[203] Rāzī also related from other Companions and Successors and applied the same methodology in terms of accepting or rejecting them.

In his work, Rāzī frequently makes linguistic analysis, referring to the famous linguist, Farrā; at times criticizing his views if they do not have a sound basis.[204] Despite the fact that he rarely mentioned Tabarī in his *tafsīr* Rāzī accepted him and benefited from the many reports of the Companions and Successors contained in his work. Being Ash'arī he also greatly benefitted from Ash'arī sources, particularly in debates relating to theological matters. One of the most important personalities Rāzī benefitted from with regard to linguistic matters was Kaffāl (d. 976 C.E.), although he did not rely on him for theological matters.[205] He also benefitted from the works of al-Ghazali and the Mutazalite scholars. When relating the Mutazalite views he utilized the work of Ali al-Jubbāī, criticizing his views and refuting them with logical arguments.[206]

Rāzī was the first exegete to highlight the importance of the thematic unity between the verses and passages of the Qur'ān. He emphasized the interrelationships between the verses and chapters, showing how each part of the Qur'ān supports and completes the other parts and reasoning that it is necessary to approach it as a whole.[207] He severely criticised the exegetes who ignore this in their interpretation.

Rāzī paid great attention to the sciences and frequently gave detailed scientific interpretations; for example, he explained some verses according to astron-

---

[201] Rāzī, *Tafsīr*, 20/ 34; 24/227–228.

[202] Rāzī, ibid, 14/199.

[203] Rāzī, ibid, 2/219–220.

[204] Rāzī, ibid, 13/107.

[205] Muhammad Rashid Rıza, *Tafsīr al-Manār*, 4/16.

[206] Rāzī, ibid, 5/81–82.

[207] Rāzī, ibid, 2/153.

omy arguments.[208] Some scholars have criticised him for focusing so much on science and following a different methodology in his *tafsīr*, however, the criticism is not valid, as many of the scientific wisdoms contained within the Qur'ān cannot be explained without resorting to science. Rāzī used scientific arguments to explain some verses and even tried to give rational explanations for the miracles in the Qur'ān.[209]

SUMMARY: FAKHR AL-DIN AL-RĀZĪ AND HIS *TAFSĪR*

1. Born in Ray in 1149 C.E. Fakhr al-Din al-Rāzī ('the praised of the religion') was a profound scholar, famous in theology, philosophy, grammar, science, logic, commentary, maths, astronomy and physics.

2. Rāzī was first educated by his father, Diya al-Din, and then in many cities; in debates he defended the Sunni position.

3. His extraordinary intellect enabled him to learn many different sciences in a short time and produce works in each field.

4. Rāzī began his scholarly career in poverty but when he died at 63 he was at the height of his fame.

5. Rāzī's book '*Tafsīr al-Kabīr*' is one of the most comprehensive in the field of reason-based (*dirāyah*) *tafsīr*.

6. Although it is a reason-based *tafsīr*, Rāzī also included many narrations in his work.

7. He often debated against materialist and naturalist scholars, challenging them on every possible occasion.

8. He approaches each chapter of the Qur'ān as if it is a separate book, interpreting it in detail.

9. At times Rāzī digresses completely from exegesis and falls into discussion of deep topics, particularly in the field of *Kalām*.

10. Rāzī often discussed moral issues and extracted lessons from the stories of pious people mentioned in the Qur'ān to bring peoples' focus to its main purpose.

11. When interpreting a verse, Rāzī investigated the Qur'ān first to see whether it held the explanation in another verse.

12. He used logical arguments without hesitation by relying on the principles of *uṣūl*.

---

[208] Rāzī, ibid, 31/158–159.
[209] Rāzī, ibid, 13/94.

13. He preferred the interpretations of Ibn 'Abbas above all others.

14. Rāzī was critical of the use of *Isra'iliyyat* sources claiming they were unreliable due to the weakness in their authenticity.

15. In his work, Rāzī frequently makes linguistic analysis.

16. Rāzī was the first exegete to highlight the importance of the thematic unity between the verses and passages of the Qur'ān.

17. Rāzī paid great attention to the sciences and frequently gave detailed scientific interpretations.

SURAH QURAYSH

بِسْمِ اللهِ الرَّحْمٰنِ الرَّحِيمِ

لِإِيلَافِ قُرَيْشٍ ﴿١﴾ إِيلَافِهِمْ رِحْلَةَ الشِّتَاءِ وَالصَّيْفِ ﴿٢﴾ فَلْيَعْبُدُوا رَبَّ هٰذَا الْبَيْتِ ﴿٣﴾ الَّذِي أَطْعَمَهُمْ مِنْ جُوعٍ وَآمَنَهُمْ مِنْ خَوْفٍ ﴿٤﴾

Surah Quraysh

In the Name of God, the All-Merciful, the All-Compassionate

1. (At least) for (God's constant) favor of concord and security to the Quraysh,

2. Their concord and security in their winter and summer journeys,

3. Let them worship the Lord of this House (the Ka'ba),

4. Who has provided them with food against hunger, and made them safe from fear.

Tafsīr

This four-verse *surah* was revealed in Mecca[210] and gives information about the favors that God has bestowed on the Quraysh.

لِإِيلَافِ قُرَيْشٍ *(At least) for (God's constant) favor of concord and security to the Quraysh.*

The Arabic particle *lam* اللام at the beginning of this verse "لإيلاف" (concord and security) has a few points that need to be noted:

1- This partical may be connected to the previous *surah* (Fīl).

2- Or, it is connected to the verses after it.

3- Or, it is not connected to the previous *surah* nor the verse after it.

---

[210] Fakhr al-Din Rāzī, *Mafātih al-Ghayb (Tafsīr al-Kabīr)*, 23/423.

If, according to the first view, it is connected with the previous *surah* (Fīl), it has three possible meanings:

First; Zajjāj and Abū 'Ubayda hold that this particle is connected to the previous *surah* and interpret it as meaning; for the security of the Quraysh God rendered them (Abraha and his army) like a field of grain, devoured and trampled. To enable the Quraysh to continue their journeys in summer and winter without fear, God destroyed the army of the elephant. Having related an opinion, Rāzī follows it with his own opinion, showing that he does not follow any scholars blindly; rather he makes his own critical analysis of their opinions and accepts or rejects them accordingly. If one claims that God destroyed the Abyssinian army (army of the elephant) because of their disbelief rather than for the security of the Quraysh, they are wrong. Rāzī refutes this claim with the following arguments:[211]

- The punishment for disbelief is postponed until Judgment Day. God would have to punish all unbelievers if He punished the army for their disbelief and this was not the case. The following two verses support this view:

  On that Day every soul will be recompensed for what it has earned; no wrong (will be done to any) on that Day. God is Swift at reckoning[212]

  If God were to take people immediately to task for their wrongdoings, He would not leave on it (the earth) any living creature (as the wrongdoings of humankind would make the earth uninhabitable). But He grants them respite to a term appointed (by Him). When their term has come, they can neither delay it by a single moment, nor can they bring it forward.[213]

  It is clear that God destroyed the people of the elephant to maintain the security of the Quraysh to enable them to understand that God honored them.

- Punishment is not the only method to deter unbelievers from their disbelief. There are other means to achieve this so it is not correct to accept one possibility above others without supporting this view with evidence.

- Even if the army of the elephant had been destroyed due to their disbelief, this does not conflict with the idea that the punishment was a favor for the Quraysh to maintain their security. We can compare this with the case of Moses; "then the family of Pharaoh picked him up only to be an adver-

---

[211] Rāzī, *Mafātih al-Ghayb*, 23/423.
[212] Qur'ān 40: 17.
[213] Qur'ān 16: 61.

sary and a source of grief for them."[214] Pharaoh's intention in taking in the child was not to raise an enemy, however, that was the result.

Rāzī uses Qur'anic verses to support his arguments, demonstrating that logic is subservient to the Qur'ān.

Second; the Arabic particle lam (اللام) may give the meaning; whatever We (God) did it was all for the Quraysh and for their safety. We destroyed them (the army of the elephant), so the Quraysh can travel safely in winter and summer.

Third; the particle *lam* (اللام) is used with the meaning of the particle *ilā* (إلى) which changes the meaning to; prior to the favor of concord and security during their winter and summer journeys, God bestowed on the Quraysh other favors and this is mentioned in the previous *surah* as the destruction of the people of the elephant.

If the particle *'lam'* (اللام) is connected to the previous *surah*, there are two other views on the intended meaning;[215]

a) Some scholars hold that Fīl and Quraysh are both parts of the same *surah* and they present the following arguments as evidence to support this view;

   - Each of the Qur'anic *surahs* is a separate entity, not relying on the preceding or following *surah*; however, these *surahs* are connected to each other for the beginning of Quraysh is related to the end of Fīl, and this shows that they are indeed one *surah*.
   - 'Ubay ibn Ka'b wrote these *surah* as one *surah* in his personal *Muṣḥāf* (personal handwritten copy of the Qur'ān)
   - Umar ibn al-Khattāb recited 'Surah Tin' in the first *rak'ah* of the Maghrib prayer and these two *surahs* (Fīl and Quraysh) in the second *rak'ah* without separating their recitation with *basmala*.[216]

b) The majority of scholars hold that the two *surahs* are separate. Whilst there is definitely a connection between the two, this is also the case for all the *surahs* of the Qur'ān; therefore, the previous arguments cannot be valid. It is not permissible for the personal transcriptions of Qur'ān to be given priority as evidence against the majority and the official Qur'ān. Finally, reciting *basmala* is controversial issue between the legal schools and according to majority; it is not recited to separate the *surahs*. There-

---

[214] Qur'ān 28: 8.
[215] Rāzī, *Tafsīr*, 23/425–426.
[216] Rāzī, *Tafsīr*, 23/426.

fore the argument that 'Umar recited them together in his prayer is not strong evidence.

After discussing different opinions, Rāzī explains that God destroyed the people of the elephant for the concord and security of the Quraysh. Mecca is situated in a desert valley whose land cannot be cultivated. When Prophet Abraham left his wife and child there, he supplicated God:

> Our Lord! I have settled some of my offspring (Ishmael and his descendants) in an uncultivable valley near Your Sacred House, so that, our Lord, they may establish the Prayer; so make the hearts of people incline towards them, and provide them with the produce of earth, so that they may give thanks.[217]

For the Quraysh and others in Mecca it was necessary to travel to different lands to trade and provide the basic needs for the Meccan residents. In their business transactions, they made great profit and were treated with respect by the kings surrounding Mecca. They would say of them; "The Quraysh are the residents of the holy land, the neighbors of God's House and the rulers of the Ka'ba."[218] They were in fact, known as the household of God. If the Abyssinians had succeeded in destroying the Ka'ba it would have ended the respect for the Quraysh, resulting in their eviction from Mecca and loss of security for their lives, property and families. In destroying the people of the elephant, God saved the Quraysh from the evil consequences and strengthened the respect of the other Arab tribes had towards them. He also proved His protection of Mecca and its residents increasing their honor and business amongst the Arab tribes. For this reason, God reminded the Quraysh of His favors and invited them to thank Him.

Another argument that supports this view is the verse at the end of this *surah*; "let them worship the Lord of this House (the Ka'ba)."[219] The intended meaning of this verse is: worship the Lord of this House that the people of the elephant wanted to destroy but God protected it. For your security and safety, the Lord of this House prevented the army of the Abyssinians from achieving their aim.

The second view about the particle 'lam' اللام in the word '*liīlaf* لإيلَٰف'; The famous linguists, Khalil and Sibawayh hold that this particle connects the verse to the verb "let them worship the Lord" فَلْيَعْبُدُوا resulting in the meaning; the Quraysh must worship the Lord of this House for their own safety and security.

---

[217] Qur'ān 14: 37.
[218] Rāzī, *Tafsīr*, 23/427.
[219] Qur'ān 106: 3.

In other words, they should perform their worship as a result of God's favors upon them. If one asks why there is the particle 'faa' (الفاء) in the word of God فَلْيَعْبُدُوا the answer for it is that it is used to mean 'condition.' It gives the meaning 'God has granted them many favors; if they ignore all other favors, they should at least worship Him for the sake of this clear favor.'[220]

The third view about the particle 'lam' اللام is that it is not related to the verses before or after it. Zajjāj explained that some scholars claim this particle means astonishment, making the meaning of the verse; 'how astonishing is the safety and security of the Quraysh!'[221] Despite the increasing paganism amongst the Quraysh that led to ignorance and deviation, God maintained His protection of them saving them from calamity and increasing their wealth. It is astonishing that God tolerated such disbelief and continued to shower His Mercy on them. Kisaī, Ahfash and Farrā also hold the same view.[222]

Scholars mentioned three opinions about the word 'iīlaf' إيلَف:

1) The word means the same as al-ilf الإلف which is familiarity and concord. There are various readings of this word but they all share the same meaning that God favored the Quraysh with security and concord in their journeys ensuring they could continually travel for the purpose of trade.

2) The word means 'to like a place for living' or 'to be familiar with that area,' or 'inspiration of God to a person to love a place so he/she could not leave it.' Situated in a desert with no means of supporting itself, Mecca was a difficult place to live; however, God warmed the hearts of the people towards Mecca so they did not leave it. This was a favor of God for the Quraysh. This is similar to the meaning of the following verses; "He has attuned their (the believers') hearts"[223] and "He reconciled your hearts so that through His favor you became like brothers."[224] Sometimes the love for a place or for a person brings familiarity and concord. The love of Meccan people for their city was increased even further after God had destroyed the army of the elephant.

3) The word, 'iīlaf' إيلَف, means to be prepared and get ready; this is the view of Farrā and Ibn Arābī. They hold that the verse means; 'in order to be

---

[220] Rāzī, Tafsīr, 23/428.

[221] Rāzī, ibid.

[222] Rāzī, Tafsīr, 23/426–428.

[223] Qur'ān 8: 63.

[224] Qur'ān 3: 103.

prepared for the journeys in summer and winter and perform them continuously.'[225]

Discussion of the repetition of 'iīlaf' (إيلاف); this word is used generally in the first instance and then with a specific meaning in the second instance. The first, general usage is when God reminds the Quraysh of His great favor of concord and security which results in peace, security, solidarity and friendship amongst them. The second usage refers specifically to the favor of concord and security in relation to their summer and winter journeys. These two journeys were of significant importance in maintaining their livelihood. This verse is similar to the following verse in terms of expression and methodology; "whoever is an enemy to God, and His angels, and His Messengers, and (so) Gabriel, and Michael, (should know that) God is surely an enemy to the unbelievers."[226] This verse uses 'His Messengers" as a general expression and then mentions Gabriel and Michael as specific examples.

The omission of a connecting particle (atf) between the two 'iīlaf' shows that the favor is a gift from God, rather than a result of their free will and achievement. This implies that they had no choice but to accept this favor. This is similar to the favor mentioned in the following verse; "God bound them (the believers) to the Word of faith, piety, and reverence for God."[227] There are two types of compulsory favor: that which prevents someone from harm and that which provides benefit. The word 'iīlaf' includes both types of favors upon the Quraysh.[228]

قُرَيْش The Quraysh;

Scholars all agreed that the Quraysh are the progeny of Nadr ibn Kinana. The Prophet (pbuh) said; "We are the offspring of Nadr ibn Kinana, we do not deny our mother or say we are not related to our father."[229] Scholars for the derivation of the name Quraysh give the following explanations:

- Quraysh is derived from the word al-qirsh القرش and it is the diminutive form of this word (ism tasghir, a diminutive form of a name).[230] Al-qirsh is big fish (probably a shark) in the sea. Ibn Abbas said; "It is a fish which eats

---

[225] Rāzī, Tafsīr, 23/428.
[226] Qur'ān 2: 98.
[227] Qur'ān 48: 26.
[228] Rāzī, Tafsīr, 23/429.
[229] Ibn Mājah, Sunan, Hudud, 37.
[230] Ism tasghir is a grammar rule in Arabic and it is used to make a name diminutive.

others but is not eaten by them, it has sovereignty over others but none has sovereignty over it."[231] As the Quraysh held the responsibility of Islam, this name was given to honor them.

- This word is derived from *al-qursh* (القرش) which means earning, because the Quraysh earned money from their business trips to other cities.
- Lays said; the Quraysh were previously scattered outside of the holy land. Qusay ibn Kilāb gathered them together into the Haram (Mecca) to reside together. They were given the name Quraysh because *taqarrush* in Arabic means 'come together.'[232]
- They were called Quraysh because they provided the needs of the pilgrims and helped the poor.

Rāzī gave the different opinions on the derivation of the word Quraysh, but he did not indicate a preference from among them, showing that he was not convinced of which view was more accurate.

رِحْلَةَ الشِّتَاء وَالصَّيْفِ, *their winter and summer journeys; This verse raises several issues that warrant discussion.*

Lays said; رِحْلَةَ *'rihla'* (journey) is a term used for the movement of a tribe. There are two views pertaining to the meaning of it in this verse:

1) According to a well-known source, the interpreters related; every year, the Quraysh used to travel to Yemen in the winter and Damascus in the summer because in those days the weather conditions were more favorable. Ata relates from Ibn Abbas:

> Whenever a person from the Quraysh was struck by famine and starvation, he would go to a place with his family and wait in a tent until death. This situation continued until Hāshim ibn Abd Manaf appeared. He was the leader of his tribe and had a son named Asad. Asad had a friend his age from the tribe of Banī Makhzum. One day, his friend complained of extreme hunger and explained his miserable situation. Upon hearing this, Asad went to his mother crying and then the mother sent them some flour and oil. This nourishment helped them for a couple days. However, the child from Banī Makhzum went to Asad again and complained about famine. This time, Hāshim ibn Abd Manaf went to the Quraysh and addressed them; 'you settled in a land which has no cultivation. Hence, you live a miserable life here. But we are the people of Haram and the most honorable among human kind.' They replied;

---

[231] Rāzī, *Tafsīr*, 23/429–430.
[232] Rāzī, ibid, 23/430.

'we will follow you without any disobedience.' As a result, Abd Manaf brought them together to make business trips to Yemen in winter and to Damascus in summer.[233]

Abd Manaf used some of the wealth of the rich residents to ease the suffering of the poor, enabling them to live better lives. Whilst they were living this way, Islam was revealed to them. The Quraysh were the richest among all Arabs and the most honorable. However, if the people of the elephant had succeeded in destroying the Ka'ba, they would have lost this position of respect, as is made clear in the following verse; "We have split them up on the earth as separate communities."[234] It is preferable for people of the same tribe to live together in one place, rather than mixing with other tribes as this will prevent disputes between them. The members of one tribe are also more likely to get on with one another during a journey. For a journey to be successful, it is essential that the travelers have a good relationship between them, as stated in the verse; "Whoever undertakes the duty of *Hajj* in them, there is no sensual indulgence, nor wicked conduct, nor disputing during the *Hajj*."[235] Good relations and manners are even more necessary when undertaking a journey than when residing in a place.

2) The other opinion is that the meaning of journey in the verse is the settlement of the Quraysh in Mecca. In this sense, the winter and summer journeys refer to the pilgrimages, *'Umrah* during the month of Rajab and *Hajj* in the month of Dhu'l Hijja. The Quraysh enjoyed the benefits associated with the pilgrims who undertook these journeys and these would have been lost if the people of the elephant had achieved their aims.[236]

فَلْيَعْبُدُوا رَبَّ هَذَا الْبَيْتِ *Let them worship the Lord of this House;*[237]

There are two ways in which a favor can be bestowed upon the people; a) preventing harm from them and b) providing some kind of benefit to them. The first form of favor is the most important and takes priority over the second. Scholars hold that it is obligatory to prevent harm from creatures but it is not obligatory to provide them with benefits; for this reason, the favor of preventing harm

---

[233] Rāzī, ibid, 23/431–432.
[234] Qur'ān 7: 168.
[235] Qur'ān 2: 197.
[236] Rāzī, *Tafsīr*, 23/431.
[237] Qur'ān 106: 3.

is mentioned first in Surah Fīl whilst the favor of providing benefit is mentioned later in Surah Quraysh.

Once people is reminded to be thankful to the One who bestows favors, God highlighted the servanthood; "Let them worship the Lord of this House."[238] This verse raises a couple of issues that need to be discussed:

First issue; worship is performed with great humility, reverence and respect. Some scholars hold that the meaning of worship here is *tawḥīd* (emphasizing on the unity of God), because He is the One who protects the Ka'ba not the idols. *Tawḥīd* is the key to all kinds of worship. Others understood worship in this context to mean the type of worship that is performed by each limb in different forms. However, it is not correct to specify and limit the definition of worship; it is in the general form and covers all kinds of worship.

The other explanation of this verse could be; let them abandon their summer and winter journeys and instead spend their time worshipping the Lord of this House because it is He who provides them with food against hunger and makes them safe from fear. The use of the word *Rabb* (the Lord) here, confirms and reminds about the words they spoke to Abraha; "There is a Lord of this House and He will protect it."[239] At that time, they did not trust the idols, rather they only trusted God and He reminded them this fact and invited them to worship Him alone. Therefore, the intended meaning of the verse would be; 'because you trust and rely on Me to protect the House you must also worship Me and serve Me alone.'[240]

Second issue; in the verse, God ascribes Himself to the House, conveying onto it honor and prestige. There are instances in the Qur'ān where God ascribes the servants to him as 'My servants'[241] and other occasions where He ascribes Himself to His servants as 'your Lord.'[242] Similarly, God sometimes ascribes Himself to the House, as in this verse, and at other times, He ascribes the House to Him, for example; "clean My House."[243]

الَّذِي أَطْعَمَهُمْ مِنْ جُوعٍ وَآمَنَهُمْ مِنْ خَوْفٍ *Who has provided them with food against hu - ger, and made them safe from fear;*[244]

---

[238] Rāzī, *Tafsīr*, 23/432.
[239] Rāzī, *Tafsīr*, 23/432.
[240] Rāzī, ibid.
[241] Qur'ān 29: 56.
[242] Qur'ān 2: 163.
[243] Qur'ān 2: 125.
[244] Qur'ān 106: 4.

There are different ways of describing the mention of food in this verse:

- God protected the Ka'ba, His holy land, making it safe for the Quraysh. As a result of this favor, they were able to make their summer and winter journeys to trade; thereby, God gave them the opportunity to feed themselves.

- Muqātil said;[245] the Quraysh struggled to make their journeys to Yemen and Damascus in winter and summer to obtain supplies including food. God inspired in the hearts of the Abyssinians to ship their food exports to Jeddah, which was an easy two-day journey by camel from Mecca. This was an example of God's favor upon them and shows that He provided them with food against hunger.

- Kalbī interpreted the verse as follows; when the Quraysh denied the message of Prophet Muhammad (pbuh) he supplicated God saying; "O God! Set these years upon them like the years of Yusuf (Joseph)."[246] Following this prayer, the Quraysh suffered from famine and starvation and they beseeched the Prophet (pbuh) to implore God for a reprieve. The Prophet (pbuh) heeded their calls and prayed to God to remove this calamity; the famine ended and abundance returned. Kalbī views that the verse is related to this incidence.[247]

There are few questions that need to be answered here;

First question, whilst worship is obligatory upon the servants for the favors that have been bestowed upon them by God, the providence of food is not one of these favors. However, compulsory worship is connected here to the provision of food, why?

Answer; There are different answers to this question:

- God reminded the Quraysh of the favor He bestowed in destroying the army of Abraha and foiling his plan to raze the Ka'ba to the ground. In doing this, He ensured their safety and security in Mecca. However, the Quraysh then asked; 'now we are commanded to worship the Lord. If we are busy with worship who will provide food for us?' To which God replied; would the One who provided food before you started worshipping not continue to provide it after you worship?

---

[245] Rāzī, *Tafsīr*, 23/433.

[246] Bukhari, *Saḥīḥ*, *Tafsīr*, 44.

[247] Rāzī, *Tafsīr*, 23/433.

- Despite the disobedience of His servants, even after all the favors they received, He continued to provide them with food. Therefore, even if they were not ashamed of disobeying God's commands, surely they should be ashamed of accepting His provision after they have chosen the path of disbelief.
- God mentioned His favors to remind them that even an animal obeys its owner who provides it with food; they are not lower than animals.[248]

Second question; God said; "...it is He who created all that is in the world for you."[249] If everything in the world was created for the servants and the earth is their property, why are they kept under obligation by being reminded with the favors of God?

Rāzī gives the following answer for this question: if one considers the stages before eating food and the benefits after eating, he will understand the value of this favor. God not only provides the food, He creates the conditions necessary for its production and the biological mechanisms necessary for digestioneHe. Therefore, by reminding us of His favors, God explains why He is the only One who deserves to be worshipped.

Third question; It is not good manners to keep someone under obligation after feeding him, however, God reminds His servants that it is He who feeds them; how this can be explained?

Rāzī's answer for this is that the reminder is not intended to humiliate the servants, rather its purpose is to guide them towards gratitude to God. The physical benefits derived from eating and drinking, in the form of energy, should be utilized in ways that serve God rather than for committing sins. The reminder serves to inform the servants that they should not use their energy for wrongdoings and invites them to worship God.[250]

Fourth question; why is it necessary to use the expression 'from hunger' (مِنْ جُوعٍ) when this meaning has already been implied by the mention of providing food?

Rāzī answers; there is much wisdom arising from mentioning hunger in the verse. Stressing it separately indicates the difficulty in experiencing hunger. The method of mentioning something separately when wishing to emphasize it is commonly used in the Qur'ān and Sunnah, for example:

---

248 Rāzī, ibid, 23/434.
249 Qur'ān 2: 29.
250 Rāzī, *Tafsīr*, 23/234.

> He it is who sends down the rain useful in all ways to rescue (them) after they have lost all hope, and spreads out His mercy far and wide (to every being)[251]

> ...who among you wakes up safe in his squadron, healthy in body, has daily sustenance he is considered as if he is given the whole world.[252]

The other benefit is that God reminds them of their hunger in previous days to enable them to better appreciate His favor in providing food. The best food is that which relieves hunger, so God brings their attention to this favor.

وَآمَنَهُم مِّنْ خَوْف *He made them safe from fear;*

The interpretation of this verse includes several points:

1) The Quraysh were always able to travel safely; their possessions on the journey and at home were never plundered whereas other people did not have these advantages. This meaning is supported by another verse; "Do they not consider that We have established (them in) a secure sanctuary while people are ravaged all around them?"[253]

2) God protected them from torture and destruction by defeating the army of the elephant.

3) God shielded them from leprosy; it never afflicted their city.

4) God bestowed them with leadership and the caliphate so they were safe from the sovereignty of others.

5) God secured them by bringing Islam to them. They knew that paganism was wrong but they did not know the true religion. God guided them to the straight path and saved them from false belief.

6) God inspired them with the revelation and saved them from ignorance. By guiding them to the straight path, they were saved from the sin of deviation. It is implied:

> O People of Mecca! You were named ignorant before the Prophethood of Muhammad (pbuh) while others were called 'the people of the book.' Then Muhammad (pbuh) became a Prophet and taught you the book and wisdom. After him, you were called 'the people of knowledge and the Qur'ān' and the others became the ignorant.

---

[251] Qur'ān 42: 28

[252] Tirmidhi, *Sunan, Zuhd*, 34.

[253] Qur'ān 29: 67.

If food can be viewed as nourishment for the body, which requires us to give thanks to God, can the revelation be viewed as nourishment for the soul? This raises a few points that require addressing:

First question; hunger and fear are expressed by using the Arabic particle 'min' (مِن) instead of 'an' (عَن); what is the wisdom in that?

Rāzī answers; using the particle 'an' would convey the meaning that they were hungry for a period of time but then they were saved; it occurred in the past but not in the present time. However, the particle 'min' implies that God saves them from hunger and fear whenever they need such favors.[254] Therefore, this Arabic particle (مِن) expresses the intended meaning more accurately.

Second question; why are the Arabic words ju' (جُوع) hunger and khawf (خَوْف) fear used in nakra (undefined) forms?

Rāzī answers;[255] in Arabic, if a word is used without a defining particle it gives the meaning the most extreme form of such word. By not defining the word 'hunger,' the verse conveys the extreme nature of their situation; they were extremely hungry due to famine to the extent that they would eat bones and carcasses. Similarly, when the word 'fear' is left undefined it indicates the severe level of fear they experienced from the threat of the people of the elephant. At other times, Arabic words are used undefined to indicate their unimportance. However, if that were the case here the verse would mean; God is All-Merciful and therefore He did not let them suffer from a little fear and hunger. So how is it possible to think that He would abandon His servants after they worship Him?

Third question; God answered the supplication of Abraham when he left his wife and child in Mecca;

> Our Lord! I have settled some of my offspring (Ishmael and his descendants) in an uncultivable valley near Your Sacred House, so that, our Lord, they may establish the Prayer; so make the hearts of people incline towards them, and provide them with the produce of earth (by such means as trade), so that they may give thanks (constantly from the heart and in speech, and in action by fulfilling Your commandments).[256]

God provided Mecca with security and abundance for Abraham's sake, so why should the Quraysh accept responsibility for this favor?

---

[254] Rāzī, Tafsīr, 23/435.
[255] Rāzī, ibid.
[256] Qur'ān 14: 37.

Answer; when God informed Abraham "indeed I will make you an imam for all people" he (Abraham) pleaded: '(Will You appoint imams) also from my offspring?' He (his Lord) answered: "I will appoint from among those who merit it but My covenant does not include the wrongdoers."[257] This verse indicates that the favor, which was bestowed as a result of Abraham's supplication, is not general and does not cover everyone. There are two types of favor; one is related to this world and the other is related to the afterlife. The favor of safety from the punishment of God on Judgment Day is only given to those who are pious and righteous, but everyone, regardless of faith, benefits from the favors of this world. Therefore, the favors of safety and sustenance for the unbelievers are not the result of the supplication of Abraham, rather they are the initial favors of God that are bestowed upon everyone in this world.[258]

God knows best, may God's mercy be upon our master Muhammad (pbuh) and his family and Companions.

SUMMARY: SURAH QURAYSH

1. This four verse *surah* was revealed in Mecca and gives information about the favors God has bestowed on the Quraysh.
2. For the first verse, Rāzī relates the opinions of other scholars then follows them with his own opinion, showing that he does not follow any scholars blindly; rather he makes his own critical analysis of their opinions and accepts or rejects them accordingly.
3. Rāzī uses Qur'anic verses to support his arguments, demonstrating that logic is subservient to the Qur'ān.
4. After discussing different opinions, Rāzī explains that God destroyed the people of the elephant for the concord and security of the Quraysh and gives the evidences for this.
5. Scholars have various views on how the name 'Quraysh' was derived. Rāzī outlines the different opinions but refrains from indicating a preference from among them, showing that he was not convinced of which view was more accurate.
6. The second verse uses terms that raise several issues; Rāzī outlines the scholars' discussions on these issues including the use of the word '*rihla*' (journey).

---

[257] Qur'ān 2: 124.
[258] Rāzī, *Tafsīr*, 23/435–436.

7. The third verse is explained with a discussion around the nature of worship, and God's relationship to the servants and the Sacred House.

8. The fourth verse warrants discussion of the nature of food, hunger and fear. The various discussion points are outlined and questions are answered by Rāzī who also utilizes linguistic analysis in his interpretation.

CHAPTER 5

Dirāyah (Reason-Based) *Tafsīr*,
Qādi Baydāwī and His *Tafsīr*

Introduction

Dirāyah tafsīr is the interpretation of the Qur'ān based on reason. *Dirāyah* literally means 'to inform' and 'to know' and is also known by the name *'tafsīr bi'l ra'y.'* *Ra'y* means 'to see,' 'to know' and 'to believe.' It is also used to mean *ijtihād*, which is juristic opinion on a new matter that has not previously been addressed in the Qur'ān or Sunnah.[259] Qualified scholars (*mufassir*) investigate the Qur'ān and extract the meanings:

> ...whereas if they would but refer it to the Messenger (pbuh) and to those among them (in the community) who are entrusted with authority, those from among them who are competent to investigate it would bring to light what it is really about.[260]

The above verse indicates that there are people of knowledge who have the ability to reveal the intended meaning of the verses. As the Qur'ān contains knowledge of the Eternal One it is essential that it is continually explained by the experts of the time.

When approaching the interpretation of the Qur'ān it is essential to begin with an investigation within the Qur'ān itself, to avoid deviation. If the verse is already explained within the Qur'ān, it is not permissible to look further. For this reason, exemplary knowledge of the Qur'ān is necessary for the *mufassir.* The second source for *tafsīr* is the Sunnah of the Prophet (pbuh). Knowledge of this can be obtained by examining the reports (traditions) of the Prophet (pbuh), known as hadith. This field requires hadith critics and methodologists to authenticate the sound hadiths from the weak and forged hadiths. If a *mufassir* is not knowledgeable in this field, he may unknowingly utilize forged hadith in his *tafsīr* that is clearly deviation. Therefore, it is essential for the *mufassir* to have a detailed knowledge of hadith and its methodology.

Another important source for *tafsīr* is the interpretation of the early scholars, The Companions and the Successors, (*Tabi'in*). They had a better understand-

---

[259] Imam Shāfi'ī, *al-Risāla*, 447.
[260] Qur'ān 4: 83.

ing of the Arabic language and were closer to the Prophet (pbuh) so their wisdom ranks above that of anyone else. Scholars from later generations did not possess such detailed knowledge of the historical background, cultural conditions and occasions behind the revelation and were more likely to mistakenly misunderstand the verses. When examining the verses, it is essential they are investigated thoroughly in the primary and secondary sources before resorting to personal opinion. Human reason should be exercised with the utmost caution when extracting the meanings from the Qur'ān. Islam, rather than preventing the use of the intellect, encourages it but with strict criteria, for if the reason is free from Islamic principles it will stray from the straight path resulting in wrong conclusions. Therefore, a *mufassir* should know *riwāyah* (tradition-based) *tafsīr* very well before adopting the *dirāyah* (reason-based) method. There is a strong relationship between the *riwāyah* and *dirāyah* methods and most scholars interchange between the two methods when making *tafsīr* even though their work is classified according to the predominately used method.

Whilst many verses of the Qur'ān can be explained using the *riwāyah* method there are more than 1000 verses that invite humanity to think and grasp the essence of the truth and therefore require the *dirāyah* method of *tafsīr*. Logical arguments have been used to understand many of the reports of the Prophet (pbuh) and even the Companions and Successors resorted to the intellect when necessary. If the content was ambiguous, they did not hesitate to explain it using logical arguments.

Verses were first approached literally; however, if the literal explanation of the meaning was against the principles of Islam, a metaphorical approach was utilized. There are certain rules and criterion that must be applied when interpreting the language of the Qur'ān due to its unique style of expression. The true meaning of the Qur'ān can only be extracted with the proper methodology and for one to be permitted to make an interpretation he must be well versed in Arabic philology, grammar, *balāghah*, etc.[261]

Islamic scholars also utilize many sciences to explain the ambiguous, *mutashābih* and brief verses of the Qur'ān. Making an interpretation of the Qur'ān by means of the *dirāyah* method necessitates knowledge of many sciences such as Arabic, grammar, *balāghah*, logic, theology, *fiqh*, *uṣūl al-fiqh*, *sīrah*, the occasions behind the revelations, the science of *qiraat* and many more. In short, *riwāyah* and *dirāyah* both complement and rely on each other in *tafsīr* because

---

[261] Suyūṭī, *al-Itqān*, 2/179.

the reason-based interpretation is only accepted when it is in accordance with the reports of the early scholars and in harmony with Islamic principles. The high objectives in the Qur'ān and Sunnah are used to examine the validity of this type of *tafsīr*.

SUMMARY: INTRODUCTION:

1. *Dirāyah tafsīr* is interpretation of the Qur'ān based on reason.
2. The Qur'ān is the primary source for *tafsīr* therefore; a *mufassir* must have an exemplary knowledge of the Qur'ān.
3. The second source for *tafsīr* is the Sunnah of the Prophet (pbuh); the *mufassir* must have a detailed knowledge of hadith and its methodology.
4. Another important source for *tafsīr* is the interpretation of the early scholars.
5. Human reason should be exercised with the utmost caution when extracting the meanings from the Qur'ān.
6. There is a strong relationship between the *riwāyah* and *dirāyah* methods and most scholars interchange between the two methods.
7. More than 1000 verses from the Qur'ān require the *dirāyah* method of *tafsīr*.
8. Making an interpretation of the Qur'ān by means of the *dirāyah* method necessitates knowledge of many sciences such as Arabic, grammar, *balāghah*, logic, theology, *fiqh*, *uṣūl al-fiqh*, *sīrah*, the occasions behind the revelations, the science of *qiraat* and many more.

Qādi Baydawī and His *Tafsīr*

His Life[262]

Abdullah ibn Umar ibn Muhammad ibn Ali Abu al-Khayr Nasir al-Din Baydāwī was born in 1252 C.E. in Bayda and was known as Baydāwī (the one who is from Bayda).[263] One of the famous scholars who grew up in the area of Azerbaijan in 4th century of *Hijrah*, his fame reached from India to Andalusia and his work circulated amongst scholars for many years.

---

[262] Please see the following references to know more about his life, books, education and books; Subkī, *Tabaqāt al-Shāfi'iyya*, 8/157–158; Ibn Kathīr, *al-Bidāya wa'l-Nihāya*, 13/309; Dāwudi, *Tabaqāt al-Mufassirīn*, 1/242–243; Zirikli, *Ālam*, 4/248–249.

[263] Omer Nasuhi Bilmen, *Buyuk Tefsir Tarihi*, 2/528.

He completed his education in Shiraz becoming the Qādi (judge) there and was later promoted to the position of chief Qādi. After leaving this position, he settled in Tabriz and lived there until his death, which occurred in either 1286 C.E. or 1319 C.E.[264]

Baydāwī followed the Shāfi'ī School of Thought (*madhhab*) and was well versed in the Islamic sciences of *tafsīr*, hadith, *fiqh*, *kalām*, *usūl*, logic and *balāghah*. He produced many valuable works in these areas that are still used by public and scholars today. Undoubtedly, Baydāwī tried to combine *Usūl al-Din* (Theology) and *Usūl al-Fiqh* (Methodology of Islamic Law) in his books and he utilized Arab philology and literature.

His Books

Baydāwī produced books almost in every field of Islamic science demonstrating that his education was received from the best scholars of his time. His well-known books are:

- *Minhāj al-Wusūl ilā Ilm al-Usūl*—a book on the methodology of Islamic law; still accepted today as an important work in this field.
- *Sharh al-Matali' Fi'l Mantiq*—a book about logic.
- *Al-Ghāyah al-Quswā*—a book on Shāfi'ī *fiqh*.
- *Sharh Masābīh al-Sunna al-Baghawī*—a book on hadith that explains the work of Baghawī in this field.
- *Tawāli al-Anwār min Metali' al Anzār*—a book on *kalām*.
- *Lubb al-Albāb fi Ilm al-I'rāb*—a book on Arabic grammar.
- *Risāla fi Mawdu'at al-Ulūm wa Teārifihā*—a book defining the sciences and their subject matter.
- *Al-Īdāh fi Usūl al-Din*—a theological work.
- *Anwar a-Tanzīl wa Asrār al-Ta'wil*—a book of *tafsīr*.

His *Tafsīr*

Baydāwī attracted fame for his seminal *tafsīr* work[265], '*Anwar a-Tanzīl wa Asrār al-Ta'wil*' (the lights of revelation and the secrets of interpretation) and is received more acknowledgement and fame than any other of his books. It has been published many times and has been used as a standard text in Islamic educational

---

[264] Zarqānī, *Manāhil al-Irfān*, 1/535.
[265] Subkī, *Tabaqāt al-Shāfi'iyya*, 8/157–158.

institutions around the Muslim world for many centuries.[266] More than 250 books have been written by scholars to explain the content of his *tafsīr* book. Baydāwī's book is not very voluminous, but it gives important information about the verses in the Qur'ān.

Baydawī gives a mainstream (in accordance with *Ahli Sunnah*) interpretation of the Qur'ān based on the rules of Arabic grammar. He explains the verses succinctly and explains their most beneficial aspects by utilizing grammar, language, logic, *qiraat*, history and *kalām*. Some readers struggle to understand some of the content of the book, but despite the difficult elements in some of the scientific explanations, it is important to remember that this book was written eight centuries ago and is one of the fruits of the Islamic civilization.

Baydawī wrote his book towards the end of his life in Tabriz; it can be seen as the culmination of his expertise in many different disciplines. The most important sources that Baydawī benefitted from to write his *tafsīr* were *Kashshāf* (Zamakhsharī's *tafsīr* book) and *Mafātih al-Ghayb* (Rāzī's book). He used *Kashshāf* to analyze, understand and demonstrate the wisdoms in the language of the Qur'ān whilst he used Rāzī's work to explain the essentials and high objectives of Islam. He also utilized Rāghib al-Isfahānī's book *Mufradaat* to indicate the secrets and wisdoms in the words of the Qur'ān.

Baydāwī analyzed the opinions of the early scholars, examining and extracting the rules from them and preferring one view above the others. His methodology was to explain the verses word by word. His work reflects his diverse literary abilities. In the section 'the occasions behind the revelations' he gives many reports from the early scholars and makes preferences between them when it is necessary. He often offers linguistic analysis and information on the various readings (*qiraat*), mainly dwelling on the seven canonical readers. He occasionally discusses legal topics, taking the Shāfi'ī position from among the different opinions.

Baydāwī uses both *riwāyah* and *dirāyah* methods in his work. At times, he relates reports from the early scholars to explain the verses and other times engages in philosophical discussions. His general approach is to outline the various views and explanations of the opinions of the early scholars. He does not always mention the sources of the view that he presents but this in no way diminishes the value of his *tafsīr*. He utilized a broad range of information obtained from various sources in a relatively short commentary.

---

[266] C. Brockelmann, GAL, 1/416–418.

Scholars trust his work and accept it as an important source in the field of *tafsīr*. However, some scholars argue that it included forged reports about the merits of *surahs* and that it is ambiguous in its expressions. It is common for famous scholars to receive criticism by others in the same field but this does not diminish their achievements. This *tafsīr* has been accepted by academics as a remarkable work and has been used in Islamic institutions as a primary text-book for centuries. Many scholars wrote explanatory books on this work, the most famous of which are:

- Muhammad ibn Yusuf al-Kirmanī (d. 1384 C.E.)
- Sayyid Sharif al-Jurjani (d. 1384 C.E.)
- Molla Husraw (d. 1480 C.E.)
- Ibn Tamjid (d. 1485 C.E.)
- Suyūtī (d. 1505 C.E.)
- Shihab al-Din al-Hafaji (d. 1659 C.E.)

Muhammad ibn Abdurrahman (d. 1469 C.E.) summarized this *tafsīr*. The best way to have knowledge of a book is from the work itself and the parts quoted below will serve to give a better insight into it.

Example; "Pilgrimage to the House is a duty owed to God by all who can afford a way to it"[267]

Baydāwī began his explanation with the word '*Hajj*' (pilgrimage) which he defined from a linguistic point of view and later gave various readings for it. He discussed the rule of pilgrimage and preferred the Shāfi'ī view to others.[268]

Baydāwī accepts the notion of abrogation in the Qur'ān and presents the following verse as evidence for his opinion:

> We do not abrogate any verse or omit it (leaving it to be forgotten) but We bring one better than it or the like of it (more suited to the time and conditions in the course of perfecting religion and completing Our favor upon you).[269]

He explains the notion of *naskh* with logical reasoning, arguing that the change is not in the rules themselves but in their application and benefits.

In order to understand Baydāwī's work in more detail, Surah Mā'un and his interpretation is presented.

---

[267] Qur'ān 3: 97.
[268] Baydāwī, *Anwar a-Tanzīl wa Asrār al-Ta'wil*, 1/221.
[269] Qur'ān 2: 106.

Summary: Qādi Baydawi and His *Tafsīr*

1. Born in 1252 C.E. in Bayda, he was known as Baydawī (the one who is from Bayda).

2. He completed his education in Shiraz becoming the Qādi (judge) there and was later promoted to the position of chief Qādi.

3. Baydāwī followed the Shāfi'ī School of Thought (*madhhab*).

4. He was well versed in the Islamic sciences of *tafsīr*, hadith, *fiqh*, *kalām*, *uṣūl*, logic and *balāghah* producing many valuable works in these areas.

5. His *tafsīr, Anwar a-Tanzīl wa Asrār al-Ta'wil,* has been published many times and has been used as a standard text in Islamic educational institutions around the Muslim world for many centuries.

6. Baydāwī gives a mainstream interpretation of the Qur'ān based on the rules of Arabic grammar.

7. He uses grammar, language, logic, *qiraat*, history and *kalām* in his explanations.

8. Baydāwī analyzed the opinions of the early scholars, examining and extracting the rules from them and preferring one view above the others.

9. Baydāwī uses *riwāyah* and *dirāyah* methods, at times relating reports from the early scholars to explain the verses and other times engaging in philosophical discussions.

10. Scholars trust his work and accept it as an important source in the field of *tafsīr* but it is not without its critics.

11. Many scholars wrote explanatory books on his work.

12. Baydāwī accepts the notion of abrogation in the Qur'ān.

Surah Al-Mā'un (Assistance)

بِسْمِ اللهِ الرَّحْمٰنِ الرَّحِيمِ

اَرَاَيْتَ الَّذِي يُكَذِّبُ بِالدِّينِ ﴿١﴾ فَذٰلِكَ الَّذِي يَدُعُّ الْيَتِيمَ ﴿٢﴾ وَلَا يَحُضُّ عَلٰى طَعَامِ الْمِسْكِينِ ﴿٣﴾ فَوَيْلٌ لِلْمُصَلِّينَ ﴿٤﴾ الَّذِينَ هُمْ عَنْ صَلَاتِهِمْ سَاهُونَ ﴿٥﴾ الَّذِينَ هُمْ يُرَاؤُنَ ﴿٦﴾ وَيَمْنَعُونَ الْمَاعُونَ ﴿٧﴾

Surah Mā'un (Assistance)

In the Name of God, the All-Merciful, the All-Compassionate

1. Have you considered one who denies the Last Judgment?
2. That is the one who repels the orphan,
3. And does not urge the feeding of the destitute.
4. And woe to those worshippers (denying the Judgment),
5. Those who are unmindful in their Prayers,
6. Those who want to be seen and noted (for their acts of worship),
7. Yet deny all assistance (to their fellowmen).

Tafsīr

This seven-verse *surah* was revealed in Mecca and is named after the word *al-mā'un* (assistance) that occurs in the final verse. It emphasizes faith in the pillars of the religion, sincerity in worship, and the importance of mutual assistance in society. In addition, it warns against hypocrisy.

أرأيت 'have you seen' is in the form of a question which conveys a surprised expression. This method is used in Arabic when denying an act, thought or attribute. Baydāwī briefly explained that this is not a real question, rather it is a surprised expression phrased in the form of question.[270] Therefore, the question is not asked to find out whether the Prophet (pbuh) saw the deniers; this information is already known. In making this statement, God is rejecting the attitude of the unbelievers and making it clear that this is not the proper conduct for humans, especially those who are favored by God to live in the holy land of Mecca.

First verse: أَرَأَيْتَ الَّذِي يُكَذِّبُ بِالدِّينِ *Have you considered one who denies the Last Judgment?*

Baydāwī holds that the expression *al-din* "بالدِّين" either means 'Judgment Day' on which occasion everyone will witness the consequences of their deeds or 'the religion of Islam.' In both cases, it warns the person or people who deny Prophet Muhammad (pbuh) and his message. The Prophet (pbuh) introduced the people to belief in an afterlife and the notion of being held accountable for one's deeds. However, they continued to commit sins, wrongdoings and injustices. They only believed in the worldly life and rejected the idea of being responsible for one's actions. Their lack of faith in Judgment Day caused them to commit evil sins. This

---

270 Baydāwī, *Anwar a-Tanzīl wa Asrār al-Ta'wil*, 3/747.

is referred to in the question, which means, 'how surprising that you thought you would be left free of your crimes without beholding their consequences.'

Baydāwī explained that the expression "one who denies" could either mean just one person or everyone who shares the same attribute.[271] Since, the Qur'ān is universal, so its message is relevant to humanity as a whole. Therefore, it is not proper method to restrict its meaning to a person or group. It is possible that the action of one person, or one occasion, was the cause for the revelation, however the content is not limited to that time or place, it is to be generally applied.

The leaders of the Quraysh denied the Prophet (pbuh) and the Qur'ān. There will be unbelievers until the end of time. The proper meaning of the verse is that God bestowed humankind with an intellect to perceive the truth, and with Prophets to guide them to the true religion. Despite these blessings, some of them deviated from the straight path and denied Judgment Day. Their disbelief resulted in the waste of their lives, as they didn't believe they would be held accountable for their deeds.

Religion established a set of rules and invited liable people to practice them by their free will to achieve contentment in this life and the afterlife. People are free to do anything but are not free of their consequences. The Arabic word '*al-din*' means to treat people as they are or to give them what they deserve. In other words, whatever treatment people receive from God on Judgment Day is a consequence of their conduct. Therefore, whatever people do in this life is indeed what they will see in the afterlife.

Second verse: فَذَلِكَ الَّذِي يَدُعُّ الْيَتِيمَ *That is the one who repels the orphan*

Baydāwī mentioned some occasions behind the revelation of this verse. The person who denied the orphan's rights might be one of these people:

- Abū Jahl was the custodian of an orphan whom he was supposed to take care of. One day, the orphan approached Abū Jahl; he was naked and in need of his own inheritance but Abū Jahl refused him and did not care about his needs. The orphan was hopeless about receiving his property. One of the leaders of the Quraysh told him to go to Muhammad (pbuh) and ask for his intercession. The other people mocked him because they knew that Abū Jahl would never listen to the Prophet (pbuh). Nevertheless, the orphan went to Muhammad (pbuh) and asked for his help. The Prophet (pbuh) who never refused anyone's request for help took the orphan and went to Abū Jahl. To everyone's surprise, Abū Jahl offered the Prophet

---

(pbuh) a seat and gave the orphan his property. When the shocked Quraysh questioned him about his unusual response, Abū Jahl replied; 'I saw two guards on the right and left of Muhammad, if I did not do what he said they would kill me right away.'[272]

- Once Abū Sufyan slaughtered an animal and in that moment, an orphan came to him to ask for a piece of meat. But he hit the orphan with his staff and rejected him.[273]

- Suddi holds that this verse was revealed about Walid ibn Mughira.

- Ibn Abbas holds that this verse was revealed about a person who combined both miserliness and hypocrisy together.[274]

As previously mentioned, Baydawī holds two views about this verse; the first is that the verse was revealed on a specific occasion, so the one who rejected the orphan was one of those mentioned in the reports. Baydawī neither examined the authenticity of the reports nor did he make preferences from among them. It seems he only related them as the occasions of revelation to help the readers understand the historical background, but he did not restrict himself to the meaning. The second view is that this verse is general rather than addressing a specific person. Even though there might be a correlation between the revelation time of the verse and a specific occasion, the content is universal and applies to any miserly person who repels orphans and this is the more appropriate view.

Third verse: وَلاَ يَحُضُّ عَلَى طَعَامِ الْمِسْكِينِ *And does not urge the feeding of the destitute*

This verse refers to the unbeliever. Unbelievers do not believe in Judgment Day or that they will be held accountable for their deeds, therefore, they don't encourage others to help the needy. Baydawī said; the Arabic particle '*fa*' الفاء is used to convey the causation between two effects. It is used in the expression, "that is the one who repels the orphan," to connect it to the previous verse, "have you considered one who denies the Last Judgment?"[275] Therefore, the reason that he does not urge the feeding of the destitute is related to the fact of denying the Judgment Day. Baydawī interprets this verse linguistically and employs grammar rules to explain the interrelations between the verses.

The commentary sheds light on the principle cause of evil acts; denying the afterlife and Judgment Day. The antidote to such immoral behavior is sound belief

---

272 Rāzī, *Tafsīr*, see the interpretation of Surah *Mā'un*.

273 Baydāwī, *Tafsīr*, 3/748.

274 Baydāwī, ibid.

275 Baydāwī, *Tafsīr*, 3/747.

that inspires the believer to perform good deeds and prevents them from engaging in evil acts. One deprived of positive motivation is more likely to commit sin and wrong others; for example, one who has false belief does not feel any compulsion to feed the destitute.

Further points can be raised here that are not contained in Baydāwī but are worthy of mention. The verse ascribes food to the destitute thereby conveying the meaning that food is their legitimate right. Not providing them with food is preventing them from their legal rights. It is obvious that only immoral and miserly people can behave in such a way. Another implication of the expression, "does not urge the feeding of the destitute," is that because he does not expect to receive any worldly benefit from feeding the destitute, he does not feel any compassion to do so. The signs for denying Judgment Day are explained in this *surah* as wronging the weak and preventing them from their rights.[276]

Fourth verse; فَوَيْلٌ لِلْمُصَلِّينَ *Woe to those worshippers*

Baydāwī did not give any analysis of this verse but there are a couple of points worth mentioning in relation to it. This verse, 'woe to the worshippers,' has a relationship with the previous verses. Repelling the orphans and not feeding the destitute are signs of hypocrisy and hypocrites cannot perform the prayers sincerely. Those who do not believe in Judgment Day cannot understand the meaning of servanthood or the importance of the prayers. They pretend to be sincere in their performance of worship but are unaware of its meaning. God has commanded the prayers, the feeding of the destitute and the care of orphans; therefore, neglecting any one of these whilst performing the others is hypocrisy.

God informed us that prayers are a prevention from performing evil deeds; "Surely, the Prayer restrains from all that is indecent and shameful and all that is evil."[277] This verse explains that hypocrisy in the prayers cannot save its performers. The hypocrites who do not believe in Judgment Day, reject orphans and neglect the needy cannot be expected to be sincere in the performance of their prayers. Their prayers do not prevent them from acting sinfully because of their hypocrisy.

Mercy is one of the essential Attributes of God. He wants his servants to be merciful and encourages them in this regard. One who does not show mercy to God's creatures, for example by repelling orphans or not feeding the destitute, is not eligible to receive God's mercy. One of the proper ways to respect God is

---

[276] Rāzī, *Tafsīr*, 23/441–442.
[277] Qur'ān 29: 45.

being merciful to His creatures. The Arabic word 'wayl' (woe) is used for the committer of the major sins, crimes and offenses. If the prayers do not lead the servants to be merciful they deserve to be addressed; "woe to those worshippers." Because, not feeding the orphans and the needy is great sin.

Fifth verse; الَّذِينَ هُمْ عَنْ صَلَاتِهِمْ سَاهُونَ *Those who are unmindful in their prayers*

Baydāwī explained that these people do not pay attention to their prayers because they are oblivious to the meaning of the prayer.[278] Verses four to seven threaten the hypocrites who do not understand the benefits of the prayers. They do not fear God; therefore, they do not perform the prayers in their homes. If they sometimes pray, they are proud of it. They are careless about whether they pray on time or prayed properly. They do not pursue God's good pleasure and approval in their prayers. They only expect worldly advantages in their acts.

One must be aware of three evil acts:

- Being unmindful in the prayers.

- Worshipping publicly with the intention of showing off.

- Preventing the basic needs of the public.

The hypocrites perform the prayer but they are unmindful in their performance. The prayer is the form of presenting one's sincere servanthood to God and sincerity in the prayers comes after true faith (*iman*). If there is a problem in the action, it signifies a problem in the belief. If one denies Judgment Day, it shows itself in the acts. The hypocrites are unmindful in their prayers because they are unmindful in their belief.

Sixth verse: الَّذِينَ هُمْ يُرَاءُونَ *Those who want to be seen and noted (for their acts of worship)*

With regard to this verse, Baydāwī only mentioned that the hypocrites perform their deeds to show off and to be appreciated by people.[279] The only valid form of worship is that which is performed with the sincere intention of achieving the pleasure of God. The worship becomes invalid if performed with any other intention. However, there is a difference between hypocrisy and showing off (*riya*). When with people, hypocrites act in the same way as believers but they hide their disbelief in their hearts. On the other hand, in the case of show off, a person wants to be seen and appreciated for his acts. When he is with other people, he seemingly worships God reverently, however when he is alone he acts differently. In other words, the hypocrite only prays when he is together with oth-

---

[278] Baydāwī, *Tafsīr*, 3/748.

[279] Baydāwī, *Tafsīr*, 3/748.

ers; when alone, he leaves the prayers. The show-off prays in the best way when he is with others but when he is alone he is careless in the performance of his prayers. He wants to gain the praise and admiration of others. The verse; "those who want to be seen and noted (for their acts of worship)"[280] is referring to those who show-off, as indicated by the use of the word 'riya' (show off).

Seventh verse: وَيَمْنَعُونَ الْمَاعُون *Yet deny all assistance (to their fellowmen)*

Baydāwi holds that the meaning of 'assistance' in this verse is either *zakat* (the obligatory charity upon those who meet the conditions) or basic things, which people borrow from each other.[281] The majority of scholars hold that the Arabic word الْمَاعُون 'assistance' means the basic things which people, (regardless if they are rich or poor), need occasionally and request from each other. To refuse such assistance is a despicable act and those who do not aid others are called miserly and immoral. The assistance could be lending tools such as an axe, hammer and bucket or it could be giving kitchen ingredients such as salt, water or a match-stick, etc. The Prophet (pbuh) said; "it is not permissible to prevent three things from people; water, fire and salt."[282]

Baydāwi connects the last verse to the previous one and explains that some people are condemned because they repel the orphans and do not feed the needy; this is due to their weakness in belief and denial of Judgment Day.[283] The following conducts are worse in the sight of God and deserve to be condemned more severely:

- Being unmindful in the prayers, (the prayers are the pillars of Islam).
- Showing off in the prayers (showing off is a branch of disbelief).
- Preventing *zakat*, which is the bridge of Islam.

God severely condemned this people by using the expression; 'woe to them.' This *surah* conveys that God also condemns anyone who shares these attributes.

In the commentary of the last verse, Baydāwi asks a question and then answers it, similar to the way in which Rāzi asks many questions and then answers them. He asked, why God not said 'woe to them' in the verse instead of 'woe to those worshippers.' He answered it, God first explains the low position of those people in worldly terms as 'ones who deny the orphan and do not urge the feeding of the destitute.' He then explains their position from the perspective of their

---

[280] Qur'ān 107: 6.

[281] Baydāwi, *Tafsīr*, 3/748.

[282] Abū Dāwud, *Sunan, zakat*, 36.

[283] Baydāwi, ibid.

spiritual life; 'woe to those worshippers (denying the Judgment) who are unmindful in their prayers and who want to be seen and noted for their acts of worship.'[284] With this interpretation, Baydāwī analyzed the evil acts concerning their addressee implying that if one violates human rights he is more likely to violate the rights of God. Someone who lives according to good morals acts in the best way in all areas of his life, both towards the creation and towards the Creator. A moral person should always display good manners if he respects God; the two are intrinsically connected, and God draws our attention to this fact.

Baydāwī finished the commentary on Surah Mā'un with the following hadith; "whoever recites Surah Mā'un will be forgiven if he is a giver of *zakat*"[285]

When quoting this hadith from Zamakhsharī, Baydāwī did not investigate its authenticity according to hadith criteria. Some hadith scholars claim that this is a forged hadith. In *dirāyah tafsīr* scholars are expected to analyze the reports and indicate their level of authenticity, comparing them if there is more than one and preferring one to the others. This is not evident in the commentary of this *surah* in Baydāwī's book and as a result, some scholars classify his work as *riwāyah tafsīr*. However, this criticism is unfounded as each type of *tafsīr* incorporates qualities of the other and may not be perfect in every aspect; therefore, despite lacking in some areas, Baydāwī's work falls under the category of *dirāyah tafsīr*.

SUMMARY: SURAH MAUN *TAFSĪR*

1. This seven-verse *surah* was revealed in Mecca and emphasizes faith in the pillars of the religion, sincerity in worship, and the importance of mutual assistance in society.

First verse:

2. Baydāwī holds that the expression *al-din* "بِٱلدِّينِ" either means 'Judgment Day' on which occasion everyone will witness the consequences of their deeds or 'the religion of Islam.'

3. Baydāwī explained that the expression "one who denies" could either mean just one person or everyone who shares the same attribute; hence the Qur'ān is universal, its message is relevant to all humanity.

Second verse:

4. He mentioned some occasions behind the revelation of this verse.

---

[284] Baydāwī, *Tafsīr*, 3/748.
[285] Baydāwī, ibid.

5. He neither examined the authenticity of the reports nor did he make preferences from among them but gave them as historical background.

Third verse:

6. Baydāwī said; the Arabic particle *'fa'* الفاء is used to convey the causation between two effects. He interprets this verse linguistically and employs grammar rules to explain the interrelations between the verses.

Fourth verse:

7. Baydāwī did not give any analysis of this verse, but there are a couple of points worth mentioning in relation to it.

8. Repelling the orphans and not feeding the destitute are signs of hypocrisy and hypocrites cannot perform the prayers sincerely.

9. Mercy is one of the essential Attributes of God. He wants His servants to be merciful and encourages merciful behavior. One who does not show mercy to God's creatures, for example by repelling orphans or not feeding the destitute, is violating the command of mercy and this is a great offense to God.

Fifth verse:

10. Baydāwī explained that these people do not pay attention to their prayers because they are oblivious to their meaning.

11. Verses four to seven threaten the hypocrites who do not understand the benefits of the prayers.

Sixth verse:

12. With regard to this verse, Baydāwī only mentioned that the hypocrites perform their deeds to show off and to be appreciated by people.

13. There is a difference between hypocrisy and showing off (*riya*). On the outside, hypocrites act in the same way as believers but they hide their disbelief in their hearts. On the other hand, someone who shows off wants to be seen and appreciated for his acts.

Seventh verse:

14. Baydāwī holds that the meaning of 'assistance' in this verse is either *zakat* (the obligatory charity upon those who meet the conditions) or basic things, which people borrow from each other.

15. Baydāwī connects the last verse to the previous one and explains that some people are condemned because they repel the orphans and do not feed the needy; this is due to their weakness in belief and denial of Judgment Day.

16. In the commentary of the last verse, Baydawī asks a question and then answers it, similar to the way in which Rāzī asks many questions and then answers them.

17. Baydāwī finished the commentary on Surah Mā'un with a hadith but did not investigate its authenticity according to hadith criteria.

18. Some scholars classify his work as *riwāyah*. However, this criticism is unfounded. Baydāwī's work falls under the category of *dirāyah tafsīr*.

CHAPTER 6

Linguistic *Tafsīr*, al-Farrā and *Ma'an al-Qur'an*

Introduction

I t is impossible to truly understand and interpret the Qur'ān without an in-depth knowledge and understanding of Arabic philology; the correlative rela-tionship between the two is apparent.[286] This is referenced in the Qur'ān itself; "We have sent down to you an Arabic Qur'ān so that you may understand."[287] The depth and richness of the Arabic language necessitates a meticulous and contemplative approach when extracting meanings from the Qur'anic verses.

In the areas of vocabulary, grammar, rhetoric, and the principles of discourse, the Qur'anic *tafsīr* must comply with the guidelines of Arabic philology. Imam Malik (d. 179 A.H.) stated; "If any person is brought to me, having interpreted the Qur'ān while he is ignorant of the Arabic language, I will make an example of him (by punishing him)."[288] Mujāhid (d. 103 A.H.) said; "It is not permissible for any person who believes in God and the Last Day to speak concerning the Book of God if he is not knowledgeable of the dialects of the Arabs."[289] Imam Shātibī (d. 790 A.H.) explained: "Whoever desires to understand the Qur'ān, then it will be understood from the speech of the Arabs, and there is no way other than this."[290]

The depth and richness of meaning in the Qur'ān are due to its miraculous authorship. In using parables, figurative and symbolic rhetoric as well as meta-phors and similes, it presents a unique creative style.[291] For this reason, a detailed knowledge of the fundamental principles of Arabic is a prerequisite for inter-preting the Qur'ān. There are verses where the wording appears general but is, in fact, specific; in other verses, words or phrases seem to be missing whereas they are inferred from the context.[292] In some verses, it seems that the logical

---

[286] Recep Doğan, *Uṣūl Tafsīr The Sciences and Methodology of the Qur'ān*, Tughra Books, Clifton USA 2014, 321.

[287] Qur'ān, 12:2.

[288] Hasanuddin Ahmed, *Introducing the Qur'an*, p. 126.

[289] Ahmed, *Introducing the Qur'an*, p. 127.

[290] Shātibī, *Muwafaqaat*, 1/ 84.

[291] Recep Doğan, *Uṣūl Tafsīr*, 321.

[292] Doğan, ibid.

sequence of the words has been reversed whereas, in fact, this reversal adds a subtle meaning that would otherwise not be present.[293] Such physiognomies are well known by the Arabs, and are indicative of the inimitability of the Qur'ān.

Qur'anic commentary centered on hadith reports is always nonpareil since it is based on the direct word of God, the words and practises of the Prophet (pbuh) and the knowledge of the Companions. These primary sources supersede the knowledge of any later linguist or grammarian. Furthermore, interpretation based on Arabic philology comes after the above three sources in its validity; it should neither contradict nor succeed the primary sources.

During the time of the Prophet (pbuh), the Qur'anic revelations served to unify the Arab tribes, enhancing and enriching their language with the addition of many different dialects. Significantly, the Quraysh tribe made concerted efforts to comprehend the various dialects and the other tribes in turn were determined to understand the Quraysh dialect.[294] Out of all the Muslims, the Prophet (pbuh) was the most eloquent and was highly admired by both his Companions and his adversaries. When questioned about his exceptional quality of speech the Prophet (pbuh) answered; "My Lord taught me this eloquence and He taught well."[295] Such was his ability the Prophet (pbuh) was able to fluently converse and make agreements with envoys from numerous tribes using their own dialect.

Over time, the Qur'ān came to be interpreted by specific groups who developed their own styles of interpretation. One of these groups was an extreme, literalist sect called Ẓāhirī (literalist). Focusing on a purely literal interpretation of the verses, this group ignored the symbolic content and the eloquent style of the Qur'ān.[296] Subsequently, another extreme sect, the Bāṭinī (esoteric) concentrated on the inner meanings of the text, completely disregarding any literal interpretations.[297] Both methods proved to be detrimental to the religion as their methods led to the inaccurate interpretation of the holy text.

It was not until after the time of the Companions that the Arabic language came to be compromised. With its borders rapidly expanding, the Islamic state embraced many different nationalities and cultures that brought with them their various traditions. Over time, the Arabic language was impacted and scholars were required to establish fundamental grammar rules in order to protect and preserve the

---

[293] Doğan, ibid.

[294] Recep Doğan, Uṣūl Tafsīr, 322.

[295] Suyūtī, Jami al-Saghīr, 1, 12.

[296] Ali Ünal, Foreword for his translation of Qur'ān.

[297] Ali Ünal, ibid.

pure Qur'anic Arabic.[298] During the Companions time, rather than providing a commentary on the whole Qur'ān, they concentrated on explaining the words that were vague, unclear, difficult, ambiguous, general or limited. The following generations, with their limited understanding of Arabic, had a greater need to understand the Qur'anic verses and so applied the linguistic methodology in accordance with the rules of Arabic grammar and in addition to the explanations of the Companions. Many books were authored according to this linguistic method, one of the most well known being 'Qarīb al-Qur'ān.'

Linguistic scholars focused their efforts on the difficult words, metaphoric expressions and ambiguous statements in their *tafsīr*, using a specific methodology. This involved identifying the root word, examining all its derivations and its placement in the sentence and explaining its usage. They would then look to Arabic poetry to discover the meanings of words.[299] However, it is important to note that some hadith and verses in the Qur'ān indicate that reliance on poetry should be limited, or even forbidden.

> And the poets the deviators follow them, do you not see that in every valley they roam, And that they say what they do not do. Except those [poets] who believe and do righteous deeds and remember God often and defend [the Muslims] after they were wronged. And those who have wronged are going to know to what [kind of] return they will be returned.[300]

The Prophet (pbuh) said, "It is better for a man's chest to be filled with pus than to be filled with poetry."[301]

Abū Bakr al-Anbari said:

> There are numerous narrations from the Companions and Successors about explaining the obscure and rare words in the Qur'ān with poetry. Yet, despite this, some who have no knowledge have criticized the grammarians, and said, 'When you do this, you make poetry a source (of understanding) rather than the Qur'ān.' He says, 'we have not made poetry a primary source over the Qur'ān, but rather we wish to clarify the meanings of the obscure and rare words in it.' [302]

---

[298] Recep Doğan, *Uṣūl Tafsīr*, 322.
[299] Doğan, ibid.
[300] Qur'ān, 42:224–227.
[301] Muslim, *Saḥīḥ, The Book of Poetry*, 5609.
[302] Zarkashī, *al-Burhān Fi 'Ulūm al-Qur'ān*, 294.

Ibn 'Abbās said, 'If you ask me about the rare words in the language, then seek it in poetry, for poetry is the record of the Arabs.[303]

Once Umar asked the Companions the meaning of the verse: "Or He will take them upon *takhawwuf*."[304] Thereupon an old man from the tribe of Hudhayl stood up and said, 'This is from our dialect. *Takhawwuf* means suffering loss little by little.' 'Umar asked him, 'Is this something that the Arabs know from their poetry?' He answered, 'Yes,' and recited to them the line of poetry. After that 'Umar said, 'Stick to the recordings, you will not be misled.' When he was asked, 'What are the recordings?' he replied, 'The poetry of pre-Islamic times. Therein are the explanations of your Book, and the meanings of your words.'[305]

Due to their limited understanding of Arabic, non-Arab Muslims had a greater need to study and understand the Qur'anic language and this resulted in the emergence of many leading non-Arab linguistic scholars. Their diligent efforts were essential in preserving the purity of Qur'anic Arabic against the influence of the different cultures and languages encountered by the expanding Islamic empire. Arab scholars focused on making the Qur'ān easy to read and understand and even consulted Arabic poetry in their efforts. On the other hand, to be able to read and understand the Qur'ān, non-Arabs needed Arabic grammar books to study and learn the language. Ibn Khaldun says:

> Influenced by other cultures and different natures, Arabs began to lose their natural ability to understand their language. The Arabic language they were familiar with was becoming unfamiliar. Afraid of reaching a point where they would be unable to understand the Qur'ān and Hadith, scholars decided to establish the essentials of Arabic, its rules, grammar and so on. This led to the first works on Arabic grammar.[306]

The second century of Islam saw the development of philology of Arabic, the most notable proponents being the scholars Abū Amr al-A'la, Isa ibn Amr as-Thaqafī, Sibawayh and al-Ahfash, who authored the earliest books on Arabic grammar. Khalil ibn Ahmad wrote the first Arabic dictionary, '*Kitāb al-Ayn*.' Linguistic scholars published vital work, such as *Gharīb al-Qur'ān*, which emphasized understanding the Qur'ān from a linguistic perspective. Whilst these books are no longer available, some of their content is known due to them being referenced in other books.

---

[303] Zarkashī, ibid.

[304] Qur'ān, 16:47.

[305] Qadi Yasir, *An introduction to 'Ulūm al-Qur'ān*, 314.

[306] Ibn Khaldun, *Muqaddima*, 3/184.

Scholars disputed about whether foreign words are used in the Qur'ān. Some scholars, such as Abū Ubayda, Ma'mar ibn al-Muthanna, Shāfi'ī and Tabarī rejected this idea, whereas others accepted the possibility due to recordings that the Quraysh tribe had met with other cultures and learned some of their words. The Qur'ān was revealed in the Quraysh dialect making it possible that some foreign expressions were included in the revelation and this is the view of most scholars. However, there are some dogmatic implications regarding this issue, especially in relation to the Arabic nature of the Qur'anic text. The scholars who wrote 'Gharīb al-Qur'ān' aimed to illustrate and explain the foreign words in the Qur'ān.

I'rāb al-Qur'ān is the investigation and analysis of sentence structure in the Qur'ān according to the rules of Arabic grammar. '*I'rāb*' is to state the type of word, its ruling and its position in a sentence and deduce the meaning accordingly. This science defines each word in a sentence; verb (*fi'il*), object (*fā'il*) or subject (*maf'ul*), and is pivotal in understanding the Qur'ān. The following examples elaborate this topic.

During the caliphate of Ali ibn Abī Tālib, a Bedouin from the desert was praying behind the imam whilst he was reciting Surah at-Tawba. The imam recited the following verse:

$$\text{أَنَّ اللهَ بَرِيءٌ مِنَ الْمُشْرِكِينَ وَرَسُولُهُ}$$

And [it is] an announcement from God and His Messenger to the people on the day of the greater pilgrimage that God is disassociated from the disbelievers, and [so is] His Messenger.[307]

When reading the last word, instead of reading '*rasuluhu*,' he made a mistake and recited it as '*rasulihi*.' With this mistake, the meaning of the verse changed to mean that God is disassociated from the pagans and from the Messenger of God (pbuh). Recognising this mistake, the Bedouin laughed. He broke his prayer and severely criticised the mistake. Caliph Ali was informed about the occurrence and, to prevent incidents of a similar nature, he ordered Abū al-Aswad ad-Dualī, an expert on the Arabic language, to write down the essentials of the Arabic language. Abū al-Aswad's reply was; 'go forth in this direction (*nahw*),' which is how the science of *Nahw* got its name.

The science of *Nahw* focuses on the Arabic words, their rules, their place in the sentence and the vowels of the last syllable of each word in a sentence. Knowl-

---

[307] Qur'ān, 9:3.

edge of *nahw* is very important as, similar to the above example, there are many other occurrences in the Qur'an where simply changing the last vowel of one word can change the whole meaning of a verse. Another example is:

$$\text{إِنَّمَا يَخْشَى اللهَ مِنْ عِبَادِهِ الْعُلَمَاءُ إِنَّ اللهَ عَزِيزٌ غَفُورٌ}$$

"Only those fear God (Allah), from among His servants, who have knowledge."[308]

In this verse if the word '*Allaha*' is read as '*Allahu*' the meaning of this verse changes to: 'God fears among his servants who have knowledge.' This is a serious mistake, which results in the prayer being nullified; if one intentionally makes this mistake, he loses his faith.

The Qur'an contains some words that have multiple meanings and groups of words that all have the same meaning. The Qur'anic science '*wujūh wan-nazāir*' focuses on this area.[309] Linguistic experts examined those words, checked their existence and use in the Arabic language and explained their meaning depending on the context in which they were used. They produced books for this purpose such as *I'rāb al-Qur'ān*, *Mushkil al-Qur'ān* and *Qarīb al-Qur'ān*. One of the earliest Qur'anic exegetes, Muqātil, wrote a book on this topic, '*Wujūh Harf al-Qur'ān*' in which he elaborates upon this topic giving examples of words which have multiple meanings and those which have different meanings in different verses.[310] He claimed that the Qur'an contains 180 words that have multiple meanings, indicating their location in the verses and explaining their meaning in each instance.[311] The following two examples illustrate this topic: in Arabic, illiterate (*ummī*) defines a person in terms of knowledge is like a newborn and is unable to read or write; it is the adjective form of *umm* (mother). In Arabic, *umm* also means the original form of something.[312] Additionally, *umm* also has some metaphorical meanings. In the Qur'an, *umm* is used as the origin, the place to be returned to, and a woman who suckles. The Arab nation was also defined as "*ummī*"; for a long time, Arabs had been known as a nation that could not read, write or calculate. "*Ummi*" also means center as it is in the expression *Ummu'l-Qura* (Mother of the Cities).

The second example is the word '*quru*' which occurs in the verse:

---

[308] Qur'ān, 35:28.
[309] Suyūtī, *al-Itqān Fi 'Ulūm al-Qur'ān*, 445.
[310] Recep Doğan, *Uṣūl Tafsīr*, 329.
[311] Doğan, ibid.
[312] Firuzābādī, *al-Qāmus al-Muhīt*, check the word "am-ma."

> Divorced women shall keep themselves in waiting for three menstrual courses, and it is not lawful for them, if they believe in God and the Last Day, to conceal what God has created in their wombs.[313]

In this verse, the word '*quru*' has two meanings; purification from menstruation and the beginning of menstruation. Islamic schools varied in their interpretations of this word, some choosing the first meaning and ruling accordingly with others choosing the second meaning and ruling based on that.[314]

The context in which a word is used can also affect the meaning; for example: "There will circulate among them young boys made eternal."[315] The word '*mukhalladun*' can be understood in one of two ways; either as they will never get older or that they will be the same age and their age won't be changed.[316]

Some Qur'anic verses can be understood as being absolute or restricted statements. For example:

> God will not impose blame upon you for what is meaningless in your oaths, but He will impose blame upon you for [breaking] what you intended of oaths. So its expiation is the feeding of ten needy people from the average of that which you feed your [own] families or clothing them or the freeing of a slave. But whoever cannot find [or afford it] - then a fast of three days [is required]. That is the expiation for oaths when you have sworn. But guard your oaths. Thus does God make clear to you His verses that you may be grateful.[317]

Abū Ḥanīfa, Thawrī and their followers understood this verse to be restricted and ruled that the fast must be three consecutive days based on the personal *Muṣḥāf* of Abdullah ibn Mas'ud. However, Imam Shāfi'ī rejected this evidence as it was not the official *Muṣḥāf*, and he ruled that it is permissible to separate the days when fasting.[318]

The Qur'ān contains some other expressions that can be understood either literally or metaphorically. For example: "And that it is He who makes laugh and weep."[319] Literally, this verse means that God created human beings who are able to laugh or cry. Metaphorically, it means that the earth laughs when plants grow

---

[313] Qur'ān, 2:228.
[314] Recep Doğan, *Uṣūl Tafsīr*, 330.
[315] Qur'ān, 56:17.
[316] Doğan, *Uṣūl Tafsīr*, 330.
[317] Qur'ān, 5:89.
[318] Doğan, *Uṣūl Tafsīr*, 331.
[319] Qur'ān, 53:43.

in it and the sky cries when it rains. The essential meaning of this verse is happiness or sadness; laughing indicates happiness and crying indicates sadness.

Some verses contain letters that strengthen the meaning of the verse. Scholars vary in their opinions about the importance of these letters; some hold that removing them does not affect the meaning of the word whilst others claim they are essential and removal would affect the essential meaning of the verse.[320] For example, in the verse: "I swear by the Day of Resurrection,"[321] the letter '*la*' at the beginning of the verse is accepted by some scholars as an additional letter which strengthens the meaning. Other linguists, however, hold that it is not additional and the meaning of this letter is prohibition, giving the meaning that Judgment Day is obvious and does not need any evidence to support it.[322]

As is apparent in the standard grammar form, pronouns are very often used in the Qur'ān and a pronoun without a reference point results in ambiguity of meaning.[323] In some verses, the reference point of the pronoun is unclear and this caused disagreement amongst scholars. For example: "And he certainly saw him in another descent."[324] In this verse, the reference point is not clear and so it is not certain whether the Prophet (pbuh) saw God or the angel Gabriel in his ascendance to the heavens.

It is clear that Qur'anic exegetes must have an exhaustive knowledge of Arabic etymology and syntax. The following scholars explained the Qur'ān by applying inclusive linguistic techniques: Zamakhsharī, Qādi Baydāwī, Nasafī, Abū as-Suud, Jalalayn, Abū Hayyan. Some of these philological works are still referenced by scholars today such as: '*al-Mufradaat fi Qarīb al-Qur'ān* (Rāghib al-Isfahānī) and *Basairu Dhaw-it Tamyiz* (Firuzābādī).

Some listed notable linguistic exegeses until the fourth Islamic century:[325]

1. Zayd ibn Ali (d. 121 A.H. / 738 C.E.), '*Tafsīr Gharīb al-Qur'ān al-Majīd.*'
2. Wāsil ibn Atā (d. 131 A.H. / 748 C.E.), '*Ma'āni al-Qur'ān.*'
3. Abān ibn Taghlab ibn Rabah al-Jarīrī (d. 141 A.H. / 758 C.E.), '*Gharīb al-Qur'ān.*'
4. Muarrij ibn Amr ibn al-Harith ibn Mani' as-Sadūsī (d. 174 A.H. / 790 C.E.), '*Gharīb al-Qur'ān.*'

---

[320] Doğan, *Uṣūl Tafsīr*, 332.
[321] Qur'ān, 75:1.
[322] Doğan, *Uṣūl Tafsīr*, 332.
[323] Doğan, ibid.
[324] Qur'ān, 53:13.
[325] Recep Doğan, *Uṣūl Tafsīr*, 324–325.

5. al-Ahfash (d. 177 A.H. / 793 C.E.), *'Kitāb Ma'ān al-Qur'ān.'*

6. Yunus ibn Habib (d. 183 A.H. / 790 C.E.), *'Ma'ān al-Qur'ān.'*

7. Abū al-Hasan Ali ibn Hamza al-Kisaī (d. 189 A.H. / 804 C.E.), *'Ma'āni al-Qur'ān.'*

8. Abū Fayd Marsad ibn al-Harith ibn Sadūs (d.195 A.H. / 810 C.E.), *'Gharīb al-Qur'ān'* and *'Ma'āni al-Qur'ān.'*

9. Abū al-Hasan Nadr ibn Shumayl an-Nahwī (d. 203 A.H. / 813 C.E.), *'Gharīb al-Qur'ān.'*

10. Muhammad ibn al-Mustanir, Abu Ali al-Qutrub (d. 206 A.H. / 821 C.E.), *'Ma'ān al-Qur'ān.'*

11. Abū Zakariyya Yahya ibn Ziyad al- Farrā (d. 207 A.H. / 822 C.E.), *'Ma'ān al-Qur'ān.'*

12. Abū Ubayda Ma'mar ibn al-Muthanna (d. 210 A.H. / 825 C.E.), *'Majāz al-Qur'ān.'*

13. Abū al-Hasan Sa'id ibn Mas'ada al-Ahfash al-Awsat (d. 221 A.H. / 835 C.E.), *'Gharīb al-Qur'ān'* and *'Ma'āni al-Qur'ān.'*

14. Abū Ubayd al-Qāsım ibn Sallam (d. 223 A.H. / 837 C.E.), *'Gharīb al-Qur'ān'* and *'Ma'āni al-Qur'ān.'*

15. Muhammad ibn Sallam ibn Abdillah ibn Sālim al-Jumahi (d. 232 A.H. / 846 C.E.), *'Gharīb al-Qur'ān.'*

16. Abū Muhammad Abd Allah ibn Muslim ibn Qutayba (d. 276 A.H. / 889 C.E.), *'Ta'wil-u Mushkil al-Qur'ān'* and *'Gharīb al-Qur'ān.'*

17. Ismail ibn Ishāq ibn Ismail ibn Ḥammad al-Azdī (d. 282 A.H. / 895 C.E.), *'Ma'āni al-Qur'ān.'*

18. Muhammad ibn Yazid ibn Abdi'l-Akbar, Abū al-'Abbās al-Mubarrad (d. 285 A.H. / 898 C.E.), *'Ma'āni al-Qur'ān.'*

SUMMARY: INTRODUCTION

1. A true understanding and interpretation of the Qur'ān requires an in-depth knowledge and understanding of Arabic philology.

2. In the areas of vocabulary, grammar, rhetoric, and the principles of discourse, the Qur'anic *tafsīr* must comply with the guidelines of Arabic philology.

3. The depth and richness of meaning are expressed through parables, figurative and symbolic rhetoric as well as metaphors and similes.

4. There are verses where the wording appears general but is, in fact, specific; in other verses, words or phrases seem to be missing whereas they are inferred from the context.

5. In some verses, it seems that the logical sequence of the words has been reversed whereas, in fact, this reversal adds a subtle meaning that would otherwise not be present.

6. The primary sources for making a commentary on the Qur'ān are the book itself, the words and practises of the Prophet (pbuh) and the knowledge of the Companions.

7. Interpretation based on Arabic philology comes after the above three sources in its validity; it should neither contradict nor succeed the primary sources.

8. During the time of the Prophet (pbuh), the Qur'anic revelations served to unify the Arab tribes, enhancing and enriching their language with the addition of many different dialects.

9. Over time, the Qur'ān came to be interpreted inaccurately by specific groups who developed their own styles of interpretation including the *Ẓahirī* (literalist) and the *Bāṭinī* (esoteric).

10. After the time of the Companions that the Arabic language came to be compromised from external influences due to the enlargement of the Islamic state.

11. Scholars were required to establish fundamental grammar rules in order to protect and preserve the pure Qur'anic Arabic. Many books were authored according to this linguistic method, one of the most well known being '*Qarīb al-Qur'ān.*'

12. Linguistic scholars focused their efforts on the difficult words, metaphoric expressions and ambiguous statements in their *tafsīr*, using a specific methodology.

13. Due to their limited understanding of Arabic, non-Arab Muslims had a greater need to study and understand the Qur'anic language and this resulted in the emergence of many leading non-Arab linguistic scholars.

14. The second century of Islam saw the development of philology of Arabic.

15. Scholars disputed about whether foreign words are used in the Qur'ān. Scholars wrote '*Gharīb al-Qur'ān*' aiming to illustrate and explain the foreign words in the Qur'ān.

16. *I'rāb al-Qur'ān* is the investigation and analysis of sentence structure in the Qur'ān according to the rules of Arabic grammar.

17. The science of *Naḥw* focuses on the Arabic words, their rules, their place in the sentence and the vowels of the last syllable of each word in a sentence.

18. The Qur'ān contains some words that have multiple meanings and groups of words that all have the same meaning. The Qur'anic science *'wujūh an-nazāir'* focuses on this area.

19. The Qur'ān contains some other expressions that can be understood either literally or metaphorically.

20. Some verses contain letters that strengthen the meaning of the verse.

21. As is apparent in the standard grammar form, pronouns are very often used in the Qur'ān and a pronoun without a reference point results in ambiguity of meaning.

22. It is clear that Qur'anic exegetes must have an exhaustive knowledge of Arabic etymology and syntax and the fourth century of Islam saw many notable linguistic scholars.

Al-Farrā and His *Tafsīr Ma'ani al-Qur'an*

His Life

One of the most profound scholars in the field of Arabic grammar was Abū Zakariyya Ziyad ibn Abd Allah ibn Mansur al-Kūfi al-Farrā (761 - 822 C.E.).[326] Born in Kūfa (Iraq), he was accomplished in linguistics, literature and other sciences.[327] He received his education from Qays ibn al-Rabi, Mandal ibn Ali, al-Kisaī and Sufyan ibn Uyayna.[328] Farrā had an exceptional memory and did not take notes while studying. He wrote books without needing to verify his work against other reference works.

The fundamentals of the Arabic language would not have survived had it not been for Farrā's work establishing its foundations and summarizing it.[329] It is reported that he wrote 3000 pages.[330] He used philosophical concepts in his work and his work revealed an inclination towards Mutazalite doctrines. Farrā is most well known for his work in the field of *nahw* (Arabic grammar), having received his education from another well-known scholar al-Kisaī, the leader of Arabic

---

[326] Ibn Nadīm, *al-Fihrist*, 99–100.

[327] Khatib Baghdadi, *Tārikh al-Baghdad*, 14/149.

[328] Recep Doğan, *Uṣūl Tafsīr*, 325.

[329] Ibn al-Anbari, *Nuzhat'ul Alifbā fi Tabaqāt al-Udabā*, 127.

[330] Ibn al-Anbar, ibid.

grammar in his time.[331] Al-Farrā produced many works on Arabic grammar and also on the linguistic aspects of the Qur'ān.[332]

His *Tafsīr*

Farrā produced his most notable work in the field of *tafsīr*; *Tafsīr al-Mushkil I'rāb al-Qur'ān wa Ma'ānihi*, more commonly known as *Ma'ān al-Qur'ān*. The following story, related by scholars, reveals the reason why he wrote this work:[333]

A companion of Farrā wrote to him and informed him that the ruler, Hasan ibn Sahl, had asked some questions about the Qur'ān that he could not answer. He asked Farrā to write a reference book to clarify and address these particular topics. Farrā gathered his students and friends and, informing them that he would write a book on the Qur'ān, he began to make a commentary. Beginning with Surah Fatiha and ending with Surah Nās, he sat in the mosque and explained the verses as the imam recited them. The tradition of interpreting the Qur'ān in the mosque began with him. It is reported that 80 copies of this *tafsīr* were written during those gatherings.[334]

Farrā wrote this book to remove the difficulties and enable a clear understanding of the Qur'ān. Initially, he addressed the ambiguous words from the *I'rāb* perspective (analyzing the words in the sentences according to the Arabic grammar), giving their meanings according to their context, then he discussed their various readings, supporting his arguments with Arabic poetry, and finally, he submitted to the true knowledge by saying "God knows best." This demonstrates a cautious reverence when interpreting the verses of the Qur'ān. For example:

> Their example is that of one who kindled a fire, but when it illuminated what was around him, God took away their light and left them in darkness [so] they could not see"[335]

Farrā asserts that the situation in this verse is a simile rather than referring to a specific person; it explains the situation of the hypocrites and the sin of hypocrisy. Farrā concludes his analysis with "God knows best."[336]

---

[331] Baghdadi, *Tārikh al-Baghdad*, 14/152.
[332] Ibn al-Anbari, *Nuzhat'ul Alifbā*, 7/278.
[333] Ibn al-Anbari, ibid.
[334] Baghdadi, *Tārikh al-Baghdad*, 14/150.
[335] Qur'ān, 2:17.
[336] Farrā, *Ma'ān al-Qur'ān*, 1/15.

In his explanations, Farrā indicates how the words are used in the Arabic language and expounds the opinions of the early scholars. For example, when interpreting the following verse, he reported the opinion of Ibn Abbas;[337]

> It is He Who created all that is in the world for you then He directed to the heaven, and formed it into seven heavens. He has full knowledge of everything[338]

Sometimes he analyses the words in the sentences from their viewpoint. For example;

> And believe in what I have sent down confirming that which is [already] with you, and be not the first to disbelieve in it. And do not exchange My signs for a small price, and fear [only] Me.[339]

In this verse, the word '*kafir*' (unbeliever) is used in its singular form despite referring to a group of people. Farrā elucidates this as a part of Arabic semantics and substantiates his view with arguments from old Arabic poetry.[340] In order to better appreciate Farrā's *tafsīr* methodology, his commentary of Surah Kawthar will be examined in line with the principles of Qur'anic exegesis.

SUMMARY: AL-FARRĀ AND HIS *TAFSĪR MA'AN AL-QUR'AN*

1. Born in Kūfa (Iraq), he was accomplished in linguistics, literature and other sciences and was known for his exceptional memory.
2. His work on the fundamentals of Arabic saved the language.
3. He used philosophical concepts in his work and inclined towards Mutazalite doctrines.
4. He is most well known for his word in the field of *nahw* and produced many works on Arabic grammar and also on the linguistic aspects of the Qur'ān.

His *Tafsīr*

5. His *tafsīr*, *Ma'ān al-Qur'ān*, was his most notable work and was written on the request of the ruler at the time to remove the difficulties and enable a clear understanding of the Qur'ān.

---

[337] Farrā, *Ma'ān al-Qur'ān*, 1/25.
[338] Qur'ān, 2: 29.
[339] Qur'ān, 2:41.
[340] Farrā, *Ma'ān al-Qur'ān*, 1/32–33.

6. He first addressed the ambiguous words from the *I'rāb* perspective then discussed their readings. He supported his views with Arabic poetry and submitted to the knowledge of God.

7. In his explanations, Farrā indicates how the words are used in the Arabic language and expounds the opinions of the early scholars.

SURAH KAWTHAR (ABUNDANT GOOD)

بِسْمِ اللهِ الرَّحْمنِ الرَّحِيم

اِنَّا اَعْطَيْنَاكَ الْكَوْثَرَ ﴿١﴾ فَصَلِّ لِرَبِّكَ وَانْحَرْ ﴿٢﴾ اِنَّ شَانِئَكَ هُوَ الْاَبْتَرُ ﴿٣﴾

Surah Kawthar (Abundant Good)

In the Name of God, the all Compassionate and the most Merciful.

1. We have surely granted you (unceasing) abundant good;

2. So pray to your Lord, and sacrifice (for Him in thankfulness).

3. Surely it is the one who offends you who is cut off (from unceasing good, including posterity).

Tafsīr

Surah Kawthar is a three-verse chapter that was revealed in Mecca. It takes its name from *al-kawthar* (unceasing, abundant good) that is mentioned in its first verse. It conveys to God's Messenger (pbuh) the good tidings that he will be favored with unceasing, abundant blessings, and that those who oppose him and determine him as one with no posterity will be cut off from every good, as well as from posterity.[341]

First verse: إِنَّا أَعْطَيْنَاكَ الْكَوْثَرَ *We have surely granted you (unceasing) abundant good.*

Farrā did not analyze this verse grammatically; he related a report from Ibn Abbas, "*kawthar* is abundant favors and the Qur'ān is one of them."[342] He then related a report from Aisha, "*kawthar* is a river in Paradise, those who want to hear its sound should place their fingers in their ears."[343]

---

[341] Ali Ünal, see footnote for Surah Kawthar.

[342] Abū Zakariyya Ziyad ibn Abd Allah ibn Mansur al-Kūfī al-Farrā, *Ma'ān al-Qur'ān*, Ālam al-Kutub, Beirut 1983, 3/295.

[343] Farrā, *Ma'ān al-Qur'ān*, 3/296.

In this verse, God conveys glad tidings to the Prophet Muhammad (pbuh) by using the Arabic word *kawthar*. This word promises an abundance of favors, a successful cause and the favor of great blessings, both in this world and the afterlife. It also implies the future success and conquests of Islam. The word also alludes to the Muslims' unending love and remembrance for their Messenger (pbuh) demonstrated through their continuous prayers and salutations. Additionally, *kawthar* indicates that the Prophet (pbuh) will be given the privilege of intercession for all humanity in the afterlife and raised to the rank of the praised (*maqam al-mahmud*).

The word *kawthar* conveys to the Prophet (pbuh) that his religion will prevail over all other religions and humanity will embrace Islam. Both the Prophet (pbuh) and the Muslims will be favored with great blessings in Paradise. *Kawthar* (the unceasing abundant favors) also implies that Prophet Muhammad (pbuh) will have the best descendants who will be dedicated in their service in the way of Islam. In fact, there is no one who could equal or be similar to him in virtue and service to Islam.

Second verse: فَصَلِّ لِرَبِّكَ وَانْحَرْ *So pray to your Lord, and sacrifice (for Him in thankfulness);*

Farrā explained this verse to mean, 'perform the Eid prayer in Eid al-Adha and then sacrifice an animal for God.'[344] Relating from Ali, he explained that the Arabic word '*nahr*' (sacrifice) means holding the left hand with the right hand in the prayer.[345] It is also reported that this verse means facing the *qibla* in the prayer.[346] Farrā said, "I heard some Arabs saying, 'our houses are facing each other from such a direction,'"[347] quoting a line of Arabic poetry to support his view.

When explaining this verse, Farrā merely mentioned some of the reports available without analyzing them or preferring one to the others. As a linguistic *mufassir*, he explains the verse philologically using Arabic poetry to support his view. He occasionally presents the opinions of the early scholars free from examination however, his preponderate stance is to provide philological analysis of the Qur'anic text.

Although Farrā did not mention the following commentary in his book, the subsequent opinion offers insight on the verse that ordered the Messenger (pbuh) to perform the *Duha* (forenoon) prayer. God made the performance of this prayer

---

[344] Farrā, ibid.
[345] Farrā, ibid.
[346] Farrā, ibid.
[347] Farrā, ibid.

obligatory for the Prophet (pbuh) whilst it was supererogatory for the rest of the Muslims. The verse also clarifies the Eid prayer, performed on the mornings of Eid al-Fitr, at the end of Ramadan and Eid al-Adha, on the tenth of Dhu'l-Hijjah. It was commanded as a form of worship during the Medina years and is performed by all Muslims.

The Prophet (pbuh) performed animal sacrifices in Mecca as an optional form of worship to express gratitude to God; however, it was made compulsory for all Muslims during the Medina years.[348] The Ḥanafī School ruled that it is compulsory at Eid al-Adha for all Muslims in possession of the agreed amount of *nisab*[349] to sacrifice an animal.

Third verse: إِنَّ شَانِئَكَ هُوَ الأَبْتَرُ *Surely it is the one who offends you who is cut off (from unceasing good, including posterity);*

In explaining this verse, Farrā elucidated[350] that the Arabic word '*abtar*' was used by the Arabs to label one who did not have a son, implying that he would not be remembered after his death as his lineage would not continue. The Quraysh used this expression to insult the Prophet (pbuh) as his sons had died at a young age and he was left with only daughters to his name. The expression in the verse إِنَّ شَانِئَكَ indicates that whoever expresses rancor and enmity towards the Proph - et (pbuh) will be the one to be cut off (*abtar*) and not remembered. God further mentions the Prophet's (pbuh) name alongside His Name as a means of glorification, and states in the Qur'ān; "We exalted your name."[351]

Farrā's method in his commentary of this verse is to initially clarify the meaning of the term '*abtar*,' giving relevant historical information to provide context. Then, he explains the verse by using another from the Qur'ān. These characteristics of *riwāyah mufassir* are perceptible in Farrā's work.

SUMMARY: SURAH KAWTHAR

1. A three-verse chapter revealed in Mecca it conveys good news to the Prophet (pbuh) that he will be favored with unceasing, abundant blessings, and that those who oppose him will be cut off from every good.

2. To explain the first verse, Farrā related reports from Ibn Abbas and Aisha and then explains the verse according to the meanings of the words.

---

[348] According to some legal schools it is recommended (Sunnah), not obligatory, but in Ḥanafī school of thought it is obligatory (*wajib*).

[349] Minimum amount to be responsible for giving *zakat*.

[350] Farrā, *Ma'ān al-Qur'ān*, 3/296.

[351] Qur'ān 94: 4.

3. To explain the second verse, Farrā mentioned some of the reports available, then explains it philologically using Arabic poetry to support his arguments.

4. The third verse is also explained according to the words used; clarifying the meaning of the word *'abtar'* then providing context through historical information and finally referring to another verse in the Qur'ān.

5. These principle characteristics of *riwāyah mufassir* are perceptible in Farrā's work.

CHAPTER 7

Theological *Tafsīr*, Imam Māturidī and *Ta'wilāt*

Introduction

After the first century of *Hijrah,* the appearance of sectarian movements in Islam, such as Mutazalite, Shia and Khārijite, was one of the main objectives that compelled scholars to produce works of *tafsīr.* Whether influenced by a political agenda or religious zeal, each group interpreted the Qur'ān to corroborate their own world-view using rational and cogent arguments to convince people of their truthfulness. These groups were selective in which verses they expounded; only quoting those that supported their agenda and ignoring others. The result was the emergence of dispute and discord amongst them that negatively impacted the Muslim community and resulted in a fallacious endorsement of these groups to the exclusion of sound knowledge.

These political conflicts that developed after the time of the Prophet (pbuh) caused great theological confusion amongst the Muslim community. Some of the more extreme groups, such as the Khārijite, accused other believers of disbelief (*kufr*), even declaring war against them, and supported their views through limited interpretations of the Qur'ān. Many ignorant Muslims deviated from the moderate Sunni path and followed false doctrines resulting in the assassination of other dissenting Muslims. The absence of a sound Islamic theology led to numerous debates taking place regarding matters of belief, with each group only focusing on verses that supported their philosophy. The deviant sects interpreted the verses without understanding the context and their relationship with other verses.[352] Islamic history has witnessed many of these sects, each of which produced *tafsīr* works based on their own religious view.

Sunni scholars felt the need to protect the Islamic faith against these extreme views. Without *tafsīr* covering the theological facets in the Qur'ān, mainstream *tafsīr* scholars were unable to satisfy the public demand for information. To address this need, they established the sound pillars of Islamic theology based on the Qur'ān and authentic Sunnah, adopting the methodology of Imam Māturidī and Ash'arī in theology and producing new *tafsīr* works. In these works, the scholars

---

[352] Shahristānī, *al-Milal Wa'n-Nihal,* Egypt 1980.

primarily elucidated the topics of belief such as free will, responsibility, destiny and the Attributes of God.

The well-known theological *tafsīr* works are:

- Abū Muslim Muhammad b Bahr al-Isfahānī (d. 934 C.E.), *'Jāmi' al-Ta'wil Muhkam al-Tanzīl.'*
- Abū Mansur Muhammad al-Māturidī (d. 944 C.E.), *'Ta'wilāt al-Qur'ān.'*
- Qādi Abd al-Jabbār (d. 1024 C.E.), *'Tanzīl al-Qur'ān an al-Matā'in.'*
- Zamakhsharī (d. 1144 C.E.), *'al-Kashshāf.'*
- Abu'l Mu'in al-Nasafī (d. 1114 C.E.), *'Tabsirat'ul Adilla.'*

SUMMARY: INTRODUCTION

1. The appearance of sectarian movements in Islam compelled scholars to produce works of *tafsīr*.

2. The groups' selective interpretations of the Qur'ān resulted in dispute and discord amongst the Muslims community and caused theological confusion.

3. Many ignorant Muslims deviated from the moderate Sunni path and followed false doctrines resulting in the assassination of other dissenting Muslims.

4. Sunni scholars felt the need to protect the Islamic faith against these extreme views. They established the sound pillars of Islamic theology based on the Qur'ān and authentic Sunnah, adopting the methodology of Imam Māturidī and Ash'arī in theology and producing new *tafsīr* works.

5. In these works, the scholars primarily elucidated the topics of belief such as free will, responsibility, destiny and the Attributes of God.

Imam Māturidī and His *Tafsīr*

His Life

Abū Mansur Muhammad ibn Mahmud al-Māturidī (d. 944 C.E.) was born in the village of Māturid in Samarkand, which gave him his name, Māturidī.[353] He was also known as Abū Mansur (father of help) due to his service to the religion; Ālam al-Huda (the scholar of world); Imam al-Huda (leader of guidance); and Imam al-Mutakallimīn (leader of theology scholars).[354] Information about his parents

---

[353] Laknawī, *Fawāid al-Bahiyya*, 195.
[354] Fethullah Hulayf, Forward in *'Kitāb al-Tawḥīd,'* Istanbul 1979.

is scarce but Baydāwī holds that his lineage comes from the Companion Abū Ayyub al-Ansari.[355] His birthday is not certain but is assumed to be 852 C.E.[356]

Māturidī was a profound scholar and strong defender of the Sunnah. He is accepted as one of the imams of *Ahli* Sunnah[357] in *Aqīda* (belief) and he followed the Ḥanafī School in practice (legal matters). He relied on the knowledge of Abū Ḥanīfa, which he learned through his teachers.[358] His contemporary, Imam Ash'arī (d. 936 C.E.), also represented *Ahli* Sunnah in *Aqīda* but due to proximity (Māturidī lived in Samarkand whereas Ash'arī lived in Baghdad), they could not benefit from each other.

Some of the most authentic information about Imam Māturidī comes from Abū Mu'in al-Nasafī who is the follower of the Māturidī School and a theology scholar. In his book *Tabsirat'ul Adillah*, he claims that Māturidī was taught by Abū Nasr al-Iyadi and Abū Bakr al-Juzjani who were the pupils of Abū Yusuf who, in turn, was a student of Abū Ḥanīfa. His other teacher was Muhammad ibn Muqātil al-Rāzī (d. 862 C.E.) who was the judge (*Qādi*) of the city of Ray.

Māturidī established the science of *Kalām* based on Abū Ḥanīfa's theology. Abū Ḥanīfa's school was distinguished in law whereas the Māturidī school specialized in the belief system, which was founded on the Qur'ān, Sunnah and logical arguments. Māturidī devoted his life to defending the belief system of *Ahli* Sunnah using logic and evidence to support his views. He died and was buried in Samarkand in 944 C.E.[359]

Using logic, Māturidī used the methodology of *Kalām* (theology) to defend *Ahli* Sunnah in the debates against the deviant sects that had emerged in his time. He interpreted the opinions of Abū Ḥanīfa and articulated them in the science of *Kalām*, explaining matters of belief using logical arguments and making them more understandable. He became known as the *Kalām* scholar of the Ḥanafī School and later this theological school of thought was ascribed to him and named the Māturidī School.[360] Subsequent scholars of this school systemized his opinions

---

[355] Hasan al-Bayadī, *Ishārāt'ul Maram min Ibārāt'ul al-Imam*, Egypt 1949, 23.
[356] Al-Māturidī, *Ta'wilāt Ahli Sunnah*, Preface, Cairo 1971.
[357] Literally translates as "people of the Sunnah and the community." They are those who hold on to the Sunnah of the Messenger (pbuh); they unite themselves upon that and are the Companions of the Messenger, the Scholars of Guidance, those who follow the Companions, and whoever travels upon their path in terms of belief, speech and action.
[358] Bayadī, *Ishārāt'ul Imam*, 23.
[359] Ibn Abī al-Wafa al-Qureshi, *Al-Jawāhir al-Mudiyya*, 1/4.
[360] Fethullah Hulayf, Forward in 'Kitāb al-Tawḥīd.'

and spread his ideas throughout Mesopotamia, central Asia, Afghanistan and other areas.

Dedicating his life to knowledge, Māturidī produced many works in various fields and became the authority for numerous fields. Not all of his books survived until the present day and those they did, have only recently been published; some of them are listed below:[361]

- *Ta'wilāt al-Qur'ān*
- *Sharh al-Fiqh al-Akbar*
- *Kitāb al-Maqālāt*
- *Radd Awail al-Adillah li'l Ka'bi*
- *Bayan Wahm al-Mu'tazila*
- *Ma'haz al-Shar'ī fi Uṣūl al-Fiqh*
- *Sharh al-Jami al-Saghīr*
- *Risāla fi'l Aqā'id*
- *Kitāb al-Tawḥīd*
- *Kitāb al-Uṣūl (Uṣūl al-Din)*
- *Risāla Fima la Yajuzu Waqfu Alayh al-Qur'ān*
- *Pendnāme-i Māturidī*
- *Risāla Shayh Abū Mansur al-Māturidī*
- *Irshād al-Mubtadain fi Tajwīd Kalami Rabb al-Alamin.*

His *Tafsīr, Ta'wilāt al-Qur'ān*

Ta'wilāt was written during the third period that marks the formation of Qur'anic exegesis. At that time, the *riwāyah* (tradition-based) method was common; however, Māturidī's *tafsīr* mainly used the *dirāyah* (reason-based) method. Despite this, in his interpretations Māturidī makes frequent references to the Qur'ān, Sunnah, the statements of the Companions and the opinions of early scholars. Additionally, he critically analyses the reports and explains them linguistically. When necessary, he indicates his preference between the reports and justifies his opinion. He uses strong arguments to refute the opinions of Mutazalite scholars [362]

Ta'wilāt encompasses all the qualifications of *dirāyah tafsīr* and is valued by scholars as a highly respected source. Beginning with the *riwāyah* method and then using the *dirāyah* method in his commentary, Māturidī is very careful not to con-

---

[361] Laknawī, *Fawāid al-Bahiyya*, 195; Zirikli, *Ālam*, 7/242.

[362] M. Ragıp İmamoğlu, *İmam Abu Mansur al-Matüridi ve Te'vilatü'l Kur'andaki Tefsir Metodu*, Ankara Üniversitesi İlahiyat Fakültesi (PhD theses) 31.

tradict the authentic reports in his interpretations. His *tafsīr* includes matters of belief classifying it an archetypal example of theological exegesis. He provides explanations of the ambiguous verses in the Qur'ān and gives details about the verses that indicate *halal*, *haram* and other legal rulings. He follows *Ahli* Sunnah in matters pertaining to belief and the Ḥanafī School in legal matters.

Māturīdī's methodology can be best conveyed using examples from his book. When interpreting the Qur'ān, his primary source was the Qur'ān itself. He demonstrates how a brief verse can be explained by another verse within the Qur'ān, and there are many examples of this in his work. For example, "Assuredly We have honored the children of Adam."[363] To explain this verse, he brings forward the verse; "surely We have created human of the best stature as the perfect pattern of creation."[364] He provides extra clarification for the first verse to convey that God prepared the earth and everything contained therein for the purpose of human beings, in this way honoring the children of Adam; "it is He Who created all that is in the world for you."[365] In addition to this, he elucidates that God bestowed humankind with free will and intellect to discern the righteous from the disbelievers and those who will benefit from His favors:

> We have sustained their traveling on the land and the sea, and provided for them (their sustenance) out of pure, wholesome things, and preferred them above many of those whom We have created with particular preferment.[366]

When explaining verses, Māturīdī mentions the various readings (*qiraat*) and personal *Muṣḥāfs* (copies of the Qur'ān) of the Companions to give a clearer interpretation. For example, the following verse; "He admits whom He wills into His Mercy,"[367] is written in the personal *Muṣḥāfs* of Ubay ibn Ka'b, Ibn Mas'ud and Hafsa as; "He devotes His Mercy to whom He wills." Māturīdī used this personal reading of the verse when giving his interpretation.

Māturīdī utilizes hadith reports to justify his argument when he uses his personal opinion to make interpretations, sometimes quoting the reports exactly and at other times merely alluding to the reports or giving their meaning. An example of this is the verse; "And (you are permitted to) eat and drink until you dis-

---

[363] Qur'ān 17: 70.
[364] Qur'ān 95: 4.
[365] Qur'ān 2: 29.
[366] Qur'ān 17: 70.
[367] Qur'ān 76: 31.

cern the white thread against the black thread."[368] Māturidī uses a hadith to explain this verse[369] and mentions that the verse is conveying how to discern the white streak of dawn against the blackness of the night.

Māturidī sometimes interprets verses from a linguistic perspective, supporting his opinions with reports from the early scholars. An example of this is the verse; "All praise and thanks are to God, *Fātir* of the heavens and the earth."[370] Māturidī gives different opinions about the meaning of the word '*Fātir*' and uses linguistic analysis to explain his own viewpoint; *Fātir* is an attribute of God Who separates the earth and heavens from the same substance. Māturidī does not rely on Arabic poetry to support his opinion; the Qur'ān is sufficient in providing explanations.[371]

Māturidī was the first *Ahli* Sunnah scholar to combine both revelation and the intellect to explicate the essentials of the Islamic faith. He used logical arguments and the Qur'ān to defend the belief system of *Ahli* Sunnah against the extreme groups.[372] He held that the *mutashābih* (ambiguous) verses could only be understood after research and their purpose was to elevate the scholars above the laymen.

Māturidī's interpretations emphasize scientific facts and the scientific content of the Qur'ān. An example is the verse; "He it is Who has created the heavens and the earth in six days, then He established Himself on the Throne."[373] In his interpretation, he explains the meaning of six days as the gradual creation and that this period saw the creation of the essential elements of earth and the heavens, not the other areas of the universe. To give a clearer and more detailed insight into Māturidī's *tafsīr* methodology, Surah Ikhlas is quoted below from his book.

SUMMARY: IMAM MĀTURIDĪ AND HIS *TAFSĪR*

1. Abū Mansur Muhammad ibn Mahmud al-Māturidī was born around 852 C.E. and died in 944 C.E.
2. He was a profound scholar and strong defender of the Sunnah specializing in matters pertaining to belief.
3. He followed the Ḥanafī School in practice (legal matters).

---

[368] Qur'an 2: 187.
[369] Bukhari, *Saḥīḥ*, 2/231.
[370] Qur'ān 35: 1.
[371] Al-Māturidī, *Ta'wilāt Ahli Sunnah*, 21.
[372] Mustafa Çetin, *Tefsirde Dirayet Metodu*, 170–174.
[373] Qur'ān 57: 4.

4. Abū Mu'in al-Nasafī, a *Kalām* scholar, claims that Māturidī was taught by Abū Nasr al-Iyadi and Abū Bakr al-Juzjani who were the pupils of Abū Yusuf who, in turn, was a student of Abū Ḥanīfa.

5. His other teacher was Muhammad ibn Muqātil al-Rāzī (d. 862 C.E.) who was the judge (*qādi*) of the city of Ray.

6. Māturidī established the science of *Kalām* based on Abū Ḥanīfa's theology.

7. He devoted his life to defending the belief system of *Ahli* Sunnah using logic and evidence to support his views.

8. Māturidī used the methodology of *Kalām* to defend *Ahli* Sunnah with logical arguments against the opinions of the deviant sects.

9. He became known as the *Kalām* scholar of the Ḥanafī School and later this theological school of thought was ascribed to him and named the Māturidī School.

10. His opinions were systemized and spread throughout the Islamic world by his students.

11. Māturidī produced many works in various fields and became the authority for numerous fields.

His *Tafsīr, Ta'wilāt al-Qur'ān*

12. Ta'wilāt was written during the third period that marks the formation of Qur'anic exegesis.

13. Māturidī's *tafsīr* mainly used the *dirāyah* (reason-based) method also referring to the Qur'ān, Sunnah, the statements of the Companions and the opinions of early scholars.

14. Additionally, he critically analyses the reports and explains them linguistically.

15. His *tafsīr* includes matters of *Kalām* classifying it an archetypal example of theological exegesis.

16. He follows *Ahli* Sunnah in matters pertaining to belief and the Ḥanafī School in legal matters.

17. When explaining verses, Māturidī mentions the various readings (*qiraat*) and personal *Muṣḥāfs* (copies of the Qur'ān) of the Companions to give a clearer interpretation.

18. Māturidī utilizes Hadith reports to justify his argument when he uses his personal opinion to make interpretations.

19. Māturidī sometimes interprets verses from a linguistic perspective, supporting his opinions with reports from the early scholars.

20. He was the first *Ahli* Sunnah scholar to combine both revelation and the intellect to explicate the essentials of the Islamic faith.

21. Māturīdī's interpretations emphasize scientific facts and the scientific content of the Qur'ān.

SURAH IKHLAS (PURITY OF FAITH)

بِسْمِ اللهِ الرَّحْمٰنِ الرَّحِيمِ

قُلْ هُوَ اللهُ اَحَدٌ ۝١ اَللهُ الصَّمَدُ ۝٢ لَمْ يَلِدْ وَلَمْ يُولَدْ ۝٣

وَلَمْ يَكُنْ لَهُ كُفُواً اَحَدٌ ۝٤

Surah Ikhlas (Purity of Faith)

In the Name of God, the All-Merciful, the All-Compassionate

1. Say: 'He, God, the Unique One of Absolute Unity.

2. God, the Eternally-Besought-of-All (Himself in no need of anything).

3. He begets not, nor is He begotten.

4. And comparable to Him there is none.'

Tafsīr

This four-verse *surah* was revealed in Mecca and takes its name from its subject matter. For this reason, it is also known as Surah at-Tawḥīd (Declaration of God's Absolute Unity).

First verse: قُلْ هُوَ اللهُ اَحَدٌ *Say: 'He, God, the Unique One of Absolute Unity';*

This *surah* was revealed to answer all the questions about God. It started with the expression '*say*' because the answer can only be given by God, not by the Prophet (pbuh). The expression does not limit the concept of *tawḥīd* (Oneness of God); rather it conveys that only God can answer these questions and that all Muslims should use these arguments to inform people about Him.

The Prophet (pbuh) is the first person who will introduce this *surah* to the people; it is the answer to his request to God to introduce Himself to His servants, therefore, he must proclaim it.

'*Say*' indicates that the verse is the answer to a previously asked question; it is being answered by God. There are two possible interpretations for the expression '*say*';[374]

- It conveys the answer to a previously asked question from God to the Prophet (pbuh).
- The Prophet (pbuh) or his followers asked a question about the topics contained within this *surah* and God responded to their question.

Prior to the word '*say*' there is no connecting particle to indicate the relationship between the question and the answer. This indicates that people are not able to see or hear God directly but must discern Him and His Presence through the examination of the causality of the universe.

هُوَ 'He'; Scholars dispute the interpretation of this word with some determining that it indicates the One who is asked. So, the meaning in this case would be, 'the One who is asked is God, and He is One.'[375] Others hold that 'He' is the greatest Name of God and the name that the children of Ali ibn Tālib used in their supplications; "O He! O there is nothing but He! O He from whom everything got its identity!" There are two ways to understand this: firstly, the expression indicates His eternal, incomparable essence; "There is nothing like unto Him."[376] It emphasizes *tawhīd*; He is One in His Essence and is exalted and can't be compared. Secondly, it is possible that 'He' refers to His Name which is not mentioned by tongue and which is not known by any of His creatures, similar to the expression of the following prayer; 'for the sake of Your name which You grant wishes when they are asked with it and answer supplications when they are made with it.'[377] If the question is related to His unknown name then the answer is merely implied, for language can neither explain it nor can the intellect comprehend it. Māturīdī's view is that the first opinion is more logical and valid in terms of being an answer for the question.[378] 'He' denotes the Divine Being in His Essence, the Necessarily-Existent One—Who is indescribable, known only by Himself.

The interpretation of the name الله God (Allah);

Linguistic scholars have disputed the root of the word '*Allah*'; it is not certain whether it derives from a known word. An aspect of every language is that there is a name for every entity that can be ascribed to it. Although the naming

---

[374] Māturīdī, *Ta'wilāt al-Qur'ān*, 10/643.
[375] Māturīdī, *Ta'wilāt*, 10/644.
[376] Qur'ān 42: 11.
[377] Māturīdī, *Ta'wilāt*, 10/644.
[378] Māturīdī, ibid.

criteria may be different across languages, the letters of a name are used to inform about the entity itself rather than its essence. In Arabic, creation is expressed with '*kun*' (be) but the letters that make up this word (*kaf* and *nun*) do not explain the reality of creation. Similarly, the names that are used for God, do not explain His Essence but merely inform us about Him. With these names, it becomes possible to know something about Him but not His Essence.

Some scholars hold the view that the Arabic word '*ilāh*' (god) is used for every deity that people worship and that this is a result of Arabic semantics rather than referencing a deity that warrants worship. The following verse illustrates the use of this word in this sense; "Have you seen the one who takes as his god (*ilāh*) his own desire? Then would you be responsible for him?"[379] This verse indicates those who venerate their own desires in place of worshipping God, despite their desires being unworthy of such reverence. Only God, whose divinity prevails over all, merits true worship. All His creatures must revere and worship Him for He creates, sustains, nourishes and educates them with His Name '*Rabb*' (Lord). He is the One true God to whom all should bow down, show their servanthood and acknowledge as the Creator (*Khāliq*). God is the Merciful and All Merciful (*Rahman* and *Rahim*), His Attributes and Names are unique and belong to Him alone. God is eternal; He has no beginning and no end and is His Names existed prior to the creation. All these aspects are implied in the verses; "Sovereign of the Day of Recompense,"[380] and "He is the Lord of everything."[381]

In the opinion of the Mutazalite scholars, God (Allah), cannot be named as One Who was worshipped before creation because nothing existed to perform this worship; therefore, before actualizing the act of worship, God could not be named 'the Worshipped' (*Ma'bud*). Māturidī does not accept this argument and refutes it in the following way:[382]

God's Attributes and Names exist alongside and at the same time as His Essence; there is no change in Him. He praised Himself before the creation and does not need others to be praised. He knew Himself as Almighty, All-Knowing, All Merciful, etc. before the creation and does not need others to affirm these names. Although the creation manifests these Attributes and Names, they exist with God and only He has the true knowledge of Himself. God, '*Allah*' is the Divine being Who manifests Himself with, and is recognized and known by His Attributes and Names.

---

[379] Qur'ān 25: 43.

[380] Qur'ān 1: 4.

[381] Qur'ān 6: 143.

[382] Māturidī, *Ta'wilāt*, 10/645.

Māturīdī analyzed the derivation of the word 'Allah' from a linguistic perspective and mentioned different views on this topic. Finding the root word for the Arabic names is significant to understanding their correct meanings.

The first view is that 'Allah' is derived from the root word 'a-la-ha' which means to seek refuge, and 'Āliha' is the one who gives refuge to those seeking it. 'Ilāh' is used in the form of 'Fa'āl' and the letter 'a' (hamza) is reduced in 'aalilāh' after which two 'lam' are combined and the word became 'Allah.'[383]

The second view is that the name 'Allah' is derived from 'wa-li-ha ya'-la-hu wila-han' meaning the source for the seekers of refuge when they fear.[384] This meaning is similar to the first view. To form the word, the letter 'waw' in wilahan is changed into 'alif' and the word became 'ilahan.' A third view is that the name is derived from 'a-la'ha' meaning to make everything bow before Him and make them servants to Him.[385] A fourth view holds that this name is related to the word 'laha' which means to be hidden,[386] whilst a fifth view relates the word to 'a-li-ha' meaning to make the hearts bewildered when they reflect upon His glory. The intellect is mystified when it contemplates His greatness.[387]

A linguistic interpretation of the words is not sufficient if the words have theological connotations. The word should also be examined according to the essentials of Islamic belief and Māturīdī goes on to discuss the meaning of 'Allah' from this perspective. When deliberating on knowledge concerning God, Māturīdī is extremely cautious, frequently concluding his statements with 'God knows best.' His view is that the name 'Allah' is only used for God Himself and He prevented His creatures from using this name for anything else. People sometimes refer to other entities as 'god' but this does not determine them as such, it is merely a linguistic expression based on their assumption. Misguided people accept these idols as intercessors between God and themselves. This is illustrated in the following verses:

> And those who take protectors besides Him [say], 'We only worship them that they may bring us nearer to God in position.'[388]

---

[383] Māturīdī, Ta'wīlāt, 10/645–646.
[384] Māturīdī, Ta'wīlāt, 10/646.
[385] Māturīdī, ibid.
[386] Ibid.
[387] Ibid.
[388] Qur'ān 39: 3.

And they worship other than God that which neither harms them nor benefits them, and they say, 'These are our intercessors with God.'[389]

Philosophers hold that God has no private name but he is recognized by the honorable names. People worship Him and address Him using the correct terminology but they cannot comprehend His Essence. God prevented people from identifying others as Creator or *Rahman* as only He has the authority to be addressed with this name. This is a favor of God upon His creatures.[390]

Say: He, God, the Unique One of Absolute Unity; the unquestionable reality about God is that He is One. This is an explanation given to a hidden question. The expression أَحَد 'One' negates all false notions and concepts about the nature of God. He is both unique and incomparable, as expressed by the word '*Aḥad*' (One) which conveys uniqueness and absolute oneness; there is no number two to follow '*Aḥad*' in numeric usage. He is *Wahid* 'One' which makes it impossible to think of a second because of the notion of *tawḥīd* (oneness). He is the only One and true God and is glorified from having no partners, rivals or anything comparable to Him.

A few points need to be mentioned regarding *tawḥīd*:
- He is absolute perfection in regards to completeness; nothing can be added to Him.
- He is the absolute One Who cannot be divided into parts.
- His Oneness is related to His Essence; the tongue cannot express, the speech cannot explain, the intellect cannot comprehend Him because He is the Lord of the worlds. He is a Divine Being, but He didn't come into being. He exists, but not from non-existence. He is with everything, but not through physical nearness. He is different from everything, but not by a physical separation. He acts, but without the accompaniment of movements and instruments.

There are some differences between God being 'the One of Absolute Unity' (*Wāḥid*) and 'the Unique One of Absolute Oneness' (*Aḥād*). God's being 'the One of Absolute Unity' (*Wāḥid*) means the manifestation of God's Names that give existence to all things and beings throughout the entire universe and are responsible for their life. God's being 'the Unique One of Absolute Oneness' (*Aḥād*) means God's concentration of the manifestations of His Names in individual things or beings. Said Nursi makes the following analogy;

---

[389] Qur'ān 10: 18.
[390] Māturidī, *Ta'wilāt*, 10/647.

The sun encompasses innumerable things in its light. This can serve to understand God's Unity. But to hold the totality of its light in our minds, we would need a vast conceptual and perceptual power. So lest the sun be forgotten, each shining object reflects its properties (light and heat) as best it can and so manifests the sun. This is an analogy for God's being the Unique One of Absolute Oneness. As related to the manifestation of God's Unity, the whole universe is a mirror to God. While as related to the manifestation of His being the Unique One of Absolute Oneness, each (shining) being is a mirror of Him.[391]

Second verse: اللهُ الصَّمَدُ *God, the Eternally-Besought-of-All (Himself in no need of anything);*

The attribute, '*al-samad*' الصَّمَدُ , is mentioned to identify *tawḥīd* (the Unity and Uniqueness of God). It conveys the meaning that everything in creation is entirely dependent on Him, but He is absolutely independent of everything; only He can meet the needs of everything in existence. He creates all beings in the most perfect form and only He can actualize the continuation of existence. Existence from non-existence and eternal life for the dependent creation is only made possible through Him. He is the only One whose existence is absolutely independent, so He is eternal. His existence is an inherent attribute of His Essence. He manifested Himself through the creation and in this way, knowledge of Him became possible.

There are two further points that need to be made about the attribute '*samad*';[392]

- He is the absolute Master. All needs are referred to Him and He is the source of all hope.
- He is absolutely void of all defects, because His Essence is whole and not a composition. This attribute is also essential for His uniqueness and oneness.

Third verse: لَمْ يَلِدْ وَلَمْ يُولَدْ *He begets not, nor is He begotten;*

God is *samad* (the Eternally-Besought-of-All and Himself in no need of anything). He begets not, because the essence of all composite things is division and giving birth. This proves that it is inconceivable to accept the notion of ascribing a child to God. How is it possible to ascribe a child for One Who does not have a womb;

> The Originator of the heavens and the earth with nothing before Him to imitate. How can He have a child, when there is for Him no consort, and

---

[391] Quoted from Ali Ünal, see the footnote for Surah Ikhlas.
[392] Māturīdī, *Ta'wīlāt*, 10/ 649.

He has created all things (i.e. nothing created can be a consort for Him)?
And He has full knowledge of everything.[393]

To be able to produce a child, one must have a partner or wife. Similarly, only those with wombs can conceive. The above verse refutes all creeds that attribute children to God. It primarily and categorically refutes the pagan doctrine that the angels are daughters and the Christian doctrine of Jesus (pbuh) being His son. Composite beings are naturally weak due to having needs. This contradicts the attribute 'samad.' If something is not a composite it cannot be divided nor increased,[394] and through this we understand His Oneness and that He is void of having a partner.

God's eternal nature means His Essence is unchanging. He needs nothing but everything is eternally dependent on Him. One of the meanings of 'samad' is 'aspiration' and in this regard, God is One who is aspired to by His servants; all creation aspires to Him to meet their needs.

Māturidī held that this verse relates to associating partners with God (shirk), which is a great sin and offense.[395] Having a child indicates that the bearer shares the same substance as the child which is obviously contrary to the notion of tawhīd. This necessitated bringing forth evidence to prove God's Uniqueness and Oneness. God created everything that exists but He is not similar to anything. The relationship between God and His creation is in no way similar to the relationship between a mother and her child. All beings other than God produce or reproduce through cause and effect, but God is beyond that; He creates everything.

In terms of substance, everything in the universe is made up of another substance or is the source of another substance. God is beyond that; nothing resembles, is similar or equal to His Essence. The creation, requiring external design and decisions, comes into existence in a time and space. This shows the need for another entity; everything needs God who designs and creates everything in a certain time and place. However, He is completely beyond all that. He was neither born nor created.

Fourth verse: وَلَمْ يَكُنْ لَهُ كُفُوًا أَحَدٌ *And comparable to Him there is none;*

The last verse of the *surah* indicates there is none comparable to God because He does not resemble His creation. To resemble means to associate and associating anything with God ruins the harmony in the universe and causes chaos.

---

[393] Qur'ān 6: 101.
[394] Māturidī, *Ta'wilāt*, 10/ 650.
[395] Māturidī, ibid.

Logic dictates that for the universe to run smoothly and harmoniously there must only be One Ruler.

Ali ibn Abī Tālib said;

> He is a Being, but not through the phenomenon of coming into being. He exists, but not from non-existence. He is with everything, but not by a physical nearness. He is different from everything, but not by a physical separation. He acts, but without the accompaniment of movements and instruments. He is the One, the only One Who is such that there is none with whom He keeps company or whom He misses when absent.[396]

The main theme of this *surah* is the Oneness and Uniqueness of God. It mentions some of His Attributes to establish a conceptual and sensory perception of *tawḥīd*. There are many different ways to understand God. One is to mention that He creates and administers His creatures, individually and as a whole. The attribution of creation to One Divine Being is an easy and logical way to explain existence. When creation is ascribed to various or random origins, insurmountable barriers are encountered. If this were the case, creating one piece of fruit would be as difficult as creating all the trees in the universe, for each and every atom has strong connections with the others and it is necessary to control, administer and provide co-ordination between them all in order to establish unity and harmony in the universe. The existence of each article requires that the atoms forming it, which are spread throughout the soil, water, and air should come together; each atom must have universal knowledge and absolute will. This is impossible because creating the heavens and the earth requires a perfect, infinite power that has no partner.

The form of the universe clearly displays Divine Unity and Oneness exhibiting clear evidence of God's Oneness. All the elements that comprise the universe are interrelated and in harmony with each other. The entire universe, from the particles to the galaxies, has been brought into existence by the same Creator, and furthermore, the motion of atoms observed in a molecule is the same as the motion of the heavenly objects observed in the solar system. This orderliness and harmony proves there is One Who has power over everything. Everything in the universe acts in strict obedience to His orders. He is God because He is the One of Absolute Unity, because He is the Eternally-Besought-of-All, because He begets not, because He is not begotten, and because comparable to Him there is none. He meets all needs but He is absolutely independent. Whatever He decrees hap-

---

[396] Ali ibn Abī Tālib, *an-Nahj al-Balāghah*, "First Sermon."

pens because His sovereignty is absolute. He is glorified and exalted above the worldly action of having a child or giving a birth because attributing this to Him destroys the belief of Divine Being.

There are two degrees of faith in God's Oneness: the first is a superficial belief that God has no partners and the universe belongs to Him alone. A believer with this degree of faith may fall into confusion or suspicion; the second degree is a firm belief in *tawḥīd*, the Oneness of God. Only He creates, maintains, provides, administers, etc. A person with his degree of faith sees God's seal on everything. They have no doubt and can feel God's Presence everywhere.

Surah Ikhlas (Purity) declares the Oneness and Uniqueness of God, at the same time, negating all false notions and concepts about the Divine Being. Everything in the universe is dependent on Him and therefore is in servitude to Him.[397] Throughout the ages, the main message and knowledge sent by God to humankind through His Prophets is the notion of *tawḥīd*. All the Prophets, including Moses, Jesus, and Muhammad (pbuh) came with the same message and invited humanity to the same belief. However, people have always deviated into polytheism or idol-worship after the death of their Prophets, forgetting their pure teachings. Their own faulty reasoning, perceptions and interpretations, have led them to the wrong path and, in order to fulfill their own worldly desires, they have ignored the Divine Being.

Summary: Surah Ikhlas

1. This four-verse *surah* was revealed in Mecca and takes its name from its subject matter.

First verse; قُلْ هُوَ اللهُ أَحَدٌ *Say: 'He, God, the Unique One of Absolute Unity';*

2. This *surah* was revealed to answer all the questions about God. The Prophet (pbuh) is the first person who will introduce this *surah* to the people.

3. The expression *'say'* has two possible meanings; it conveys the answer to a previously asked question from God to the Prophet (pbuh); the Prophet (pbuh) or his followers asked a question about the topics contained within this *surah* and God responded to their question.

4. The lack of a connecting particle before *'say'* indicates that people are not able to see or hear God directly.

5. هُوَ 'He'; Scholars dispute the interpretation of this word but with some determining that it indicates the One who is asked. So, the meaning in this

---

[397] Māturidī, Ta'wilāt, 10/652.

case would be, 'the One who is asked is God, and He is One.' Māturidī's views this as the most valid opinion.

6. Linguistic scholars have disputed the root of the word 'Allah'; it is not certain whether it derives from a known word.

7. The names that are used for God, do not explain His Essence but merely inform us about Him.

8. Some scholars hold the view that the Arabic word 'ilāh' (god) is used for every deity that people worship and that this is a result of Arabic semantics rather than referencing a deity that warrants worship.

9. Māturidī analyzed the derivation of the word 'Allah' from a linguistic perspective and mentioned different views on this topic.

10. Māturidī goes on to discuss the meaning of 'Allah' from the perspective of Islamic belief. His view is that the name 'Allah' is only used for God Himself and He prevented His creatures from using this name for anything else.

11. The expression أَحَد 'One' negates all false notions and concepts about the nature of God. He is both unique and incomparable, as expressed by the word 'Aḥad' (One) which conveys uniqueness and absolute oneness.

12. He is the only One and true God and is glorified from having no partners, rivals or anything comparable to Him.

13. God's being 'the One of Absolute Unity' (Wāḥid) means the manifestation of God's Names, which give existence to all things and beings throughout the entire universe and are responsible for their life.

14. God's being 'the Unique One of Absolute Oneness' (Aḥād) means God's concentration of the manifestations of His Names in individual things or beings.

Second verse; اللہ الصَّمَدُ *God, the Eternally-Besought-of-All (Himself in no need of anything);*

15. The attribute, 'al-samad' الصَّمَدُ, is mentioned to identify tawḥīd (the Unity and Uniqueness of God). It conveys the meaning that everything in creation is entirely dependent on Him, but He is absolutely independent of everything.

16. There are two further points that need to be made about the attribute 'samad': He is the absolute Master. All needs are referred to Him and He is the source of all hope; He is absolutely void of all defects, because His Essence is whole and not a composition. This attribute is also essential for His uniqueness and oneness.

Third verse; لَمْ يَلِدْ وَلَمْ يُولَدْ *He begets not, nor is He begotten;*

17. God is *samad* (the Eternally-Besought-of-All and Himself in no need of anything). He begets not, because the essence of all composite things is division and giving birth. This proves that it is inconceivable to accept the notion of ascribing a child to God.

18. To be able to produce a child, one must have a partner or wife. Similarly, only those with wombs can conceive. The above verse refutes all creeds that attribute children to God.

19. Māturidī held that this verse relates to associating partners with God (*shirk*), which is a great sin and offense.

20. In terms of substance, everything in the universe is made up of another substance or is the source of another substance. God is beyond that; nothing resembles, is similar or equal to His Essence.

Fourth verse; وَلَمْ يَكُنْ لَهُ كُفُوًا أَحَدٌ *And comparable to Him there is none;*

21. The last verse of the *surah* indicates there is none comparable to God because He does not resemble His creation.

22. The main theme of this *surah* is the Oneness and Uniqueness of God. It mentions some of His Attributes to establish a conceptual and sensory perception of *tawhīd*.

23. The form of the universe clearly displays Divine unity and oneness exhibiting clear evidence of God's Oneness. All the elements that comprise the universe are interrelated and in harmony with each other.

24. There are two degrees of faith in God's oneness: the first is a superficial belief that God has no partners and the universe belongs to Him alone and the second degree is a firm belief in *tawhīd*, the Oneness of God.

25. Surah Ikhlas (Purity) declares the Oneness and Uniqueness of God, at the same time, negating all false notions and concepts about the Divine Being. Everything in the universe is dependent on Him and therefore is in servitude to Him.

CHAPTER 8

Theological *Tafsīr*, Zamakhsharī and His *Tafsīr*

Introduction

The Mutazalite theological sectarian movement was initiated by Wāsil ibn Ata (d.131 A.H.) during the Amawi Caliphate.[398] Known for an excessive use of logic and continual debates in interpreting religious texts, this school of thought emphasized the human intellect and repudiated the methods of the early Islamic scholars. For this group, the intellect, God, religion, *halal* and *haram* held equal value and they only accepted reports from the Prophet (pbuh) and the Companions that did not contradict the intellect; in the event of an apparent contradiction, the intellect was preferred. The Mutazalite scholars concentrated on interpreting the *mutashābih* (unclear) verses in the Qur'ān rather than the *muhkam* (clear) verses and produced *tafsīr* books in this way.[399]

Wāsil disputed with his contemporaries over whether the term disbelief was applicable to Muslims who committed major sins. His views opposed the majority on the matter and he ended up separating from Hasan Basrī and his friends. Wāsil's view was that Muslims who committed major sins were in a place between belief and disbelief and he left the debate on those terms. Hasan Basrī affirmed that Wāsil parted company from the other scholars and after that incident was known as *Mu'tazila* (one who separated himself).[400]

The Mutazalite scholars denied the notion of destiny, believing instead in absolute free will. They hold that human beings determine their own destiny and God does not have knowledge of the progressive design. Censuring these views, Sunni scholars considered the Mutazalite an extreme group.

There are five essential points to note about the Mutazalite doctrine;[401]

1) *Tawḥīd* (Oneness of God). The most significant concept in the Mutazalite school of thought is *tawḥīd* and they strongly oppose anything that may contradict this, including the Attributes of God that are independent of His Essence. In other words, the Attributes of God are distinct from the

---

[398] Ibn Taymiyya, *Muqaddima fī Uṣūl al-Tafsīr*, s. 21.
[399] İgnaz Goldziher, *Madhāhib al-Tafsīr al-Islamī*, Cairo 1955, 152–153.
[400] Dhahabī, *al-Tafsīr wa'l Mufassirīn*, 1/368–369.
[401] Dhahabī, *al-Tafsīr wa'l Mufassirīn*, 1/371.

Divine Essence. The Mutazalite held that God can be called by names like "living," "knowing," and "powerful," but He cannot be qualified by "life," "knowledge," and "power."[402] Their view is that the Eternal God has neither names nor attributes; these were ascribed to Him after the creation and, therefore, they are created.[403] Mutazalite scholars hold that God is One, Unique, has no likeness, is beyond place and time and is not comparable to anyone. He has no physical form and His being can only be perceived through revelation or reason but not through the senses.[404]

2) *'Adl* (Justice); Humans beings are independent and responsible from their own decisions and actions. God does not create their deeds or limit their free will.

3) *Al-Wa'd wa'l wa'īd* (Warning and Promise); God will reward good deeds and punish bad deeds in relation to justice.

4) *Al-Manzila bayn al-Manzilatayn* (a place between two stages); A Muslim who commits major sins is neither a believer nor a non-believer but is between the two.

5) *Al-Amr bi'l Ma'ruf wa'n Nahy anil Munkar* (commanding the good and prohibiting the evil); Muslims are obliged to convey the message of Islam to guide people to the straight path. They can do this by praying sincerely, preaching verbally or by using force. They forced other Muslims to accept their views and persecuted those who refused.

Summary: Introduction

1. The Mutazalite theological sectarian movement was initiated by Wāsil ibn Ata during the Amawi Caliphate.

2. The movement emphasized the human intellect and repudiated the methods of the early Islamic scholars.

3. The Mutazalite scholars concentrated on interpreting the *mutashābih* (unclear) verses in the Qur'ān rather than the *muhkam* (clear) verses and produced *tafsīr* books in this way.

---

[402] Ibn Sallum, *Mukhtaṣar Lawāmi'*, 96.

[403] Abū Ya'lā Muhammad ibn al-Ḥusayn al-Farrā, *Al-Mu'tamad fī Uṣūl al-Dīn*, ed. Wadī' Zaydān Ḥaddād (Beirut: Dār al-Mashriq, 1974), 70–71.

[404] Kifayat Ullah, M.A., *Al-Kashshāf: Al-Zamakhsharī's (D. 538/1144) Mutazalite Exegesis of the Qur'ān*, A Dissertation submitted to the Faculty of the Graduate School of Arts and Sciences of Georgetown University, Washington D.C. 2013, 165.

4. Wāsil's views on belief opposed the majority on the matter and he ended up separating from the other scholars and became known as *Mu'tazila* (one who separated himself from others).

5. The Mutazalite scholars denied the notion of destiny, believing instead in absolute free will, and due to this Sunni scholars considered the Mutazalite an extreme group.

6. There are five essential points to note about the Mutazalite doctrine: *Tawḥīd* (Oneness of God); *'Adl* (Justice); *Al-Wa'd and wa'l wa'īd* (Warning and Promise); *Al-Manzila bayn al-Manzilatayn* (a place between two stages); *Munkar* (commanding the good and prohibiting the evil).

Zamakhsharī and His *Tafsīr*

His Life and Education

Abū al-Qāsım Mahmud Ibn 'Umar al Zamakhsharī (1075 - 1144 C.E.) was born in the province of Zamakhshar/Kharizm in Central Asia.[405] He specialized in Arabic grammar, lexicography and the notion of *i'jāz* (the eloquence of the Qur'ān),[406] giving priority to the use of reason over narration. He ascribed to the Mutazalite school of thought and promoted these views through his *tafsīr*.

At the time of his birth, Kharizm was one of the important centers in the development of Islamic thought. The famous vizier, Niẓām al-Mulk, supported scholars financially thus relieving them of daily responsibilities and enabling them to dedicate themselves to study. Coupled with an unprecedented freedom of thought, religion in that region flourished, yielding the advancement of great scholarship.

The limited information available about Zamakhsharī's parents suggests they were righteous people.[407] As an adult, Zamakhsharī travelled to Bukhara, the center of knowledge, to continue his education and was greatly influenced by the well-respected scholar, Mahmud ibn Jarir al-Dabbi al-Isfahānī (d. 1113 C.E.). Al Dabbi was an expert in language, Arabic grammar, *balāghah* (eloquence) and Arab literature.[408] Dabbi taught Zamakhsharī Arabic grammar and imparted his views of the Mutazalite scholars. Well versed in philosophy and logic, he was very passionate in promoting Mutazalite views.[409] He supported Zamakhsharī financially and introduced him to Niẓām al-Mulk to be promoted by the government.

---

[405] Yakut al-Rumi, *Mu'jam al-Buldan*, Beirut 1957, 3/147.
[406] Recep Doğan, *Uṣūl Tafsīr*, 153.
[407] Ibn Hallikān, *Wafayāt al-Ayān*, 4/254–260.
[408] Ibn Kathīr, *al-Bidāya wa'n-Nihāya*, 12/219.
[409] Dhahabī, *Mīzān al-I'tidāl*, 4/78.

Zamakhsharī travelled to Khorasan and Isfahan to make his fortune but on becoming seriously ill, he denounced material benefits and dedicated his life to God,[410] first learning Hadith from the famous scholars in Baghdad and later moving to Mecca where he produced his *tafsīr*.[411] Whilst in Mecca, Zamakhsharī produced many other valuable works but severe homesickness caused him to return to Kharizm where he died in the Jurjan province around 1144 C.E.[412]

Zamakhsharī forwent marriage to dedicate himself to scholarly activities; his students becoming more beloved to him than his own kin. He produced many works in various Islamic disciplines, following the Ḥanafī School in *fiqh* but defending the Mutazalite views in belief.

His Books

Zamakhsharī wrote many books in different fields, some of which were published and others of which can still be found in libraries in their original handwritten form. Some of his books are:[413]

- *Al-Kashshāf an Haqāiq al-Tanzīl wa Uyūn al-Aqāwil fi Wujūh al-Ta'wil*
- *Al-Fāiq fī Gharīb al-Hadith*
- *Kitāb al-Jibāl wa'l Amkina wa'l Miyāh*
- *Nawābigh al-Kalim*
- *Maqāmāt*
- *Rabi' al-Abār wa Nusus al-Akhbār*
- *Al-Anmuzaj*
- *Al-Mufassal fī San'ah al-I'rāb*
- *Al-Mudrad wa'l Muallaf*
- *Al-Muhajjāt wa'l Mutammam*
- *Asās al-Balāghah*
- *Muqaddima al-Adab*
- *Al-Qistās al-Aẕīm fī Ilm al-Arūz*
- *Al-Mustaqsa fī Amthal al-Arab*
- *Ajab al-Ajab fī Sharh Lamiya al-Arab*
- *Hasāis al-Ashara al-Kiram al-Barara*
- *Sharh Kitāb al-Sibawayh*
- *Sharh al-Mufassal*

---

[410] Ibn Athīr, *al-Kāmil fī Akhbār al-Bashar*, 3/ 16.
[411] Zarqānī, *Manāhil al-Irfān*, 1/538.
[412] Zirikli, *Ālam*, 8/55.
[413] Dhahabī, *al-Tafsīr wa'l Mufassirīn*, 1/429–482.

His *Tafsīr*

The Mutazalite scholar Zamakhsharī produced his *tafsīr* in Mecca over a period of two years,[414] beginning it with the phrase; "all praise is due to God, who created the Qur'ān."[415] When interpreting verses he presented the views of the Mutazalite, emphasizing the sciences of *ma'an* (the science of concepts) and *bayān*[416] and maintaining the view that all *mufassirs* must have a detailed knowledge of these sciences. Zamakhsharī benefitted from abundant sources as evident in his *tafsīr* works and the broad knowledge expressed in other Islamic sciences.

He related information from many other scholars including: Mujāhid (d. 722 C.E.), Amr ibn Ubayd al-Mu'tazili (d. 761 C.E.), Abū Bakr al-Asam (d. 849), Zajjāj (d. 923) and al-Rummani (d. 994 C.E.). He was well versed in the science of *qiraat* (various Qur'anic readings) and frequently referred to the following sources in this regard; Abdullah ibn Mas'ud's *Muṣḥāf*, Ubay ibn Ka'b's *Muṣḥāf*, the *Muṣḥāfs* in Hejaz and Damascus.[417] Zamakhsharī praised the contributions of Sibawayh in the field of Arabic grammar and often utilized his work when analyzing verses from a linguistic perspective. He also mentioned the views of other linguists such as al-Mubarrad (d. 898 C.E.) and Abū Ali al-Farisi (d. 987 C.E.).[418] He benefitted from Jāhiz (d. 869 C.E.), Abū Tammam (d. 846 C.E.) and Abu'l Ala al-Ma'arri (d. 1057 C.E.) in Arab literature.

Zamakhsharī's work is greatly admired for his emphasis on the eloquence of the Qur'ān. He explained the semantics of the words, statements and the verses from a *balāghah* (the science of eloquence) perspective. In elucidating the miracle of the Qur'ān, he concentrated on two aspects; the eloquence in its expression and the news about the unseen (*ghayb*).[419] In understanding the eloquence of the Qur'ān, one can access the secrets in it words, the richness in its meaning, the wisdom in its expressions and the deep and various knowledge contained therein.[420] Another miraculous aspect of the Qur'ān is the information about unseen events and some of these verses prove the truthfulness of Muhammad's (pbuh) Prophethood since the predictions became factual events, for example:

---

[414] Zamakhsharī, *al-Kashshāf*, Cairo 1973 4/ 659.
[415] Recep Doğan, *Uṣūl Tafsīr*, 153.
[416] It is a branch of Arabic rhetoric dealing with metaphorical language, connecting idea and verbal expression or writing, and interpreting knowledge.
[417] Zamakhsharī, *al-Kashshāf*, 1/347,399,437.
[418] Zamakhsharī, ibid, 2/369; 3/278; 1/17.
[419] Zamakhsharī, ibid, 2/273.
[420] Zamakhsharī, ibid, 4/104.

> Alif. Lam. Mim. The Byzantine Romans have been defeated in the lands close-by, but they, after their defeat, will be victorious within a few (nine) years—to God belongs the command (the absolute judgment and authority) both before and after (any event)—and at the time (when the Romans are victorious), the believers will rejoice.[421]

The Romans were Christians who followed Divine Scripture and this shared commonality meant the Muslims felt a close affinity to them as opposed to the pagan Quraysh who, like the Persians, worshipped fire and other idols. The revelation of this *surah* consoled the persecuted Muslims of Mecca by predicting the unexpected victory of the Romans against the Persians only nine years after having suffered a great defeat.[422]

Zamakhsharī emphasized and valued the human intellect above Sunnah, *ijma* (general consensus) and *qiyās* (analogy). In his interpretation of verse 111 in Surah Yusuf, Zamakhsharī mentioned the intellect as a necessary component of religion, equal to the Sunnah, *ijma* and *qiyās*, since the human intellect is necessary for their comprehension. This conviction in the significance of the intellect underpins the framework of his *tafsīr* methodology. He implemented a reason-based approach to the Qur'ān and used scientific methods as well as logical arguments to interpret the verses. For example, his explanation of the following verse is based on logical arguments:

> Do not (O believers) revile the things or beings that they have, apart from God, deified and invoke, lest (if you do so) they attempt to revile God out of spite, and in ignorance.[423]

Zamakhsharī interpreted this verse to mean that the human intellect necessitates the prohibition of any cause that produces a harmful effect. Sometimes good deeds can result in something that is harmful. An example of this is speaking badly about the deities of others. This could result in them speaking badly of God. Therefore, this must be prohibited to prevent such an evil consequence.[424]

Despite his *tafsīr* being reason-based, Zamakhsharī also benefited from *riwāyah* methods and used reports from the early scholars to explain some verses. If a report clarifies the '*asbāb al-nuzūl*' (occasions of revelations) of certain verses, he first checked the authenticity and, if authentic, he used it to explain the verse.

---

[421] Qur'ān 30: 1–4.
[422] Zamakhsharī, ibid, 3/368.
[423] Qur'ān 6: 108.
[424] Zamakhsharī, ibid, 2/44.

For example, he related from Hasan and Qatāda when interpreting verse 26 in Surah Baqara.[425]

Zamakhsharī's unique *tafsīr* methodology differed from the traditional commentary format and can be understood in the analysis of *muhkam* and *mutashābih*:

> It is He Who has sent down on you this (glorious) Book, wherein are verses absolutely explicit and firm: they are the core of the Book, others being allegorical. Those in whose hearts is swerving pursue what is allegorical in it, seeking (to cause) dissension, and seeking to make it open to arbitrary interpretation, although none knows its interpretation save God. And those firmly rooted in knowledge say: 'We believe in it (in the entirety of its verses, both explicit and allegorical); all is from our Lord'; yet none derive admonition except the people of discernment.[426]

Zamakhsharī's interpretation of '*muhkamāt*' (translated above as 'verses absolutely explicit and firm') is 'the verses that are preserved from speculation and doubt.' He held that the debates over the *muhkam* and *mutashābih* verses constitute the foundation of *tafsīr* and that it is impossible to make Qur'anic commentary before understanding these verses. Forming the core of the Qur'ān, the *muhkam* have a firm meaning and are perfectly arranged; as such, they do not require any extra explanation but serve as the basis for explaining the *mutashābih* verses. Zamakhsharī emphasized the importance of *tafsīr*, stating that it is the duty of scholars to scrutinize the verses and to struggle hard to expose the meaning of the *mutashābih* verses by referring them to the *muhkam* ones. The following examples clarify how he used *muhkam* verses to explain the *mutashābih* ones:

"Some faces on that Day will be radiant (with contentment), looking up toward their Lord."[427] This verse is *mutashābih* and Zamakhsharī explained it according to the Mutazalite view that God will not be seen in the afterlife. Therefore, he used the following verse to shed light on the former; "eyes comprehend Him not, but He comprehends all eyes."[428] In his opinion, the second verse is *muhkam* and explains the previous one.

As a result of its Mutazalite views, Sunni scholars have criticized the *tafsīr Kashshāf*, however, they have still cited, adopted and commented on it, sometimes extensively. The eminent scholar Baydāwī tried to explain the content of this *tafsīr* in his work *Anwar al-Tanzīl wa-Asrār al-Ta'wīl* but excluded all content that con-

---

[425] Zamakhsharī, ibid, 1/84.
[426] Qur'ān 3: 7.
[427] Qur'ān 75: 23.
[428] Qur'ān 6: 103.

tradicts Sunni views. Ibn al-Munayyir (d. 683 A.H./1284 C.E.) in his *Kitāb al-Intiṣāf min al-Kashshāf*, Fakhr al-Dīn al-Rāzī (d. 606 A.H./1209 C.E.) in his *Tafsīr al-Kabīr*, Abū Ḥayyān al-Andalusī (d. 745 A.H./1344 C.E.) in his *Baḥr al-Muḥīṭ* and Ibn Khaldun (d. 808 A.H./1406 C.E.) in his *Muqaddima and Jalal al-Dīn al-Suyūtī* (d. 911 A.H./1505 C.E.) all criticized Zamakhsharī's Mutazalite views.[429]

In order to understand his technique and methodology better, Surah Kafirun is quoted and analyzed below.

SUMMARY: ZAMAKHSHARĪ AND HIS *TAFSĪR*

1. Abū al-Qāsım Mahmud Ibn 'Umar al Zamakhsharī (1075 - 1144 C.E.) specialized in Arabic grammar, lexicography and the notion of *i'jāz* (the eloquence of the Qur'ān), giving priority to the use of reason over narration.

2. He ascribed to the Mutazalite school of thought and promoted these views through his *tafsīr*.

3. Zamakhsharī travelled to Bukhara for his education and was greatly influenced by the well-respected scholar, al Dabbi, an expert in language, Arabic grammar, *balāghah* and Arab literature.

4. Dabbi taught Zamakhsharī Arabic grammar and imparted his views of the Mutazalite scholars.

5. After becoming ill, Zamakhsharī dedicated his life to God, learning Hadith from the famous scholars in Baghdad and later moving to Mecca where he produced his *tafsīr*.

6. He produced many works in various Islamic disciplines, following the Ḥanafī School in *fiqh* but defending the Mutazalite views in belief.

His *Tafsīr*

7. His *tafsīr* expounded Mutazalite views, emphasizing the sciences of *ma'an* and *bayān*.

8. He related information from many other scholars and was well versed in the science of *qiraat* and frequently referred to the varied sources in this regard.

9. Zamakhsharī praised the contributions of Sibawayh in the field of Arabic grammar and often utilized his work when analyzing verses from a linguistic perspective.

---

[429] Kifayat Ullah, M.A., *Al-Kashshāf: Al-Zamakhsharī's (D. 538/1144) Mutazalite Exegesis of the Qur'ān*, 12.

10. Zamakhsharī's work is greatly admired for his emphasis on the eloquence of the Qur'ān, concentrating on the eloquence in its expression and the news about the unseen (*ghayb*).

11. Zamakhsharī emphasized and valued the human intellect above Sunnah, *ijma* (general consensus) and *qiyāṣ* (analogy) and this underpins the framework of his *tafsīr* methodology.

12. He implemented a reason-based approach to the Qur'ān and used scientific methods as well as logical arguments to interpret the verses.

13. Despite his *tafsīr* being reason-based, Zamakhsharī also benefited from *riwāyah* methods and used reports from the early scholars to explain some verses.

14. Because of its Mutazalite views, Sunni scholars have criticized the *tafsīr*, *Kashshāf*, however, they have still cited, adopted and commented on it, sometimes extensively.

SURAH KAFIRUN (THE UNBELIEVERS)

بِسْمِ اللهِ الرَّحْمٰنِ الرَّحِيمِ

قُلْ يَا اَيُّهَا الْكَافِرُونَ ۙ ﴿١﴾ لَا اَعْبُدُ مَا تَعْبُدُونَ ۙ ﴿٢﴾

وَلَا اَنْتُمْ عَابِدُونَ مَا اَعْبُدُ ۚ ﴿٣﴾ وَلَا اَنَا عَابِدٌ مَا عَبَدْتُمْ ۙ ﴿٤﴾

وَلَا اَنْتُمْ عَابِدُونَ مَا اَعْبُدُ ۙ ﴿٥﴾ لَكُمْ دِينُكُمْ وَلِيَ دِينِ ﴿٦﴾

Surah Kafirun (The Unbelievers)

In the Name of God, the All-Merciful, the All-Compassionate

1. Say: 'O you unbelievers (who obstinately reject faith)!
2. I do not, nor ever will, worship that which you worship.
3. Nor are you those who ever worship what I worship.
4. Nor will I ever worship that which you worship.
5. And nor will you ever worship what I worship.
6. You have your religion (with whatever it will bring you), and I have my religion (with whatever it will bring me).'

This six-verse *surah* was revealed in Mecca and takes its name from the word '*al-kafirun*' which is present in the first verse. '*Kafir*' is the term used to describe a person who rejects the principles of the faith of Islam, either partially or wholly. This *surah* instructs the Prophet (pbuh) and his followers to be determined and steadfast in the faith against the unbelievers and to avoid coercing the unbelievers to accept their faith.

Tafsīr

Removing hypocrisy and establishing firmness in belief, this *surah* symbolizes sincerity and purity in faith.

First verse: قُلْ يَا أَيُّهَا الْكَافِرُونَ *Say: "O you unbelievers (who obstinately reject faith);*

This verse addresses the unbelievers who refuse to believe in God. God knows that they will not believe in the future and therefore, He uses word 'unbeliever' to describe them.[430] In his commentary, Zamakhsharī differed from other Mutazalite scholars who maintained that God is unaware of a person's absolute destiny. They believed that each person creates his own destiny; therefore, if they remain in a state of disbelief it is due to their own free will since God does not interfere with a person's decisions.

In interpreting this verse, Zamakhsharī used the *riwāyah* method by quoting the following report:

> A group from the Quraysh said; O Muhammad! Let us follow both religions; you follow our religion and we will follow your religion. You worship our gods for a year and we will worship your God for a year.' The Prophet was greatly offended by this offer and said; may God protect me from associating any partner with Him.' They said; 'Greet some of our gods and revere them and we will believe in you and worship your God.' Thereupon this *surah* was revealed. The Prophet went to the Ka'ba which was full of people. He recited to them the *surah*; "Say: 'O you unbelievers (who obstinately reject faith)! I do not, nor ever will, worship that which you worship. Nor are you those who ever worship what I worship. Nor will I ever worship that which you worship. And nor will you ever worship what I worship. You have your religion (with whatever it will bring you), and I have my religion (with whatever it will bring me).'"[431] It was at that point that they despaired of him.[432]

Wāḥidī related this incident as follows:

---

[430] Zamakhsharī, *Kashshāf*, 4/423.
[431] Qur'ān 109: 1–6.
[432] Zamakhsharī, ibid.

These verses were revealed about a group of people from the Quraysh who said to the Prophet (pbuh): 'come follow our religion and we will follow yours. You worship our idols for a year and we will worship your God the following year. In this way, if what you have brought us is better than what we have, we would partake of it and take our share of goodness from it; and if what we have is better than what you have brought, you would partake of it and take your share of goodness from it.' The Prophet (pbuh) said; 'may God forbid that I associate anything with Him.' After that, God revealed all the verses of this *surah*. Then The Messenger of God (pbuh) went to the Ka'ba. It was full of people. He recited to them the *surah*. They despaired of him after this incident.[433]

Knowing the historical context of the revelation of the verses helps in understanding the intended meaning. The occasions behind the revelations provide insight into the conditions at the time the verses were revealed and also helps to prevent misunderstandings. Zamakhsharī quoted this report to describe the historical context at the time of the revelation, but he did not analyze the authenticity of the report according to Hadith criteria. His methodology shows that when reports seem reasonable and do not defy logic, he did not examine them, however, in every other case, he checked their authenticity. The above report was quoted with no further commentary, as this is not essential in Zamakhsharī's methodology.

Second verse: لاَ أَعْبُدُ مَا تَعْبُدُونَ *I do not, nor ever will, worship that which you worship;*

The particle '*la*' لَا is used to express the phrase 'I do not worship' and conveys an absolute negative meaning. This particle is only used at the beginning of *muḍāri'* (present tense) verbs to convey the negative meaning about them in the future.[434] Use of this particle conveys that the Prophet (pbuh) will never worship that which the Quraysh worship. The meaning is firm and closes all other possibilities. Similarly, if the Arabic particle '*ma*' comes at the beginning of *muḍāri'* verbs it gives the meaning of present tense. According to this grammatical rule, مَا تَعْبُدُونَ 'the gods which you worship' is understood to mean that the Prophet will never worship the gods that the Quraysh worship now. This Arabic particle shows that the current belief of the Quraysh is wrong and therefore, the Prophet (pbuh) will never agree with them on this issue. However, the grammatical use of the Arabic particle '*ma*'

433 Wāḥidī, *Asbāb al-Nuzūl*, see the Surah Kafirun.
434 Zamakhsharī, ibid.

does not disregard the possibility that they may, in the future, change their belief to be in line with Islam.

Third verse: وَلاَ أَنْتُمْ عَابِدُونَ مَا أَعْبُدُ *Nor are you those who ever worship what I worship;*

Relating from the great linguistic scholar Khalil, Zamakhsharī informed about another particle, the use of which conveys a negative meaning in Arabic. The particle 'lan' لَنْ is composed of 'la' and 'an'[435] and in using this the verse means; 'I will never do now, nor in the future, what you ask of me with regard to worshipping your gods. Similarly, you never do what I ask of you regarding worshipping my Lord.'

Zamakhsharī's skillful analysis of this verse showed his abilities as an outstanding scholar of linguistic science. His opinion was that as God had chosen the Arabic language for conveying the revelation, it is necessary to all the Islamic sciences.[436] In his commentary, he constantly made use of grammatical analysis to explain the verses.

Zamakhsharī strictly adhered to Mutazalite principles when defining belief, transgression, disobedience and guidance.[437]

- Unbelief (*kufr*); concealing God's favors and being ungrateful to Him.
- Transgression (*fusūq*); committing major sins and therefore leaving the religion.
- Disobedience (*'iṣyān*); disobeying the commandments of God.
- Guidance (*rushd*); steadfastness and firmness on the path of truth.
- Belief (*īmān*); confirmation with certainty.
- Submission (*Islām*); verbal affirmation without an agreement of the heart.

Fourth verse: وَلاَ أَنَا عَابِدٌ مَا عَبَدْتُمْ *Nor will I ever worship that which you worship;*

This verse conveys that the Prophet (pbuh) never worshipped the pagan gods in the past, despite living amongst the Quraysh (polytheists) for forty years before announcing his Prophethood. Therefore, if he had never worshipped their gods before, how could they expect him to do so during his Prophethood? The fundamental essence of Islamic belief is *tawḥīd*; belief in the Oneness of God and the rejection of any other deities. During the time of ignorance (*jahiliyyah*), the Prophet (pbuh) avoided the idols and refused to acknowledge them, even when his uncles

---

[435] Zamakhsharī, ibid.

[436] Kinga Dévényi, "I'rāb," *Encyclopedia of Arabic Language and Linguistics*, 2:401–6.

[437] Kifayat Ullah, M.A., *Al-Kashshāf: Al-Zamakhsharī's (D. 538/1144) Mutazalite Exegesis of the Qur'ān*, 146.

requested him to visit them. His firm rejection meant that he was never asked again and this incident clearly demonstrates his consistent anti-pagan stance even before the dawn of Islam. For the Quraysh to believe that the Prophet (pbuh) could ever accept their offer, which would mean him compromising his beliefs, was quite illogical.

Fifth verse: وَلَا أَنْتُمْ عَابِدُونَ مَا أَعْبُدُ *And nor will you ever worship what I worship;*

This verse elucidates that the polytheists never worshipped what the Prophet (pbuh) worshipped, instead constantly rejecting his invitation to Islam and exerting inordinate efforts to sway him from his path. The character and attitude of the Quraysh towards Islam was so harsh it was inconceivable to think they could ever accept the religion as God had commanded. This demonstrates that paganism is contrary to *tawḥīd* in its essence and the two concepts can never be reconciled. The two are mutually exclusive; one contradicts the other and therefore if one exists the other cannot. Without rejecting all other deities, polytheists cannot believe in One God and worship Him alone. Similarly, a Muslim cannot worship idols without denouncing the belief in *tawḥīd*.

Here Zamakhsharī anticipates a question and provides the answer for it:

Question: In the verse; وَلَا أَنْتُمْ عَابِدُونَ مَا أَعْبُدُ "and nor will you ever worship what I worship" the Arabic word '*a-ba-da*' (worship) is used in the past tense when indicating the unbelievers but in the present tense when referring to the Prophet (pbuh). What is the wisdom in the variance of the tenses?

Answer: The Quraysh had been worshipping idols for a long time before Muhammad (pbuh) announced his Prophethood and this is indicated with the use of the past tense of the verb 'worship.' However, the Prophet (pbuh) never worshipped idols, either in the past or at the time of this dialogue, therefore, for him the verb 'worship' is used in the present tense.

Zamakhsharī analyzed and explained this verse from a linguistic perspective and used similar techniques as Rāzī in using theoretical questions and answers. In order to understand the textual syntax of the words and the use of different tenses it is necessary to be an authority on Arabic grammar and philology. The Qur'ān comes from eternal knowledge, contains eternal knowledge and its meanings are preserved in its original words. The principal method of extracting the meanings is through a sound application of sciences such as hermeneutics, philology and semantics. The words are the molds of the meanings and the Qur'ān can only be understood from its original words and original language. For this reason, Zamakhsharī emphasizes the linguistic aspect of the Qur'ān, as demonstrated in the following question;

Question: What is the answer if one asks why the Arabic particle 'ma' is used as a conjunction to the verb 'worship' instead of the particle 'man'?

Answer: Firstly, for the benefit of readers it is necessary to identify these two particles before giving Zamakhsharī's answer. The conjunctive particle 'ma' means 'that' or 'which' and is used to identify a specific person or a thing, but the particle 'man' means 'who' or 'whom' and is used to identify a specific person. This verse indicates an attribute not an actual subject so the meaning is that the Prophet (pbuh) does not worship 'false' deities, nor do the Quraysh worship the 'true' God.[438] Using grammatical analysis, Zamakhsharī implied that the true God has true Divine Attributes and therefore He deserves to be worshipped; the Attributes of God are true and real so worshipping Him is true and valid. However, the idols are deprived of such attributes; therefore worshipping them is false and invalid.

Question: If the Arabic article 'ma' is accepted as a subordinating conjunction what would the meaning of the verse be?

Answer: If the particle is accepted as a subordinating conjunction the meaning would be; 'I will never practice your pagan rituals nor will you ever practice the rituals of Islam.'[439] If one is to perform sound worship then the belief system behind it also needs to be sound. Any lack in this area means that the rituals of belief, such as prayer, will be deficient. A person whose belief is sound cannot condone the practice of the rituals of false belief. A religion's foundation lies in its belief system; any falseness present in the belief system leads to false rituals and immoral actions. Therefore, morality and good manners are the result of a sound belief system.

Sixth verse: لَكُمْ دِينُكُمْ وَلِيَ دِينِ *You have your religion (with whatever it will bring you), and I have my religion (with whatever it will bring me);*

Religion determines the identity of those who follow it. The unbelievers are known by their religion, as are the believers, since religion has a great impact on the development of the worldview. Associating partners with God is an aspect of the unbelievers whilst *tawḥīd* belongs to the Prophet (pbuh). Prophet Muhammad (pbuh) was sent to invite the Quraysh to the truth and save them from deviation. Even if they refuse this invitation and do not follow the Prophet (pbuh) they are entitled to freedom of religion, as are the believers. In this regard, the verse can be interpreted to mean; "I am Muhammad (pbuh) and I was sent to you as a Prophet to invite you to Islam. If you accept Islam, you will be saved. However,

---

[438] Zamakhsharī, ibid.
[439] Zamakhsharī, ibid.

if you reject it and do not follow me, let me convey my message and never invite me to associate partners with God."[440]

Zamakhsharī ends his commentary of Surah Kafirun with the following hadith from the Prophet:

> Whoever recites this *surah* is accepted to have recited a quarter of the Qur'ān. Also, the chiefs of Satan will be driven away from him, he will be protected against *shirk* (associating partners with God) and will be safe from the tremendous fear of Judgment Day.[441]

SUMMARY: SURAH KAFIRUN

1. Surah Kafirun was revealed in Mecca and was named from the word '*al-kafirun*' which is present in the first verse; '*kafir*' meaning 'unbeliever.'

2. This *surah* instructs the Prophet (pbuh) and his followers to be determined and steadfast in the faith against the unbelievers and to avoid coercing the unbelievers to accept their faith.

Tafsīr

First verse; قُلْ يَا أَيُّهَا الْكَافِرُونَ *Say: "O you unbelievers (who obstinately reject faith);*

3. This verse addresses the unbelievers who refuse to believe.

4. In his commentary, Zamakhsharī differed from other Mutazalite scholars who maintained that God is unaware of a person's absolute destiny.

5. In interpreting this verse, Zamakhsharī used the *riwāyah* method quoting a report to describe the historical context at the time of the revelation, but he did not analyze the authenticity of the report according to hadith criteria.

6. His methodology shows that when reports seem reasonable and do not defy logic, he did not examine them, however, in every other case, he checked their authenticity.

Second verse; لَا أَعْبُدُ مَا تَعْبُدُونَ *I do not, nor ever will, worship that which you worship;*

7. The particle '*la*' لا is used to express the present tense phrase 'I do not worship' and conveys an absolute negative meaning about them in the future.

8. Use of this particle conveys that the Prophet (pbuh) will never worship that which the Quraysh worship. The meaning is firm and closes all other possibilities.

---

[440] Zamakhsharī, ibid.
[441] Zamakhsharī, ibid.

9. The Arabic particle 'ma' gives the meaning of present tense and means that the Prophet will never worship the gods that the Quraysh worship now.

10. However, the grammatical use of the Arabic particle 'ma' does not disregard the possibility that they may, in the future, change their belief to be in line with Islam.

Third verse; وَلاَ أَنْتُمْ عَابِدُونَ مَا أَعْبُدُ *Nor are you those who ever worship what I worship;*

11. Relating from Khalil, Zamakhsharī informed about another particle 'lan' which gives the verse the meaning; 'I will never do now, nor in the future, what you ask of me with regard to worshipping your gods. Similarly, you never do what I ask of you regarding worshipping my Lord.'

12. Zamakhsharī's skillful analysis of this verse showed his abilities as an outstanding scholar of linguistic science.

13. Zamakhsharī strictly adhered to Mutazalite principles when defining belief, transgression, disobedience and guidance.

Fourth verse; وَلاَ أَنَا عَابِدٌ مَا عَبَدْتُمْ *Nor will I ever worship that which you worship;*

14. This verse conveys that the Prophet (pbuh) never worshipped the pagan gods in the past and never would in the future as it is against *tawḥīd*.

Fifth verse; وَلاَ أَنْتُمْ عَابِدُونَ مَا أَعْبُدُ *And nor will you ever worship what I worship;*

15. This verse elucidates that the polytheists never worshipped what the Prophet (pbuh) worshipped, instead constantly rejecting his invitation to Islam and exerting inordinate efforts to sway him from his path.

16. Zamakhsharī analyzed and explained this verse from a linguistic perspective and used similar techniques as Rāzī in using theoretical questions and answers.

17. In order to understand the textual syntax of the words and the use of different tenses it is necessary to be an authority on Arabic grammar and philology.

Sixth verse; لَكُمْ دِينُكُمْ وَلِيَ دِينِ *You have your religion (with whatever it will bring you), and I have my religion (with whatever it will bring me);*

18. Religion determines the identity of those who follow it. Associating partners with God is an aspect of the unbelievers whilst *tawḥīd* belongs to the Prophet (pbuh).

19. Each side is entitled to freedom of religion.

CHAPTER 9

Juristic *Tafsīr*, Jassās and His *Tafsīr*

Introduction

As an eternal source of knowledge, the Qur'ān contains knowledge of many different sciences and each interpreter approached the text according to his own field. Accordingly, Muslims jurists focused on its legal content, trying to understand the verses related to worship (*ibadāt*), legal relationships (*muamalāt*) and penal law ('*uqubāt*). Although these works encompass additional methods in their commentaries they are classified as juristic *tafsīr* since they predominantly focus on the legal aspects of the Qur'ān. These works reflect the views of certain legal schools and their related *tafsīr* methodology.[442]

Scholars dispute the actual number of verses purely dealing with legal issues, due to the nature of the verses, some of which clearly deal with legal content whereas other merely imply it.[443] For the most part, the verses indicating legal content were revealed in Mecca in chapters Baqara, Nisā and Maida amongst others. The prominent jurist, Jassās (d. 981 C.E.), holds that there are more than 1000 legal verses in the Qur'ān[444] whereas Ghazzalī (d. 1111 C.E.) and Rāzī (d. 1209 C.E.) maintain that this number is only 500.[445] These are just a few of many views about the number of legal verses,[446] the minimum of which holds the number to be 200, and this figure identifies the verses which purely deal with legal content. Similarly, the scholars who accept a higher number of legal verses in the Qur'ān within their classification have included the verses that deal with legal content both directly and indirectly.

Scholars have classified two types of legal verses depending on the clarity with which they expound legal rules; a) the verses that clearly and directly explain legal rules and b) the verses that imply legal rules and require interpretation from expert jurists through *ijtihād*. The second type of verses consists of two categories; the verses from which legal rules can be extracted without resorting to other

---

[442] Mevlüt Güngör, *Kur'an Tefsirin de Fıkhi Tefsir Hareketi ve İlk Fıkhi Tefsir*, Kur'an Kitaplığı, İstanbul 1996, s. 51

[443] Bedreddin Çetiner, "*Ahkânıu>l-Kur>ân*", DİA, İstanbul 1988, 1/551.

[444] Mevlüt Güngör, *Cassās ve Ahkāmu'l-Kur'ān'ı*, Elif Matbaası, Ankara 1989, s. 49.

[445] Zarkashī, *al-Burhān fī 'Ulūm al-Qur'ān*, Dār al-Fikr, Beirut 2001, 2/ 5.

[446] Suyūtī, *Kanz al-Irfān fī Fıqh al-Qur'ān*, s. 29

verses and the verses that must be referred to other verses in order to extract their rules.[447]

Beginning in the second century after *hijrah,* the scholars who produced juristic *tafsīr* were known as '*Aḥkām al-Qur'ān,*' '*Fiqh al-Qur'ān*' and '*Tafsīr Āyāt al-Qur'ān.*' The most acknowledged juristic exegetes are listed below;

- Imam Shāfi'ī (d. 819 C.E.), '*Aḥkām al-Qur'ān*'
- Taḥawī (d. 933 C.E.), '*Aḥkām al-Qur'ān*'
- Jassās (d. 980 C.E.), '*Aḥkām al-Qur'ān*'
- Abū Bakr ibn Arābī (d. 1148 C.E.), '*Aḥkām al-Qur'ān*'
- Al-Qurtubī (d. 1272 C.E.), '*al-Jāmi' li Aḥkām al-Qur'ān.*'

Summary: Introduction

1. Muslims jurists focused on the legal content of the Qur'ān, trying to understand the verses related to worship (*ibadāt*), legal relationships (*muamalāt*) and penal law ('*uqubāt*) and are classified as juristic *tafsīr*.

2. Scholars dispute the actual number of verses purely dealing with legal issues, due to the nature of the verses, some of which clearly deal with legal content whereas other merely imply it.

3. Scholars have classified two types of legal verses: a) those that clearly and directly explain legal rules and b) those that imply legal rules and require interpretation through *ijtihād.*

4. The second type has two categories; a) verses from which legal rules can be extracted without resorting to other verses, b) verses which must be referred to other verses.

5. Beginning in the second century after *hijrah,* the scholars who produced juristic *tafsīr* were known as '*Aḥkām al-Qur'ān,*' '*Fiqh al-Qur'ān*' and '*Tafsīr Āyāt al-Qur'ān.*'

Jassās and His *Tafsīr*

His Life and Education

Abū Bakr al-Jassās al-Ḥanafī, a famous jurist of the Ḥanafī School, was born in the city of Ray in 917 C.E.[448] He went to Baghdad to complete his education, which at

---

[447] Bedreddin Çetiner, "*Ahkānıu>l-Kur>ān*", DİA, İstanbul 1988, 1/551.
[448] To know more about his life and education please refer to Mevlüt Güngör, *Cessās ve Ahkāmu'l-Kur'ān'ı,* 100–178.

that time was the center of scholarly and political activities. After learning many Islamic disciplines, he became an authority in the Ḥanafī School. Jassās's teachers were renowned for their expertise in the fields of hadith, *fiqh*, Arab philology and others. Jassās was highly esteemed for his profound knowledge in the science of Islamic Jurisprudence as well as for being well versed in the hadith sciences, the knowledge of which he evidently employed in his juristic discussions.

Jassās is accepted as a *mujtahid* in the third category of *ijtihād* (*mujtahid fi'l mas'ala*). This title identifies him as capable of extracting rules in certain areas using the Ḥanafī School methodology. He had a strong, noble character, was intolerant of injustice and quick to criticize the erroneous actions of his contemporary rulers. To maintain the independence of his scholarly opinions he refused all official government positions that were offered him. His opponents accused him of partiality towards Mutazalite opinion, but this claim is baseless and was clearly refuted in his *tafsīr*.[449]

Jassās's many students emanated from different cities and some later became famous jurists in Ḥanafī *fiqh*. His extraordinary memory, logic and intellect are clearly apparent on analysis of his work. The majority of Jassās's writing explains the work of the early Ḥanafī scholars such as Taḥawī and al-Karkhī, which required an in-depth knowledge of their *fiqh*. It is reported that he produced 12 works.[450]

His Methodology in *Tafsīr*

The most important work of Jassās is his final book '*Aḥkām al-Qur'ān*,' an accumulation of his expertise and a summary of his previous work.[451] In his book, he explains verses in the order they appear in the Qur'ān, concentrating on verses dealing with legal matters rather than interpreting the whole book. The total number of verses explained in his book is 1050.

Jassās used five categories of source in '*Aḥkām al-Qur'ān*': *tafsīr*, hadith, *fiqh*, Arab philology and history. He benefitted from many *tafsīr* books in his work but only mentions by name those of Shāfi'ī and Taḥawī.[452] He benefitted from the books of famous hadith scholars such as Tabaranī (d. 971 C.E.) and Ḥākim Nisaburī (d. 1014 C.E.). In the field of *fiqh* he benefitted almost from all early scholars.[453] His sources in linguistic sciences are the famous scholars Kisaī, Hamza, Asma'i, Farrā,

[449] Mevlüt Güngör, *Cessās ve Ahkāmu'l-Kur'ān'I*, 138–148.
[450] Güngör, ibid, 152–178.
[451] Abū Bakr Ahmad ibn Ali al-Rāzī al-Jassās, *Aḥkām al-Qur'ān*, Dār al-Fikr, Beirut 1993.
[452] Jassās, *Aḥkām al-Qur'ān*, 1/52,164,370,470; 2/358; 3/47,372,453.
[453] Güngör, *Cessās ve Ahkāmu'l-Kur'ān'I*, 183–196.

Abū Ubayda, Ahfash and Zajjāj.[454] Occasionally, he relates historical information about specific events but does not mention his sources. He also mentions the famous historians, Ibn Isḥāq (d. 768 C.E.), Wāqidī (d. 822 C.E.) and Muhammad ibn Umar (d. 823 C.E.).[455]

Similar to the majority of scholars in this field, Jassās uses both the *riwāyah* and *dirāyah* methods in his *tafsīr*. When interpreting the verses he refers to the Qur'ān first and then to the Sunnah, following which he relates the opinions of the Companions and Successors about the occasions of the revelations (*asbāb nuzūl*), the abrogating-abrogated (*nāsikh-mansukh*) verses and the various Qur'anic readings (*qiraat*). Jassās's interpretation of the verses containing legal matters exposes the practical aspect of the Qur'ān.

In his *tafsīr*, he often explains the ambiguous verses by referring to other verses.[456] The brief nature of the legal verses necessitated detailed explanations in the light of the hadith of the Prophet (pbuh). Therefore, Jassās significantly benefitted from these explanations, referring to them in virtually every legal verse in his *tafsīr*. He generally mentioned all the hadiths related to a particular subject and held the opinion that the explanations of the Prophet (pbuh) are in themselves revelations which must be taken in to consideration when practicing the commands.

Jassās analyses the verses according titles that are characteristically associated with jurisprudence rather than *tafsīr*. He first explains the verses literally, and then refers to related verses. On occasion, he presents various opinions regarding unusual words in the Qur'ān, indicating his preference and supporting this with evidence from Arabic poetry. He also provides supplementary material about the verse such as *qiraat*, Arabic grammar, *balāghah* and *asbāb al-nuzūl*.

In explaining abrogated verses, Jassās elucidates all the abrogated rulings applicable to the verse, mentions the different opinions and indicates his preference from among them. In explaining the verses, he relates the evidence of the Prophet (pbuh), the Companions and the Successors, as mentioned earlier. Any conflict between the early scholars is analyzed and reconciled. Any disputes between the legal schools are elucidated by giving the Ḥanafī view followed by the stance of the other main schools of thought. He defends the view of his own school and tries to refute the others. In justifying the Ḥanafī position, Jassās uses supporting arguments from the Qur'ān and Sunnah and logical arguments, including any possi-

---

[454] Jassās, *Aḥkām al-Qur'ān*, 1/365; 2/218, 345; 3/29.
[455] Jassās, ibid, 1/449; 2/6, 38, 40, 43.
[456] Jassās, ibid, 3/114.

ble counter arguments in his discussions, and thereby ensuring his methodology as sound and valid.

In explaining verses, Jassās offers various perspectives, often extracting numerous rulings from a single verse. In this sense, he is at times quite exclusive in his findings. Occasionally he summarizes the topic after an extended discussion ensuring the reader does not lose the intended context. Before analyzing or giving a literal meaning for a word, he examines the statements of the Prophet (pbuh) to discover his use and intended meaning of the word. For example, he explains the use Arabic word 'edha' in the following verse from the point of Prophetic explanation:[457]

> They also ask you about (the injunctions concerning) menstruation. Say:
> It is *a state of hurt* (and ritual impurity), so keep away from them during
> their menstruation and do not approach them until they are cleansed. [458]

The Prophet used the same word (*edhā*) in one of his statements: "If one's shoe is inflicted with filth (*edhā*) he should rub it to the earth and then pray, because soil cleans it."[459] In this hadith, the word 'edhā' is used to mean filth; therefore, in his interpretation of the above verse, Jassās preferred this meaning.

Jassās believed that if the science of the occasions of the revelations was neglected it would lead to the erroneous interpretation of verses. He utilized this science to ensure a sound understanding of the verses. For example, the verse; "O you who believe! Prescribed for you is retaliation in cases of (deliberate, unjust) killing: freeman for freeman, slave for slave, female for female,"[460] was revealed after a specific incident. Jassās relates the following incident from Sha'bī and Qatāda as the reason behind the revelation of this verse: Two Arab tribes were engaged in fighting and one of them was richer and more powerful than the other. They demanded capital punishment of a freeman for a murdered slave of theirs, and a freeman for their women. This incident caused the revelation of this above verse.[461]

Jassās holds the opinion that abrogation of verses was a necessary tool to manage the adjustment of the Islamic society to the new lifestyle. God aided them by changing and removing some commands and prohibitions gradually, to prepare them for the final stages of Islam. There is much unresolved dispute among scholars about this science and it is a vital topic of Islamic jurisprudence. Jassās

---

[457] Jassās, ibid, 1/336.
[458] Qur'ān 2: 222.
[459] Jassās, *Aḥkām*, see the interpretation of 2: 222.
[460] Qur'ān 2: 178.
[461] Jassās, ibid, 1/134.

explained this matter expansively used evidence from the Qur'ān and Sunnah to refute the arguments of his opponents.[462] In his opinion, the Sunnah is also revelation and as such he supports the notion that the *mutawātir* Sunnah has the authority to abrogate verses of the Qur'ān.[463]

In his *tafsīr*, Jassās occasionally mentions the various readings of the Qur'ān. He explains the meaning and legal aspects of the verses according to the style of the imams of *qiraat* if there is any difference between them. He not only gives the various readings of the verse but also analyzes each and makes preferences between them. However, he neglects to identify the imams with the respective readings and does not identify the chain of reporters.[464]

Jassās's *tafsīr* combines both *riwāyah* (tradition-based) and *dirāyah* (reason-based) concepts. He accepts the importance of personal opinion in the process of interpreting verses and criticizes scholars who only accept literal meanings. He benefits from *uṣūl al-fiqh*, *fiqh*, *kalām*, Arabic and its grammar, *balāghah*, etc. indicating his preferences based on these sciences. In order to identify authentic hadiths he examines them in the light of *uṣūl hadith* (the methodology of hadith) attempting to reconcile any apparent contradictions between them. Jassās established the principles of methodology and then interpreted the verses accordingly;[465] hence, he is a jurist who considerably benefits from the principles and methodologies of Islamic law in his *tafsīr*. He sometimes discusses and tries to prove the validity of the secondary sources of Islamic law such as *qiyās* (analogy), *istiḥsān* (juristic preference) and *'urf* (custom).

To understand the characteristics of his method, his commentary on the *basmala* (the Name of God) is examined below.

Summary: Jassās and his *Tafsīr*

1. Abū Bakr al-Jassās al-Ḥanafī, a famous jurist of the Ḥanafī School was born in the city of Ray in 917 C.E.
2. He was educated in Baghdad by famous scholars and became an authority for all Ḥanafī scholars particularly in the areas of Islamic Jurisprudence and hadith sciences.
3. Jassās is accepted as a *mujtahid* in the third category of *ijtihād*.

---

[462] Jassās, ibid, 1/85.
[463] Jassās, ibid, 1/22.
[464] Jassās, ibid, 2/168–169.
[465] Jassās, ibid, 1/19, 161, 429.

4. The majority of Jassās's writing explains the work of the early Ḥanafī scholars.

His methodology in *tafsīr*

5. The most important work of Jassās is his final book '*Aḥkām al-Qur'ān*' which deals with 1050 legal verses from the Qur'ān.

6. He used *tafsīr*, hadith, *fiqh*, Arab philology and history in his work.

7. Jassās uses both the *riwāyah* and *dirāyah* methods in his *tafsīr* referring to the Qur'ān first and then to the Sunnah, following which he relates the opinions of the Companions and Successors.

8. He often explains the ambiguous verses by referring to other verses.

9. Jassās significantly benefitted from hadith explanations, referring to them in virtually every legal verse in his *tafsīr*.

10. Jassās analyses the verses according titles that are characteristically associated with jurisprudence rather than *tafsīr*.

11. In explaining abrogated verses, Jassās elucidates all the abrogated rulings applicable to the verse, mentions the different opinions and indicates his preference from among them.

12. In explaining the verses, conflicts between the early scholars are analyzed and reconciled.

13. He defends the view of his own school and tries to refute the others using supporting arguments from the Qur'ān and Sunnah and logical arguments.

14. In explaining verses, Jassās offers various perspectives, often extracting numerous rulings from a single verse.

15. Before analyzing or giving a literal meaning for a word, he examines the statements of the Prophet (pbuh) to discover his use and intended meaning of the word.

16. Jassās believed that if the science of the occasions of the revelations was neglected it would lead to the erroneous interpretation of verses.

17. Jassās holds the opinion that abrogation of verses was a necessary tool to manage the adjustment of the Islamic society to the new lifestyle.

18. In his *tafsīr*, Jassās occasionally mentions the various readings of the Qur'ān, elucidating, analyzing and explaining them before making a preference between them. However, he neglects to identify the imams with the respective readings and does not identify the chain of reporters.

THE INTERPRETATION OF *BASMALA*

بِسْمِ اللهِ الرَّحْمَنِ الرَّحِيمِ

Basmala

In the Name of God, the All-Merciful, the All-Compassionate

Tafsīr

When discussing the *basmala* there are several points that need to be covered[466] including: the meaning of the pronoun in *basmala*; whether it is a verse of the Qur'ān or not; whether it is a verse of Surah Fatiha; whether it is a verse of each *surah* in the Qur'ān; whether it is in itself a complete verse; its recitation in the prayers and its related rulings.

The meaning of the pronoun in *basmala*

Basmala contains a secret pronoun; the beginning particle, 'ba' is only used when connected to a manifest verb or a secret one that has been removed for certain wisdoms. In this instance, the pronoun has two meanings; information or command. If it is used to mean information then the meaning of *basmala* becomes; 'I begin with the Name of God.' However, the expression 'I begin' is reduced because someone reciting begins with its recitation anyway, therefore removing the need to say, 'I begin.' If however, the pronoun is used to convey a command, it means; 'Begin with the Name of God.' Both of these meanings have equal possibility, but the context of Surah Fatiha implies that it is used as a command in this case.

Supporting this idea, the verse of Surah Alaq which reads; 'Read with the name of your Lord'[467] also implies that *basmala* is a command, because God commanded the believers to start reciting the Qur'ān with His Name. Even if the pronoun is taken to mean information, it still in fact conveys the meaning of a command, for God informs His servants that He starts with His Name, and this becomes a command for believers to do the same. It is also possible that the pronoun intends both meanings as the expression can be understood either way.

---

[466] This part is quoted from Abū Bakr Ahmad ibn Ali al-Rāzī al-Jassās, *Ahkām al-Qur'ān*, Dār al-Fikr, Beirut 1993, 1–15.

[467] Qur'an 96: 1

Question: If one disputes the idea of accepting two meanings of a word (metaphorical and literal) at the same time when it is expressed openly, should the same rule also be valid when referring to pronouns?

Answer: If a word is expressed clearly in an informative form, it is not permissible to accept two meanings; this is because a word cannot mean a command and information at the same time. When a command is intended, the informative form becomes metaphorical. Similarly, when a word conveys a literal meaning, it cannot be interpreted metaphorically; one word cannot be understood both literally and metaphorically at the same time. A word's true meaning is its literal meaning, whereas the metaphorical meaning is secondary to it. Therefore, a word cannot be taken as a command and information simultaneously. However, in the case of a pronoun it is different due to the word not being mentioned openly. A pronoun's meaning is related to the intention of the speaker and therefore, it is permissible to convey both meanings because the intended meaning is expressed through use of the pronoun. In this light, *basmala* can be understood as follows: 'I begin with the Name of God (informative), so you must start with it (command) to ensure you receive its blessings.' It is not necessary to prove one meaning over the other unless there is supporting evidence.

Basmala is not a general expression and so there is no need to declare one meaning as preferable to another. However, when a pronoun is connected to a word, which can be understood in two ways, it is necessary to find the reference point based on evidence. For example, "for my followers' mistakes, forgetfulness and actions which they performed under duress are removed."[468] In this case, two meanings are possible; firstly, the sin is removed for an offence committed mistakenly, forgetfully or by force; secondly, there is no compensation for acts of this nature. Here either meaning, or both, can be intended but it is necessary to prove it with evidence.

There are occasions when the pronoun can be interpreted in both ways, but it is not permissible to accept both meanings simultaneously. For example, the Prophet (pbuh) said, "the deeds are according to the intentions."[469] When using this hadith as evidence for extracting a rule, it is clear that the interpretation of 'the deeds' is pivotal. However, it is unknown what 'the deeds' refers to. In addition, it is not known whether this statement intends to convey that the greatest rewards can only be achieved with a superior intention, or whether the intention is a precondition for the validity of the deeds. It is not permissible to accept

---

[468] Ibn Mājah, *Sunan*, 2045.
[469] Bukhari, *Saḥīḥ*, Waḥy, 1.

both meanings (superiority or a precondition) at the same time, therefore, if the intention is a precondition for an act the meaning of superior rewards is ignored, and vice versa.

If mentioning the Name of God is proved as a command for an action then this action must be performed immediately after uttering it. For example, it is a precondition of the prayers to utter 'Allahu Akbar' (iftitah takbir) at the beginning. This is based on the verse; "prosperous indeed is he who purifies himself and who mentions the Name of his Lord and performs the prayer."[470] These verses connect the performance of the prayers with the utterance of God's Name (Allahu Akbar) without indicating any break between the two; therefore, the prayers must begin immediately after uttering the name.

The following verses indicate the obligation of uttering basmala prior to slaughtering an animal; "When they (the camels) are lined up in standing position for sacrifice, pronounce God's Name over them"[471] and "And do not eat of that which is slaughtered in the name of other than God and over which God's Name has not been pronounced (at the time of its slaughtering), for that is indeed a transgression."[472] On the other hand, uttering basmala is only recommended, not commanded, for acts of purification (ghusl and wudu), before consuming food and drink.

Question: If one disputes this view and believes that uttering basmala before performing wudu is obligatory for its validity based on the following hadith; "there is no wudu for a person who does not mention God's Name," how do you answer?

Answer: In the hadith, the meaning of the pronoun is not clear and there is no evidence to indicate that it is binding, therefore, it is understood generally and the rule for wudu and its preconditions are extracted from other sources of evidence. Therefore, the meaning of this hadith is: "the best reward in wudu can only be achieved with the intention"; i.e. to gain the greatest reward for wudu one should utter basmala before the act.

If basmala is from the Qur'ān

Muslim scholars unanimously agree that basmala forms part of a verse in Surah Naml; "Indeed, it is from Solomon, and indeed, it reads: *In the Name of God, the All-Merciful, the All-Compassionate.*"[473]

---

[470] Qur'ān 87: 14–15.
[471] Qur'ān 22: 36.
[472] Qur'ān 6: 121.
[473] Qur'ān 27: 30.

Reports state that when Archangel Gabriel brought the revelation of the first five verses of Surah 'Alaq, the *basmala* was not revealed as part of it. During the early years of Islam, the Prophet (pbuh) used to start reading the *surahs* by saying *'bismika Allahumma'* باسمك اللهم . This continued until the revelation of the verse, "And [Noah] said, "Embark therein; in the Name of God is its course and its anchorage. Indeed, my Lord is Forgiving and Merciful"[474] Following this revelation, the Prophet (pbuh) recited بسم الله *'bismillah.'* With the revelation of the verse, "Say, 'call upon God or call upon the Most Merciful,'"[475] the Prophet added *'al-Rahmān'* الرحمن to *bismillah*. Finally, when Surah Naml was revealed the Prophet (pbuh) started to recite بِسْم الله الرَّحْمَن الرَّحِيم in the Name of God, the All-Merciful, the All-Compassionate at the beginning of *surahs*. This is supported by hadiths that are related by Sha'bī, Malik and Qatāda. When the Hudaybiya treaty was about to be signed the Prophet (pbuh) instructed Ali ibn Abī Tālib to write *'bism Allah al-Rahman al-Rahim'* at the beginning. The Quraysh representative, Suhayl, objected as he did not know Rahman, and told Ali to write *'bismika Allahumma.'* All these arguments prove that *'bism Allah al-Rahman al-Rahim'* in Surah Naml is not a full verse; rather it is only part of the verse.

If *basmala* is a verse of Surah Fatiha

Jaṣṣāṣ gave information of a dispute over whether or not *basmala* is a verse of Surah Fatiha. Kūfī Qur'ān experts hold that it is a verse whilst Baṣrī experts disagree. The early scholars of the Ḥanafī School never indicated an acceptance of *basmala* as a verse of Surah Fatiha. Abu'l Hasan al-Karkhī holds that it must be recited silently in the prayers proving that he does not accept it as a verse otherwise, along with the other verses of Surah Fatiha, it would be recited loudly. Imam Shāfi'ī holds that it is a verse of Surah Fatiha and its omission necessitates repetition of the prayer.

The position of *basmala* in every *surah* of the Qur'ān

Scholars dispute whether the position of *basmala* at the beginning of the *surahs* is intended to be a verse of each *surah*. Ḥanafī scholars hold that it is not a verse of any *surah* for it is not recited loudly when reciting Surah Fatiha in the prayers, so the rule is the same for other *surahs*. Shāfi'ī holds that it is a verse of every *surah*. Early scholars only discussed whether it is a verse of Surah Fatiha; none

---

[474] Qur'ān 11: 41.
[475] Qur'ān 17: 110.

of them held the view that it was a verse of any other *surah* so this was not a matter of debate.

Hadith evidence reported by Abū Hurayra proves that *basmala* is not a verse of Surah Fatiha;

> God, the Glorious and Exalted, said, 'I have divided the prayer between Myself and My servant equally and My servant shall be granted what he asked for.' Therefore when the servant says, 'all praises and thanks are due to God, the Lord of the universe,' God says, 'My servant has praised Me.' When he says, 'the Most Beneficent, the Most Merciful,' God says, 'My servant has extolled Me.' When he says, 'Master of the Day of Judgment,' God says, 'My servant has glorified Me.' When he says, 'You Alone we worship and Your aid Alone do we seek,' God says, 'this is between Me and My servant and My servant shall have what he requested,' When he says, 'guide us to the Straight Path, the Path of those whom You have favored, not of those who have incurred Your wrath, neither of those who have gone astray,' God says, 'this is for My servant and My servant shall have what he asked for.'[476]

If *basmala* was a verse of Surah Fatiha, this hadith would mentioned it as every single verse of that *surah* is referred to here. This hadith proves that *basmala* is not a verse of Surah Fatiha.

The expression 'the prayer' indicates Surah Fatiha and it is a well-known fact that the Prophet (pbuh) intended this meaning as it is recited in every prayer. There are two reasons why *basmala* cannot be accepted as a verse of Surah Fatiha. Firstly, it is not mentioned in the above hadith where God divided the prayer for Him and His servant equally. Secondly, and related to the first point, if the prayer is divided equally, the inclusion of *basmala* would upset the balance, making God's share more than that of the servant.

Jassās refutes those who hold the opinion that *basmala* is a verse of Surah Fatiha due to its inclusion in the second verse of the *surah* that includes al-Rahman and al-Rahim. This claim is unfounded because if *basmala* were a verse in its own right, it must be mentioned separately and it is not permissible to reduce its form. The opponents supported their claim with a hadith which stated that the verse 'Master of the Day of Judgment; is apportioned between God and His servant. However, this hadith is clearly a mistake of the hadith reporters as this verse belongs to God alone; there is no share in it for the servant. The verse that is apportioned between God and the servant is, "You Alone do we worship and

---

[476] Muslim, *Saḥīḥ*, Salah, 38.

Your aid alone do we seek."⁴⁷⁷ In this verse, the servant supplicates God and He accepts their supplication. The verses after the fourth verse are apportioned to the servant and this is clear from their meaning.

As previously mentioned, the *basmala* at the beginning of each *surah* is not a verse; it is a separator to indicate the end of one *surah* and the beginning of another. Ibn Abbas reports;

> I asked 'Uthman ibn 'Affan (third Caliph of Islam): 'Why did you include Surah Anfal and Surah Tawba in the long seven *surah* even though Surah Anfal has less verses than the others and you skipped the writing of *basmala* (In the Name of God the Merciful) between them?' 'Uthman said: 'Whenever the Messenger of God (pbuh) received a group of verses he would call some of his scribes and inform them where to position the verses among the other verses. Anfal was among the early *surahs*, which were revealed in Medina, but Tawba was among the *surahs* that were revealed later. The context of Anfal was similar to the context to Tawba and therefore I thought they were the same *surah*.⁴⁷⁸

It is clearly expressed by 'Uthman that *basmala* is not a verse of every *surah*; it is only written to separate the *surahs* one from another.

The Prophet (pbuh) assigned the placement of the verses within each *surah* but there is no evidence to prove that this is the case for *basmala*. The knowledge of the verse placement is equal to knowledge of the verse and this is only known through *mutawātir* reports. Changing the position of any verse is not permissible as the Prophet (pbuh) established the order himself. If *basmala* was a verse at the beginning of each *surah* this would be known from the *mutawātir* reports just as we know the place of *basmala* in Surah Naml. Since this is not the case, it is not permissible to accept it as a verse of every *surah*.

Question: *Basmala* is written in all the early *Mushāfs* (the Companions' personal copies of the Qur'ān) and this should be sufficient evidence to accept it as a verse of every *surah*. How do you answer this?

Answer: The manuscript of the Qur'ān has been reported to us inclusive of the *basmala*, however, it was not related that the *basmala* is a verse of every *surah*. The evidence on which we base our knowledge conveys that *basmala* is written as a separator at the beginning of each *surah*. As proved earlier, only Surah Naml includes *basmala* in a verse. Its placement at the beginning of each *surah* does not indicate that it is a part of the *surah*. A report from Abu Hurayra, related from

---

⁴⁷⁷ Qur'ān 1: 4.

⁴⁷⁸ Abu Dāwud, *Sunan*, hadith no: 786–787

the Prophet (pbuh) is further evidence that *basmala* is not a part of the beginning verse of every *surah*.

> Abu Hurayra relates from the Prophet (pbuh): 'The Surah in the Qur'ān which has thirty verses will intercede for its owner until he is forgiven: 'Blessed is He in whose hand is dominion' (Surah Mulk).'[479]

Qur'ān experts and other scholars agree that the number of verses in Surah Mulk is 30 without the *basmala*. With its inclusion, the number of verses would be 31, which clearly contradicts the above hadith. All Qur'ān experts agree that Surah Kawthar has three verses and Surah Ikhlas has four verses. If the *basmala* was included as a verse of these *surahs* the number would increase.

Jassās analyses a hadith that accepts *basmala* as a verse of Surah Fatiha. He concludes that the hadith is not authentic as it was the hadith transmitters who added the expression '*basmala* is one of the verses of Fatiha' to the report. Additionally, according to the principles of hadith, there is a serious problem in the chain of narrators. He concludes that there is no strong evidence that can be used as basis to accept *basmala* as a verse of Surah Fatiha or of any other *surahs*.

If *basmala* is a complete verse of the Qur'ān

Scholars agree that in Surah Naml, *basmala* is only part of, not a complete verse. The beginning of the verse is, 'Indeed, it is from Solomon.' However, this does not prevent *basmala* from being a complete verse in other places in the Qur'ān. The second verse of Surah Fatiha is part of the *basmala*; '*al-Rahman al-Rahim*' and it is a complete verse.

Whilst *basmala* is not a verse of Surah Fatiha, there is evidence indicating that it is a complete verse of the Qur'ān.[480] Umm Salama reports; 'the Prophet (pbuh) recited *basmala* in the prayer and counted it as a complete one verse.' In another narration: 'The Prophet (pbuh) accepted '*bism Allah al-Rahman al-Rahim*' as a complete verse.' There are reports which indicate that Ali ibn Abī Tālib and Abdullah ibn 'Abbas accepted *basmala* as a complete verse of the Qur'ān. Abū Burda relates from his father:

> The Prophet (pbuh) said; 'Do not leave the *masjid* unless I inform you about a verse or a *surah* which was not revealed to any Prophet after the Prophet Solomon except me. He walked and I followed him to the door of the *masjid*.

---

[479] Qur'ān 67: 1.
[480] To see these evidences please check Jassās, *Ahkām al-Qur'ān*, 1/7–8.

He put one foot outside of the door while the other was inside and turned his face to me and said; 'What do you recite from the Qur'ān first in the prayer?' I said; '*Bism Allah al-Rahman al-Rahim.*' After that, the Prophet left the *masjid*' (without adding or saying anything).[481]

If there is no report contradicting that *basmala* is a complete verse of the Qur'ān, then the claim is considered proven. So, *basmala* is accepted as a complete verse of the Qur'ān for there is no opposing evidence to it.

Question: It is mentioned earlier that the place of each verse in the Qur'ān has to be proved with *mutawātir* reports and by using this criteria it may be confirmed that the *basmala* is not accepted as the first verse of every *surah* even though it is written at their beginning. How do you now accept *basmala* as a verse of the Qur'ān with *āḥād* (single source) reports?

Answer: Proving the place of a verse in the Qur'ān equates to proving that it is a verse of the Qur'ān and therefore, it is only accepted with *mutawātir* reports. However, the discussion here is not about the placement of *basmala*. It is not necessary for the Prophet (pbuh) to obtain the approval of Muslims in regards to placing *basmala* at the beginning of *surahs*; rather the Muslims learns from him and practice accordingly. The beginning and end of verses do not require consensus and are therefore the subject of dispute amongst scholars. So, it is permissible to accept *basmala* with *khabar wāḥid* as a verse of the Qur'ān without ascribing it to the certain *surah* or certain place in specific *surahs*. From this viewpoint, we can deduce that as *mutawātir* reports from the Prophet (pbuh) do not indicate the beginning and end of verses, it is not obligatory upon us to know the exact number of each verse.

Although the *basmala* is not a verse of any specific *surah*, it is a verse of the Qur'ān. It is a single verse that was revealed repeatedly and is placed at the beginning of each *surah* to afford its reader the utmost benefit from its blessings. It is logical to accept *basmala* as a separate verse wherever it is written and there is no sound reason to reject this claim since there are many verses in the Qur'ān which are repeated many times but counted as a separate verse each time. For example, the following verse is repeated 31 times in Surah Rahman and each time is counted as a separate verse; "So which of the favors of your Lord would you deny?"[482] Similarly, *basmala* is a separate verse wherever it is written and therefore, it should be counted separately.

---

[481] To see these evidences please check Jassās, *Aḥkām al-Qur'ān*, 1/7–8.
[482] Qur'ān 55: 13.

The rule of *basmala* in the prayers

Abū Ḥanīfa, Ibn Abī Layla, Thawrī, Abū Yusuf, Muhammad, Zufar and Imam Shāfi'ī hold that *basmala* is recited in the prayers after *isti'adha* (*audhu billahi min-ash shaytan al-rajim*) and before Surah Fatiha. However, scholars dispute whether it should be recited in every *rak'ah* and before each *surah* in the prayers. Abu Ḥanīfa holds that it is recited in every *rak'ah* before Surah Fatiha but not before the *surahs* that come after Surah Fatiha. For him, its recitation before Surah Fatiha is sufficient. Imam Shāfi'ī holds that *basmala* is recited before every *surah* in the prayers. It is reported from Ibn Abbas and Mujāhid that reciting *basmala* once at the beginning of every *rak'ah* is sufficient. Imam Malik holds that *basmala* is not recited in the prescribed prayers whether the recitation of the Qur'ān is loud or silent (the Qur'ān is recited loudly in the *Fajr*, *Maghrib* and *'Isha* prayers and silently in the *Ẓuhr* and *'Asr* prayers). According to Imam Malik, it is permissible to recite *basmala* in the optional (*nāfila*) prayers.

An analysis of the evidence about the recitation of *basmala* is beneficial.[483] Umm Salama and Abū Hurayra report; 'the Prophet (pbuh) recited *basmala* and Surah Fatiha in the prayers.' Anas ibn Malik reports; 'I performed the prayers behind the Prophet (pbuh), Abū Bakr, 'Umar and 'Uthman; all recited *basmala* silently.' It is a well-known fact that the obligatory prayers are performed in congregation. Anas ibn Malik reports; 'the Prophet (pbuh) opened the prayers with Surah Fatiha.' This hadith does not contradict the previous hadiths, because the Prophet (pbuh) recited the *basmala* silently in the prayers where the Qur'ān is recited loudly. It is reported from 'Ali, 'Umar, Ibn Abbas and Ibn 'Umar that they all recited *basmala* at the beginning of the prayers and the Companions did not dispute them in this matter. This evidence proves that *basmala* is recited in both the obligatory and the optional prayers.

Abū Ḥanīfa deems the recitation of *basmala* once at the first *rak'ah* of the prayers as sufficient. This is related to his opinion that *basmala* is not the first verse of the *surahs* or it would be recited with them. Additionally, the rules pertaining to the prohibition of regular actions within the prayer form a complete set. In this regard, the prayer is considered as one action with *basmala* recited before performing the action. One *basmala* is sufficient for the whole action, even if the prayer is long. This can be viewed as similar to writing *basmala* just once at the beginning of a book regardless of its length. Similarly, *basmala* is not repeated for any other actions of the prayer such as bowing or prostrating. This proves

---

[483] To see these evidences please check Jassās, *Aḥkām al-Qur'ān*, 1/7–8.

that rather than being part of the *surahs, basmala* is used to separate them from one another. Another hadith also supports this view: 'The Prophet (pbuh) does not know the end of the *surahs* until *basmala* is revealed.' This evidence proves that *basmala* is placed to separate the *surahs* but it is not included in their verses.

Question: If the purpose of the *basmala* is to separate the *surahs* from each other, surely it must be recited in the respective places. How do you explain this?

Answer: This is not necessary because the separation between the *surahs* was known when *basmala* was revealed. Its recitation at the beginning of the prayers is to benefit from its blessings. Therefore, reciting it once before the prayers is sufficient for the rest of the prayer. However, it is encouraged to recite *basmala* at the beginning of each *rak'ah* as each can be considered a unique part in its own right. However, reciting it at the beginning of each *surah* in each *rak'ah* is not necessary. It is only recited before Surah Fatiha in each *rak'ah*.

There are two groups of scholars who hold that *basmala* must be recited before every *surah.* The first group accepts *basmala* as the first verse of each *surah* whereas the second group refutes this but still insists that it should be recited before each *surah.* They support their opinion with evidence, purporting that as the Prophet (pbuh) recited *surahs* by beginning with *basmala* outside the prayers, the same should be done within the prayers: Anas ibn Malik reports; 'The Prophet (pbuh) said that a *surah* was revealed a little while ago and he recited *basmala* and after that recited Surah Kawthar until its end.'[484]

Reciting *basmala* loudly in the prayer

Scholars vary in their opinions about the rule of reciting *basmala* in the imam-led prayers which are performed out loud. Ḥanafī scholars and Thawrī hold that *basmala* is recited silently; Ibn Abī Layla holds that it is optional to recite it loudly or silently whereas Imam Shāfi'ī maintains that the *basmala* is recited loudly. Reports from the Companions contradict each other. For example, 'Umar ibn Dharr reports from his father; 'I prayed behind ibn 'Umar and he recited *basmala* loudly.' Ibrahim reports; "Umar recited *basmala* silently and then recited Surah Fatiha loudly in the prayers.' Abdullah ibn Mas'ud was reciting *basmala* silently in the prayers. There are contradicting reports from Ibn 'Abbas about the rule of reciting *basmala* in the prayers, therefore it is difficult to make a preference between them. Abī Wail reports; "Umar and 'Ali did not recite *basmala, ta'awwudh* (*audhu billahi min-al-shaytan al-rajim*) and *amin* loudly in the prayers.' Anas reports; 'the

---

[484] To see these evidences please check Jassās, *Aḥkām al-Qur'ān*, 1/7–8.

Prophet (pbuh), Abū Bakr, 'Umar and 'Uthman recited *basmala* silently in the prayers.' A'isha reports; 'the Prophet (pbuh) starting the prayer with *takbir* (*Allahu Akbar*), after that he recited Surah Fatiha and then finished the prayer with *salām*.'[485] This report indicates that the *basmala* is not recited loudly, otherwise A'isha would have heard it.

This confirms that the *basmala* is not a verse of Surah Fatiha and is recited silently. If someone disagrees with this and says it is permissible to recite a verse silently whilst reading other verses out loud in the prayer, they can be answered as follows: There are other verses which it is Sunnah to start the prayers with. These are not recited loudly, but are said silently, for example; "Indeed, I have turned my face toward He who created the heavens and the earth, inclining toward truth, and I am not of those who associate others with God."[486] When this has been recited silently, it is followed with Surah Fatiha and the other verses, which are spoken aloud.

Jassās holds that if the *basmala* was a verse of Surah Fatiha the Prophet (pbuh) would have recited it loudly as he did the Fatiha. Although some reports indicate that the Prophet (pbuh) recited the *basmala* in the prayer, they do not confirm whether he recited it loudly or silently. Sometimes, Companions heard the Prophet (pbuh) recite it because they were standing close to him, but others did not hear it because they were positioned further away from him. This indicates that he recited it quietly and only the people next to him could hear it. The Companions who stood near him in the prayer could hear him reciting the verses in the *Ẓuhr* and *'Asr* prayers despite those prayers being performed silently. This does not mean that he spoke those verses aloud; rather it means they heard his whispered recitation as they were close to him.

The following report clearly proves that *basmala* is not the verse of Surah Fatiha. Abū Hurayra reports; 'When the Prophet (pbuh) stood up for the second *rak'ah* he would start reciting '*al-hamd'u lil-lahi rabbi'l-alamin*' (all praise and gratitude belong to the Lord of the worlds) without waiting.' If *basmala* was a verse of Surah Fatiha the Prophet (pbuh) would not omit it in the prayer. When Umm Salama, the wife of the Prophet (pbuh), was asked about the prayer of the Prophet (pbuh) she described it word by word but she did not mention him reciting *basmala* in the prayer. Jassās holds that this report describes the optional prayers which the Prophet (pbuh) sometimes performed in her room, because he always performed the obligatory prayers in congregation. Additionally 'Ali, the

---

[485] To see these evidences please check Jassās, *Aḥkām al-Qur'ān*, 1/7–8.
[486] Qur'ān 6: 79.

fourth caliph and one of the earliest Muslims did not recite *basmala* loudly in the prayer. 'Ali learned the prayer directly from the Prophet (pbuh) and performed it together with him countless times. If *basmala* was supposed to be recited loudly 'Ali would never oppose it.

Even if the evidences supporting and refuting the recitation of *basmala* silently in the prayer are of equal weighting, there are two reasons why its silent recitation is still preferable. Firstly, the prominent Companions such as Abū Bakr, 'Umar, 'Uthman, 'Ali, 'Abdullah ibn Mas'ud and Anas ibn Malik did not recite it loudly. In the case of conflicting reports about a certain matter, we look to the practice of the Companions to clarify it, and, in this case, their practice is reciting *basmala* silently. Secondly, if there was a correct rule pertaining to the loud recitation of *basmala* it would be supported by *mutawātir* reports as is the case for the rule of reciting the Qur'ān in the prayer. Since no mutawātir reports in this regard, the *basmala* is not recited loudly in the prayer.

The rules of *basmala*

The rules contained within the *basmala* can be explained from different perspectives. *Basmala* is full of blessings and Muslims are commanded to utter it before performing every action; for example, it is obligatory to utter it before slaughtering animals. This command is in the form of a recommendation and conveys the necessity of glorifying and exalting God in every act, not just those for which it is obligatory. It is a symbol of Islam by which Muslims are recognized.

Basmala should be recited to expel Satan. The Prophet (pbuh) said; "If a servant mentions God's Name (*basmala*) before eating, Satan cannot sit with him at the table for food, however if he doesn't mention it, Satan takes his share from the food." Uttering *basmala* is considered a form of opposition to the polytheists who began each action by uttering the names of their idols, whereas Muslims begin every action with the Name of God.

Basmala is a refuge for the people who fear. Nothing in the universe happens without God's permission and He has encompassed His creatures with the Mercy that is expressed in *basmala*. Reciting *basmala* indicates that the utterer abandons all worldly powers and seeks refuge with God alone. It provides tranquility and inner peace to those who utter it.

Basmala, and the Mercy contained therein, announces the Divinity of God over everything that is created, administered, sustained, nourished, etc. Its utterance is the expression of recognition of the favors of God and conveys thankfulness and gratitude to Him. By uttering *basmala* the Muslims ask for God's help and seek protection against all kinds of evil. *Basmala* contains two unique and unequivocal Names of God that are not permitted for use anywhere else: Allah and Rahman.

SUMMARY: *TAFSĪR* OF *BASMALA*

The meaning of the pronoun in *basmala*

1. *Basmala* contains a secret pronoun; the beginning particle, *'ba,'* which in this case has two meanings; information or command.

2. The context of Surah Fatiha implies that it is used as a command in this case.

3. Even if the pronoun is taken to mean information, it still in fact conveys the meaning of a command, for God informs His servants that He starts with His Name, and this becomes a command for believers to do the same.

4. A pronoun's meaning is related to the intention of the speaker and therefore, it is permissible to convey both meanings because the intended meaning is expressed through use of the pronoun rather than openly.

5. *Basmala* is not a general expression and so there is no need to declare one meaning as preferable to another. However, when a pronoun is connected to a word that can be understood in two ways, it is necessary to find the reference point based on evidence.

6. There are occasions when the pronoun can be interpreted in both ways, but it is not permissible to accept both meanings simultaneously.

7. If mentioning the Name of God is proved as a command for an action then this action must be performed immediately after uttering it.

8. To gain the greatest reward for *wudu* one should utter *basmala* before the act.

If *basmala* is from the Qur'ān

9. Muslim scholars unanimously agree that *basmala* forms part of a verse in Surah Naml.

10. When Surah Naml was revealed the Prophet (pbuh) started to recite بِسْمِ اللهِ الرَّحْمَنِ الرَّحِيمِ in the Name of God, the All-Merciful, the All-Compa - sionate at the beginning of *surahs*. This is supported by hadith evidence related by Sha'bi, Malik and Qatāda.

If *basmala* is a verse of Surah Fatiha

11. Jassās related a dispute over whether or not *basmala* is a verse of Surah Fatiha. The early scholars of the Ḥanafī School never indicated an acceptance of *basmala* as a verse of Fatiha.

The position of *basmala* in every *surah* of the Qur'ān

12. Scholars dispute whether the position of *basmala* at the beginning of the *surahs* is intended to be a verse of each *surah*.

13. Ḥanafī scholars hold that it is not a verse of any *surah* for it is not recited loudly when reciting Surah Fatiha in the prayers. Shāfi'ī holds that it is a verse of every *surah*.

14. Hadith evidence supports that *basmala* is not a verse of Surah Fatiha.

15. Jassās refutes those who hold the opinion that *basmala* is a verse of Surah Fatiha because it is already included in the second verse of the *surah* which includes al-Rahman and al-Rahim.

16. The *basmala* at the beginning of each *surah* is a separator to indicate the end of one surah and the beginning of another.

17. The placement of the verses in each *surah* was assigned by the Prophet (pbuh) but there is no evidence to prove that this is the case for *basmala*.

18. The manuscript of the Qur'ān has been reported to us inclusive of the *basmala*, however, it was not related that the *basmala* is a verse of every *surah*. The evidence on which we base our knowledge conveys that *basmala* is written as a separator at the beginning of each *surah*.

19. Jassās analyses a hadith which accepts *basmala* as a verse of Surah Fatiha but concludes that it is not authentic and has a problem in the chain of transmission.

If *basmala* is a complete verse of the Qur'ān

20. Scholars agree that in Surah Naml, *basmala* is only part of, not a complete verse.

21. The second verse of Surah Fatiha is part of the *basmala*; 'al-Rahman al-Rahim' and it is a complete verse.

22. Whilst *basmala* is not a verse of Surah Fatiha, there is evidence indicating that it is a complete verse of the Qur'ān.

23. If there is no report contradicting that *basmala* is a complete verse of the Qur'ān, then the claim is considered proven.

24. The beginning and end of verses do not require general consensus and are therefore the subject of dispute amongst scholars. So, it is permissible to accept *basmala* with *khabar wāḥid* as a verse of the Qur'ān without ascribing it to the certain *surah* or certain place in specific *surahs*.

25. Although the *basmala* is not a verse of any specific *surah*, it is a verse of the Qur'ān. It is a single verse that was revealed repeatedly and is placed

at the beginning of each *surah* to afford its reader the utmost benefit from its blessings.

The rule of *basmala* in the prayers

26. Abū Ḥanīfa, Ibn Abī Layla, Thawrī, Abū Yusuf, Muhammad, Zufar and Imam Shāfi'ī hold that *basmala* is recited in the prayers after *istiadha* (*audhu billahi min-ash shaytan al-rajim*) and before Surah Fatiha.

27. Scholars dispute whether it should be recited in every *rak'ah* and before each *surah* in the prayers.

28. An analysis of the evidence about the recitation of *basmala* is beneficial and proves that *basmala* is recited in both the obligatory and the optional prayers.

29. The prayer is considered as one action with *basmala* recited before completing the action. One *basmala* is sufficient for the whole action, even if the prayer is long. This view is supported by hadith evidence.

30. There are two groups of scholars who hold that *basmala* must be recited before every *surah.*

Reciting *basmala* loudly in the prayer

31. Scholars vary in their opinions about the rule of reciting *basmala* in the imam-led prayers which are performed out loud.

32. Reports from the Companions contradict each other but indicate that the *basmala* is not a verse of Surah Fatiha and is recited silently.

33. Jassās holds that if the *basmala* was a verse of Surah Fatiha the Prophet (pbuh) would have recited it loudly as he did the Fatiha.

34. The prominent Companions such as Abū Bakr, 'Umar, 'Uthman, 'Ali, 'Abdullah ibn Mas'ud and Anas ibn Malik did not recite it loudly.

35. There is no *mutawātir* report pertaining to the loud recitation of *basmala* in the prayer.

The rules of *basmala*

36. *Basmala* is a command in the form of a recommendation and conveys the necessity of glorifying and exalting God in every act.

37. *Basmala* should be recited to expel Satan.

38. *Basmala* is a refuge for the people who fear. Nothing in the universe happens without God's permission and He has encompassed His creatures with the Mercy which is expressed in *basmala*.

39. *Basmala*, and the Mercy contained therein, announces the Divinity of God over everything that is created, administered, sustained, nourished, etc.

CHAPTER 10

Sufi *Tafsīr*

Introduction

The Prophet (pbuh) lived an exceedingly spiritual life, abandoning worldly pleasures in the struggle to achieve the pleasure of God. However, he warned his Companions away from extreme worship that would make practicing Islam difficult for them, such as remaining unmarried, forbidding lawful things to oneself and spending the night in prayer with no sleep.[487] The Companions of the Prophet (pbuh) lived very spiritual lives, deprived themselves of worldly pleasures and endured tremendous hardships however; they did not give this lifestyle a name. The term 'Sufism' was applied by later Muslim scholars who lived during the *hijrī* third century. They articulated the principles of Islamic Sufism as a separate discipline defining Sufism as the path to reaching the highest level of servanthood to God.

Sufism has many different definitions: the annihilation of the individual's ego, will, and self-centeredness by God and the subsequent spiritual revival with the light of His Essence; the continuous striving to cleanse one's self of all that is bad or evil in order to acquire virtue.[488] Tabarī describes Sufism as resisting the temptations of the carnal, (evil-commanding) self (*nafs al-ammara*) and evil qualities and acquiring laudable moral qualities.[489] Some scholars describe Sufism as seeing behind the "outer" or surface appearance of things and events, and interpreting whatever happens in the world in relation to God, therefore every act of God becomes a window through which to "see" Him.[490] M. Fethullah Gülen describes Sufism as the path followed by an individual who, having been able to free himself or herself from human vices and weaknesses in order to acquire angelic qualities and conduct pleasing to God, lives in accordance with the requirements of God's knowledge and love, and in the resulting spiritual delight that ensues.[491]

---

[487] Recep Doğan, *Uṣūl al-Tafsīr*, 294.
[488] M. Fethullah Gulen, *Sufism*, (tr: Ali Ünal) New Jersey 2006, *Sufism and Its Origins* (Introduction).
[489] Gulen, ibid.
[490] Recep Doğan, *Uṣūl al-Tafsīr*, 293.
[491] Gulen, ibid.

Worshipping God as if seeing Him even though one does not see Him, in the awareness that He sees everyone, is the essential meaning of Sufism. There are three levels of attainment for the perfection of human beings; *īmān* (faith), Islam (submission to the Will of God) and *iḥsān* (worshipping God as if seeing Him). This is clearly expressed in the Prophetic tradition which known as the Gabriel hadith;

> One day, while we were sitting with the Prophet (pbuh), a man came up to us whose clothes were extremely white, whose hair was extremely black, and upon whom no traces of travelling could be seen. None of us knew him. He sat down close to the Prophet (pbuh), so their knees rested against each other and placed his two hands upon his thighs and said, 'Muhammad, tell me about Islam.' The Messenger of God (pbuh) said, 'Islam is witnessing that there is no god but God and that Muhammad is His Messenger, and you establish the prayer, and you give *zakat*, and you fast Ramadan, and you perform the *Hajj* of the House if you are able to journey to it.' He said, 'You have told the truth,' and we were amazed at him asking him and then telling him that he told the truth. He said, 'Tell me about *īmān* (faith). He said, 'That you affirm God, His angels, His books, His Messengers, and the Last Day, and that you affirm the Decree, the good of it and the bad of it.' He said, 'You have told the truth.' He said, 'Tell me about *iḥsān*.' He said, 'That you worship God as if you see Him, for if you don't see Him then truly He sees you.'[492]

The religion of Islam is easy to practice and if one makes it difficult, he cannot carry out his duties continuously. Some of the Companions abstained from some permissible acts to achieve a superlative level of *iḥsān* but God warned them with the verse: "O you who have believed, do not prohibit the good things which God has made lawful to you and do not transgress. Indeed, God does not like transgressors."[493] With consideration to this verse, living Islam on a spiritual level is never prohibited; indeed, it was encouraged by the Prophet (pbuh) and his Companions.

In the early days of Islam, religious commandments were not written down; rather, the practice and oral circulation of commandments related to belief, worship, and daily life led the people to memorize them.[494] Since religious commandments were vital issues in a Muslim's individual and collective life, scholars prioritised these and compiled them into books. Legal scholars collected and codi-

---

[492] Bukhari, *Saḥīḥ*, Belief, 47; Muslim, *Saḥīḥ*, *The Book of Faith*, 1.

[493] Qur'ān, 5: 87.

[494] Doğan, *Uṣūl al-Tafsīr*, 294.

fied books on Islamic law, its rules and principles pertaining to all fields of life; hadith scholars established the Prophetic traditions (hadith) and way of life (Sunnah), and theologians dealt with issues concerning Muslim belief.[495] In conjunction, Sufi masters primarily concentrated on the pure, spiritual dimension of the Islamic truth. They sought to reveal the essence of humanity's being, the real nature of existence, the inner dynamics of humanity and the cosmos by calling attention to the reality of that which lies beneath and beyond their outer dimension.[496]

With the expansion of the borders of the Islamic world, Muslims encountered many new customs, cultures and races resulting in the development of Islamic thought and discussion on different issues, which led to the establishment of many Islamic disciplines.[497] Scholars were named according to the field they studied, so those who studied the spiritual side of Islam were termed Sufi and their respective works of Qur'ān interpretation were known as *Sufi tafsīr*. Sufism is not separate from Islam; rather it is the spiritual facet. Despite winning many battles and achieving the spoils of war, the Prophet (pbuh) and his Companions lived very simple and spiritual life. The Prophet (pbuh) never completely abandoned this world but he focused on the afterlife while living in this world and, following his example, the Companions did the same.[498]

Islamic spiritual life, based on asceticism, regular worship, abstention from all major and minor sins, sincerity, purity of intention, love, yearning and the individual's admission of his or her essential impotence and destitution, became the subject matter of Sufism, a new science possessing its own method, principles, rules, and terminology.[499] Fear and love are the two essential themes of Sufism. Hasan Basrī (d. 110 A.H. / 728 C.E.) who lived in Baghdad epitomised the fear component while Rabia al-Adawiyah (d. 135 A.H. / 752 C.E.) represented love of God.

Some biased scholars claim that Sufism evolved out of other cultures with the expansion of the Islamic borders, and that Islam and Sufism are mutually exclusive. This unfortunate view ignores the fact that Sufism has its roots in the very earliest days of Islam and is merely the spiritual side of the religion and

---

[495] Gulen, *Sufism and Its Origins*, Introduction.
[496] Gulen, *Sufism and Its Origins*, Introduction.
[497] Doğan, *Uṣūl al-Tafsīr*, 295.
[498] Doğan, *Uṣūl al-Tafsīr*, 295.
[499] Gulen, ibid.

not different from it.[500] Sufism is living Islam on the deepest level, since it requires austerity, self-control self-criticism and the continuous struggle to resist the temptations of Satan and the evil-commanding self in order to fulfill religious obligations.

Sufi exegeses fall into two categories; 1) theoretical and 2) *ish'ārī*. The first type bases a reading of the Qur'ān on pre-existing ideas and theories and attempts to interpret the book according to those; the second is interpretation born of the personal inspiration of the *mufassir* and therefore cannot be corroborated by any evidence.[501] There are difficulties with each of these types of exegeses. It is important to note that in Islam, all scholars are in the service of the Qur'ān and therefore they cannot use the Qur'ān for their personal aims. Even though theoretical Sufi *mufassir* interpreted the Qur'ān in line with their philosophical and theological opinions, it is sometimes difficult to understand their interpretations. For example, Muhyiddin ibn 'Arābī interpreted some verses in his books 'Futuḥāt Makkiyya' and 'Fusūs al-Ḥikam' in a way that cannot be understood easily. He interpreted the following verse; "Whoever is an enemy to God and His angels and His Messengers and Gabriel and Michael, then indeed, God is an enemy to the disbelievers"[502] as follows; Gabriel is the active reason, Michael is the soul of the sixth firmament and *Israfil* is the soul of the fourth firmament. He sees the angels, who are in the charge of the plants, which are intended for human beings, as 'reason' and the angels who are in the charge of animals as 'trusted reason.'[503]

The founder of theoretical *tafsīr* is generally acknowledged to be Muhyiddin ibn 'Arābī whose main theory is based on 'wahdat-i wujud' (similar to pantheism). A reader may mistakenly believe that Arabi's *tafsīr* is heavily influenced by pantheism, despite this being an incorrect assessment; however, a layman would have difficulties in discerning the difference. For example, the verse "Our Lord, You did not create this aimlessly; exalted are You"[504] is interpreted as: "O Lord, You didn't create anything but Yourself, whatever besides You is not real. You created everything as reflection of Your Names and Attributes. We glorify and exalt You from the existence of anything else other than You."[505] For him, everything in existence is destined to perish, so it they are not real.

---

[500] Doğan, *Uṣūl al-Tafsīr*, 295.

[501] Doğan, *Uṣūl al-Tafsīr*, 296.

[502] Qur'ān, 2: 98.

[503] Dhahabī, *at-Tafsīr wal-Mufassirun*, v.3 pp. 6–7.

[504] Qur'ān, 3: 191.

[505] Dhahabī, *at-Tafsīr*, v.11 p. 340.

In attempting to interpret the verses in tandem to their theoretical under-standing, they disregarded any correlation between their explanations and the Arabic rules and strayed from the fundamental purpose of the Qur'ān.[506] As a result, the clear, understandable Qur'ān became ambiguous and difficult to understand. The interpretation of the whole Qur'ān or the whole verse in the theoretical *tafsīr* was rare, rather the *mufassir* focused on the parts of verses that fit their own ideas: for example, Muhyiddin ibn 'Arābī rarely interpreted a whole verse in his books *Futuḥāt-i Makkiyya* and *Fusūs al-Ḥikam*.[507] Sadr al-Din Konawī and Abd al-Razzaq al-Kāshānī adopted the style of Muhyiddin ibn 'Arābī in their *tafsīr, Kitāb al-I'jāz –al-Qur'ān* and *Ta'wilāt*.[508]

The other type of Sufi exegesis is known as *ish'ārī tafsīr*. This type of *tafsīr* was named '*ish'ārī*' because it can only be achieved through a deep meditation on the verses rather than through a literal reading of them. It is the interpretation of the Qur'ān based on inspiration. The scholars do not try to prove their ideas by using the Qur'ān for their personal opinions; rather they give meanings to the Qur'ān with the help of their inspiration.[509] They do not deny the literal meanings of the verses but believe that each verse has many levels and that the inner meanings are hidden in the words and letters.[510] In order to extract the inner meanings from the Qur'ān through this process, they purify their heart from worldly things. The Qur'ān mentions the story of Moses with a man (Khādir) who was endowed with special knowledge from God;[511] and Sufi's aim to achieve that special knowledge by applying certain methods.[512] This special knowledge is mostly related to the inner dimension of things, events and beings. They conceal this knowledge and use a specific language composed of symbols, signs and metaphoric expressions.

Sufi scholars bring some arguments to defend their approach to the Qur'ān. Some of them are;

> Do you not see that God has made subject to you whatever is in the heavens and whatever is in the earth and amply bestowed upon you His favors, [both] *apparent and unapparent*? But of the people is he who dis-putes about God without knowledge or guidance or an enlightening Book [from Him].[513]

---

506 Doğan, *Uṣūl al-Tafsīr*, 297.
507 Dhahabī, *at-Tafsīr*, v.11 p. 340.
508 Doğan, *Uṣūl al-Tafsīr*, 297.
509 Dhahabī, *at-Tafsīr wal-Mufassirun*, v.3 p. 18; Zarqānī, *Manāhil al-Irfān*, v.1 p. 546.
510 Dhahabī, *at-Tafsīr wal-Mufassirun*, v.3 p. 18.
511 See *Surah Kahf*.
512 Doğan, *Uṣūl al-Tafsīr*, 297.
513 Qur'ān, 31: 20.

The expression '*ẓāhir-bāṭin*,' ('apparent' and 'unapparent'), indicates there are inner and outer dimensions of the Qur'ān. Imam Shāṭibī (d. 1388 C.E.), a prominent grammarian and legal theorist, held that the outer meaning of the verses is just the literal reading of them and the inner meaning of the verses gives the real understanding.[514] The Prophet (pbuh) said:

> In every verse there are outer meanings (*ẓāhir*), inner meanings (*bāṭin*), the last border [rulings] (*hadd*) and it's beyond [warnings of the last day and the afterlife] (*muttala'*). Each of these categories has twigs and branches.[515]

Ẓāhir is the literal meaning of the verse, *bāṭin* is its inner dimensions, *hadd* is the rulings within the verse pertaining to *halal* or *haram* and *muttala'* is the warnings and good tidings contained in the Qur'ān.[516] Sufi scholars focused on the inner dimensions of the verses rather than their literal meanings.

The Bāṭinī (esoteric) sects interpret the Qur'ān as Sufi scholars do but they ignore its literal meaning and rules of Islam and so are regarded as deviants. Alternately, *ish'ārī* scholars never ignore Shari'ah and its rules. They believe that it is necessary to implement all the Islamic principles to achieve God's pleasure and access the inner dimension of the Qur'ān. The Bāṭinī scholars emphasized the inner meanings in their interpretations and favored their own views in the event of any contradiction between the literal and esoteric explanations. They clearly disregarded Islamic obligations and rules in their view that if a person has a pure heart he/she is not required to perform religious acts. Alternately, *ish'ārī* scholars never interpret the Qur'ān in a manner which annul its rules; rather they accept the literal meanings, and use their inspiration to discern the inner meanings to produce a harmonised outcome.

Ibn Taymiyya (1263—1328 C.E.) of the Hanbalī School accepts *ish'ārī tafsīr* based on certain conditions;

There are two types of inner knowledge; the first compromises the literal meaning of the verses and the second does not. If the inner meaning does not compromise the literal meaning of the verse it is rejected. Whoever claims: "I know one inner meaning but it contradicts the literal meaning" is wrong, either he is ignorant or corrupt. On the other hand, if the inner meaning complements the literal meaning, it is like the literal meaning. This can be proved with the words

---

[514] Shāṭibī, *al-Muwafaqaat*, v.3 pp. 382–383.
[515] Ibn Hibban, *Saḥīḥ* 1:146.
[516] Doğan, *Uṣūl al-Tafsīr*, 298.

of the Qur'ān and Sunnah, but it is not accepted as the only meaning of the verse. Those who say that it is the only meaning of the verse are wrong. If they do not claim this, it can be accepted as part of the interpretation.[517]

Ibn Ḥazm (994—1064 C.E.), a leading proponent and codifier of the Ẓahirī School, does not accept *ish'ārī tafsīr* because the Prophet (pbuh) explained everything in Qur'ān and nothing is hidden in the religion.[518] The scholars put forward some conditions to accept Sufi interpretations;[519]

1) It is not contrary to the literal meaning of the Qur'ān
2) There is evidence from the Qur'ān or Sunnah that supports the interpretation.
3) Islam and logic do not contradict it.
4) There is no claim that this is the only meaning of the verse.

Inspiration is the main source for this type of *tafsīr* and this is not sufficient evidence by itself. The experience is subjective since it is a particularized event between the individual scholar and God; therefore, the knowledge is applicable to the individual and cannot be imposed upon others.

In short, Islamic Sufism is neither philosophy, nor merely theory; but an experienced knowledge. Without one personally experiencing these intuitions, inspirations and spiritual ecstasies, it remains a difficult concept to comprehend. The famous *tafsīr* works in this manner are;

- Sahl ibn Abdullah al-Tustarī (d. 986 C.E.), '*Tafsīr Qur'ān al-Aẓīm*'
- Abū Abdurrahman Muhammad ibn Musa as-Sulami (d. 1021 C.E.), '*Haqāiq al-Tafsīr*'
- Muhammad al-Qushayrī (d. 1072 C.E.), '*Latāif al-Ishārat bi Tafsīr al-Qur'ān*'
- Abū Muhammad Ruzbahan, '*Arāisu Bayan fi Haqāiq al-Qur'ān*'
- Najmuddin Dāya, '*Ta'wilāt an-Najmiyya*'
- Ni'matullah Nahjivānī, '*al-Fawātīh al-Ilāhiyya wa'l-Mafātih al-Ghaybiyya*'

SUMMARY: INTRODUCTION

1. Despite leading a deeply spiritual life, the Prophet (pbuh) warned his Companions away from extreme worship that would make practicing Islam difficult for them.

---

[517] Ibn Taymiyya, *Risāla Fi Ilm al-Bātin*, pp. 231–236.

[518] Ibn Ḥazm, *al-Fasl*, v.2 pp. 91–92.

[519] Doğan, *Uṣūl al-Tafsīr*, 300.

2. The Companions of the Prophet (pbuh) lived very spiritual lives however; they did not give this lifestyle a name.

3. The term 'Sufism' was applied by later Muslim scholars who articulated the principles of Islamic Sufism as a separate discipline.

4. Sufism has many different definitions: the annihilation of the individual's ego, will, and self-centeredness by God and the subsequent spiritual revival with the light of His Essence; the continuous striving to cleanse one's self of all that is bad or evil in order to acquire virtue.

5. Worshipping God as if seeing Him, even though one does not see Him, in the awareness that He sees everyone, is the essential meaning of Sufism.

6. There are three levels of attainment for the perfection of human beings; *īmān* (faith), Islam (submission to the Will of God) and *iḥsān* (worshipping God as if seeing Him).

7. Religious commandments were vital issues in a Muslim's individual and collective life, scholars prioritised these and compiled them into books; Sufi masters primarily concentrated on the pure, spiritual dimension of the Islamic truth and their respective works of Qur'ān interpretation were known as *Sufi tafsīr*.

8. Sufism is not separate from Islam; rather it is the spiritual facet.

9. Sufism is living Islam on the deepest level, since it requires austerity, self-control self-criticism and the continuous struggle to resist the temptations of Satan and the evil-commanding self in order to fulfill religious obligations.

10. Sufi exegeses fall under two categories; 1) theoretical and 2) *ish'ārī*.

11. Even though theoretical Sufi *mufassir* interpreted the Qur'ān in line with their philosophical and theological opinions, it is sometimes difficult to understand their interpretations.

12. The founder of theoretical *tafsīr* is generally acknowledged to be Muhyiddin ibn 'Arābī.

13. In attempting to interpret the verses in tandem to their theoretical understanding, they disregarded any correlation between their explanations and the Arabic rules and strayed from the fundamental purpose of the Qur'ān.

14. The other type of Sufi exegesis is known as *ish'ārī tafsīr*. This type of *tafsīr* was named '*ish'ārī*' because it can only be achieved through a deep meditation on the verses rather than through a literal reading of them. It is the interpretation of the Qur'ān based on inspiration.

15. Sufi scholars bring some arguments to defend their approach to the Qur'ān including the apparent and unapparent meanings in the verses.

16. *Ẓāhir* is the literal meaning of the verse, *bātin* is its inner dimensions, *hadd* is the rulings within the verse pertaining to *halal* or *haram* and *muttala'* is the warnings and good tidings contained in the Qur'ān. Sufi scholars focused on the inner dimensions of the verses rather than their literal meanings.

17. The Bātinī (esoteric) sects interpret the Qur'ān as Sufi scholars do but they ignore its literal meaning and rules of Islam and so are regarded as deviants.

18. *Ish'ārī* scholars never ignore Shari'ah and its rules. They believe that it is necessary to implement all the Islamic principles to achieve God's pleasure and access the inner dimension of the Qur'ān.

19. Some scholars accept *ish'ārī tafsīr* based on certain conditions whilst other refute it completely.

20. Inspiration is the main source for this type of *tafsīr* and this is not sufficient evidence by itself.

21. In short, Islamic Sufism is neither philosophy, nor merely the theory; but an experienced knowledge.

Tustarī and His Work

His Life and Education

One of the most important scholars of *ish'ārī tafsīr* is Abū Muhammad Sahl ibn Abdullah at-Tustarī. Born in Tustar in 818 C.E. in Khūzistān, south-western Iran,[520] Tustarī began his education at a young age and had memorized the whole Qur'ān by the time he was six or seven. He had a very good character and treated people kindly during his whole life. At an early age, he was introduced to Sufism by his uncle Muhammad ibn Sawwā. Tustarī would rise in the early hours and watch his uncle performing his nightly vigil[521] and it was from him that he learned the Sufi practice of remembrance of God when one night his uncle told him to recite

---

[520] To know more about his life, education and books please check Abū Nuaym, *Hilyatu>l Awliya*, Egypt 1351, 10/139–213; Sulami, *Tabaqāt al-Sufiyya*, Egypt 1372, s. 206; Sharani, *Tabaqāt al-Kubra*, Egypt 1954 1/77; Ibn Nadīm, *al-Fihrist*, s. 263.

[521] Abū al-Qāsim al-Qushayrī, *al-Risāla al-Qushayriyya*, Cairo, 1966, 83.

inwardly without moving his tongue, 'God is with me, God is watching over me, God is my Witness.'[522]

From his childhood, Tustarī displayed a strong inclination towards Sufi life and it was related that he lived on barley bread alone until the age of twelve.[523] Experiencing a spiritual crisis at a young age, he travelled to 'Abbādān (in present-day south-western Iran) to find the answer from the scholars there.[524] There he met with Abū Habib, staying with him for some time to benefit from his Sufi teachings.[525] After returning home, Tustarī lived a solitary and ascetic life for twenty years, disciplining himself by eating less, speaking less, sleeping less, avoiding the consumption of animal products, etc.

In 834 C.E., Tustarī went to Mecca to perform *Hajj* and came across the great Sufi Master Dhū'l-Nūn al-Miṣrī (d. 245 A. H. / 860 C.E.).[526] He stayed with him and benefitted from his knowledge, in particular the true trust in God, which is one of the key concepts in his *tafsīr*.[527] His great respect for Dhū'l-Nūn led him to say, 'I do not like to engage in discourse concerning mystical knowledge as long as Dhū'l-Nūn is alive.'[528]

Following the death of Dhū'l-Nūn in 860 C.E., Tustarī began publicly teaching large groups of followers. He was driven out of his town following accusations of evil acts or heresy and moved to Basra with his disciples. It is most likely that a jealous scholar stirred people against him using false accusations.[529] After settling in Basra, he was challenged by two jurists from the Shāfi'ī School. Convincing them that he was merely a servant of God, they acknowledged his spiritual superiority[530] and he lived out his remaining days in Basra until his death in 896 C.E.

Tustarī had many pupils some of who remained with him for many years. Muhammad ibn Sālim was one of his well-known students responsible for transmitting and expounding his sayings and teachings. Abū Bakr al-Sijzī transmitted his *tafsīr* and 'Umar ibn Wāsil al-'Anbarī narrated anecdotes about him and elu-

---

[522] Sahl ibn 'Abd Allāh al-Tustarī, *Great Commentaries on the Holy Qur'ān*, translated: Annabel Keeler and Ali Keeler, Fons Vitae, Kentucky 2011, Introduction.

[523] Qushayrī, *Risāla*, 84.

[524] Muḥyī al-Dīn Ibn Arābī, *al-Futūḥāt al-Makkiyya*, Beirut, 2007, 1/101.

[525] Qushayrī, *Risāla*, 85.

[526] Sulami, *Tabaqāt*, 199.

[527] Ibn Athīr, al-*Lubab fī Tahdhīb al-Ansāb*, 1/176.

[528] Abū Naṣr 'Abd Allāh ibn 'Alī (al-Ṭūsī) al-Sarrāj, *Kitāb al-Luma fī'l-Taṣawwuf*, London 1914, 181.

[529] Ibn al-Jawzī, *Talbīs Iblīs*, Cairo, 1950, 162.

[530] Sha'rānī, *Tabaqāt al-Kubrā*, 1/6.

cidated some of his Qur'anic interpretations.[531] As well as transmitting his teachings, these disciples also related what they observed about the spiritual states of their master, including reports of some miraculous events (*karamaat*), which Tustarī either described to them, or they themselves witnessed.[532] These events included the description of a night when Tustarī held his finger in the flame of a lamp for two hours without feeling any pain and, a day when he vanished mysteriously after the 'Asr prayer. He reported that he had encountered and conversed with a *jinn* of such a great age that he had met both Jesus and Muhammad (pbuh) and he had also conversed with wild beasts and birds.[533] However, Tustarī did not pay any attention to these *karamaat* (wonders) for they might be tricks of Satan. He believed that if a person abstains from the world for forty days in true faith and sincerity, he will be given special gifts from God.[534]

Tustarī was very humble and whenever he was praised, he would refer the person to God and emphasize His Majesty. His life was in a state of continual awareness of God. Tustarī claimed; "My state in the prayer and outside of the prayer is the same."[535] He endured extreme starvation and when questioned about his provision, he replied that a believer's daily bread is God, his sustenance is the remembrance of God and his nourishment is religious knowledge.[536] Tustarī valued a life of austerity; he found that wisdom is in hunger and ignorance is in satiety and so advised his disciples accordingly;

> Let your food be barley, your sweetmeat dates, your condiment salt and your fat yoghurt. You should let your clothes be of wool, your houses be the mosques, your source of light the sun, your lamp the moon, your perfume water, your splendor be in cleanliness.[537]

Tustarī was loyal to the Sunnah when establishing the principles of his teaching;

> One should always adopt hardship for oneself, but when giving counsel to others, one should choose what is bearable and easy. To do this is to follow in the footsteps of the Prophet (pbuh), who, when confronted with a particular matter concerning the community, used to choose what was

---

[531]   al-Tustarī, *Great Commentaries on the Holy Qur'ān*, Introduction.

[532]   Tustarī, *Tafsīr*, 2:25.

[533]   Sarrāj, *Kitāb al-Luma*, 316.

[534]   Qushayrī, *Risāla*, 703.

[535]   Sarrāj, *Kitāb al-Luma*, 293

[536]   Abū Tālib al-Makkī, *Qūt al-Qulūb fī Mu'āmalat al-Maḥbūb*, Beirut 1997, 2/282.

[537]   Tustarī, *Tafsīr*, 7: 172.

light and gentle, but when the matter concerned himself, would apply that which is hardest and most severe.[538]

Tustarī had some knowledge of medicine and treated people but at the same time, he suffered from an illness which he used to treat in others for thirty years.[539] Towards the end of his life, he became very weak from illness but never complained. His disciple reported:

> It was his way and his conduct to be full of gratitude to God and remember Him. He was also constant in observing silence and reflection. He would dispute little and was of a generous spirit. He led people through his good character, mercy and compassion for them, and by giving good counsel to them. Truly, God filled his heart with light and made his tongue speak with wisdom. He lived a praiseworthy life and died as a stranger in Basra, may God have mercy upon him.[540]

Tustarī was considered a moderate Sufi leader who defined *ma'rifa* (knowledge of God), *yaqin* (certainty in faith), soul and life based on the fundamentals of Islam.[541] For him, the nourishing soil for the worship of God is *ma'rifa*, its seed is *yaqin* and its water is knowledge; life is also knowledge and therefore, if one is ignorant he/she is metaphorically dead.[542] Tustarī believed that continual repentance was just as important as the other tenets of worship such as performing the five daily prayers, giving *zakat* or fasting during Ramadan.[543] He held that to be a good servant of God, one must only earn and consume what is *halal*; if one worships God, his money should be earned from *halal* methods and he should only provide *halal* for his family.[544]

Following his death, his student, Ibn Sālim, transmitted his teachings. They reached Abū Tālib al-Makkī (d. 996 C.E.) through *the tariqa of Salimiyya* (the path of Salimiyya). Tustarī wrote many books few of which have survived until the present time. Some of his books are *'Daqāiq al-Muhibbīn,' 'Mawāiz al-Ārifīn,' 'Jawābāt-u Ahlil Yaqīn,' 'Qiṣaṣ al-Anbiya,' 'al-Qāya Li Ahli'n Nihāya,' 'Risāla'* and *'Tafsīr al-Qur'ān al-Aẓīm.'*[545] Besides his own works, Tustarī's teachings have been pre-

---

[538] al-Tustarī, *Great Commentaries on the Holy Qur'ān*, Introduction.

[539] Sarrāj, *Kitāb al-Luma*, 203.

[540] Tustarī, *Tafsīr*, 10: 62.

[541] Doğan, *Uṣūl al-Tafsīr*, 302.

[542] Doğan, ibid.

[543] Doğan, ibid.

[544] Doğan, ibid.

[545] L. Massignon, *Encydopedie de l'Islam*, (Sahl at-Tustarī), IV. 65.

served in works of Sufism such as the '*Kitāb al-Luma*' of Abū Naṣr al-Sarrāj and the '*Qūt al-Qulūb*' of Abū Ṭālib al-Makkī.

His *Tafsīr*

Tustarī's *tafsīr* book is '*Tafsīr al-Qur'ān al-Aẓīm*.' Published in Egypt in 1908, it was not written by him but was orally delivered to his pupils who preserved and transmitted it. Some years later, it was compiled and written with additional notations[546] leading some scholars to argue that the text we have today is not his original work but the collective work of various other scholars.[547] Ibn Nadīm doesn't mention this book and for this reason some scholars suspect its authenticity, however, most scholars accept it as Tustarī's work and consider it to be the first *ish'ārī tafsīr*.[548]

The *tafsīr* is composed of three layers; the first comprising Tustarī's actual comments on the verses; the second includes a number of his comprehensive maxims on mystical topics as well as illustrative material taken from the stories of the Prophets, probably added by Tustarī's disciples; the third represents further insertions by later scholars and includes exegetical proof texts taken from the Qur'ān and hadith, the lengthy explanation of a poem, and anecdotes about Tustarī.[549]

Rather than interpreting the whole Qur'ān, Tustarī's work includes comments on 1000 verses sourced from all the *surahs*. The nature of the exegetical content is varied and includes both exoteric interpretations as well as providing additional information about the context of the verses.[550] As well as explaining the literal meanings of the verses, Tustarī gives additional explanations that could be considered as ethical in nature. The book also includes discussions of mystical topics, anecdotes about early mystics and Tustarī's own views concerning different aspects of the mystical path.

Methodology in His *Tafsīr*

To understand Tustarī's approach to Qur'anic commentary some statements are analysed below. When discussing the process of revelation, Tustarī states that God sent down the Qur'ān in five parts at a time: five clear verses (*muḥkam*), five

---

[546] al-Tustarī, *Great Commentaries on the Holy Qur'ān*, Introduction.
[547] L. Massignon, ibid.
[548] Doğan, *Uṣūl al-Tafsīr*, 302.
[549] Böwering, *Mystical Vision*, 128–135.
[550] Tustarī, *Tafsīr*, 5:83, 14:25, 42:7.

ambiguous verses (*mutashābih*), five verses concerning what is permissible (*halal*), five verses concerning what is prohibited (*haram*), and five parabolic verses (*amthal*).[551] The believers firmly attach to what is clear and believe what is ambiguous in it. They accept *halal* as permissible and *haram* as prohibited.

In his work, Tustarī also mentions knowledge of both the inner and outer levels of meaning in the Qur'ān. He explains that God used Arabic as the language of the Qur'ān and expounded it in a clear Arabic tongue in the letters of the alphabet to convey the knowledge of its inner (*bātin*) and outward (*zāhir*) meanings.[552] Tustarī holds that every verse has four levels: an outward (*zāhir*) and an inward sense (*bātin*), a limit (*hadd*) and a level that enlightens the heart by understanding the purpose of the verse (*matla'*). The outward sense is the recitation and the inward sense is the understanding of the verse; the limit defines what is lawful and unlawful, and the point of transcendence is the heart's elevation to the intended meaning, which is knowledge of God. *Zāhir* is the literal meaning of the verse that can be achieved through reading it, but *bātin* requires intentional struggling to understand it. Tustarī holds that if God wants one of his servants to be closer to Him, He teaches him the *zāhir* and *bātin* meanings of the Qur'ān together.

In commenting on the verse below, Tustarī warns against interpreting the Qur'ān according to one's own whims or desires:

> It is He Who has sent down on you this (glorious) Book, wherein are verses absolutely explicit and firm: they are the core of the Book, others being allegorical. Those in whose hearts is swerving pursue what is allegorical in it, seeking (to cause) dissension, and seeking to make it open to arbitrary interpretation, although none knows its interpretation save God. And those firmly rooted in knowledge say: 'We believe in it (in the entirety of its verses, both explicit and allegorical); all is from our Lord'; yet none derives admonition except the people of discernment.[553]

He explains that the expression, 'desiring its interpretation' is referring to the desire of the lower self or the *nafs*.[554] He quotes from 'Ali ibn Abī Tālib to explain the expression 'those firmly rooted in knowledge':

> They are the ones whom knowledge has protected them from plunging into the interpretation of the Qur'ān according to some whim (or with set arguments) without awareness of the unseen mysteries. This is due

---

[551] Tustarī, *Tafsīr*, Introduction.
[552] Tustarī, *Tafsīr*, Introduction.
[553] Qur'ān 3: 7.
[554] Tustarī, *Tafsīr*, 3: 7.

to God's guidance of them, and His disclosing to them His unseen secrets
from within the treasure chests of knowledge.[555]

The hidden or esoteric meanings of the Qur'ān are the unseen mysteries
contained therein and are only exposed to special servants of God. Tustarī holds
that the secrets contained within the Qur'ān are infinite and cannot possibly be
encompassed all together; the Qur'ān represents the knowledge of God which is
unlimited and therefore, if a person is given a thousand ways of understanding
each letter of the Qur'ān, he could not reach the end of God's knowledge within
it.[556] The Qur'ān comes from the speech of God (*Kalām*) and His speech is eternal. Hence, there is no end to any of His Attributes. His servants are only able to
comprehend of His speech as much as He opens it to them.

> The people of Moses made, after [his departure], from their ornaments a
> calf, an image having a lowing sound. Did they not see that it could nei-
> ther speak to them nor guide them to a way? They took it [for worship],
> and they were wrongdoers.[557]

For Tustarī, this verse symbolised anything that separates people from worshipping the one true God. The golden calf represents family, children, worldly
things and idols. Human beings can only get close to God by ridding themselves
of these obstacles or false loves. The Jews overcame their carnal desires (and
destroyed the golden calf) saving themselves from idol worship and becoming
closer to God.[558]

> Who created me, and He [it is who] guides me. And it is He who feeds me
> and gives me drink. And when I am ill, it is He who cures me. And who
> will cause me to die and then bring me to life. And who I aspire that He
> will forgive me my sin on the Day of Recompense.[559]

He interprets this verse as: God created me to worship Him alone and guided me to the straight path to bring me closer to Him. He is the One who feeds me
with the pleasures of faith and gives me the drink of contentment. He protected
me when I inclined to worldly pleasures and He prevented me from following
my carnal desires. He kills and revives me by His Names. When mentioning them

[555] Tustarī, ibid.
[556] Tustarī, *Tafsīr*, 18: 109.
[557] Qur'ān, 7: 148.
[558] Tustarī, *Tafsīr*, 39–40.
[559] Qur'ān, 26: 78–82.

I experience death and I experience life. I am kept at a point between fear and hope. He judges me with His Mercy and Forgiveness.[560]

"We ransomed him with a great sacrifice."[561]

Tustarī interprets this verse to mean: Due to his human nature, Abraham loved his son greatly. When God commanded Abraham to kill his own son in return for His favors and protection, he did not intend Abraham to literally sacrifice his son. It was a symbolic act and a test of Abraham's devotion to God. God wanted Abraham to sacrifice his love of the world and anything that would become between him and God. The best way of testing him was to command him to kill his greatest worldly love, his son. Abraham understood the nature of God's command and renouncing all worldly loves, he committed himself to God. In return, his son was spared; at the moment of sacrifice, God replaced him with a ram.[562]

> Your Lord has decreed upon Himself mercy: that any of you who does wrong out of ignorance and then repents after that and corrects himself, indeed, He is Forgiving and Merciful.[563]

Tustarī's interpretation of this verse is that God revealed to Prophet David the following: 'O David, whoever knows Me, he desires Me. Whoever desires Me, he loves Me. Whoever loves Me, he searches for Me. Whoever searches for Me, he finds Me. Whoever finds Me, he struggles not to lose Me.' Thereupon David said, 'O my Lord, where can I find You when I search for You?' God replied: 'You can find Me in the broken hearts that fear Me a lot.'[564]

Through his interpretations, Tustarī struggles to purify the hearts, discipline the desires and embellish the minds with good thoughts. To this end, he employed the stories of pious people from early generations as examples to prove his interpretations.[565] For Tustarī, practising Islam and its obligations are preconditions for understanding the inner meanings of the verses of the Qur'ān and is it only if one listens to the Qur'ān wholeheartedly and practices it in his life that God distinguishes him with the special ability to extract the inner meanings.

These examples illustrate that Tustarī's interpretations are neither illogical nor against Islamic principles and are therefore accepted.

---

[560] Tustarī, 69–70.
[561] Qur'ān, 37: 107.
[562] Tustarī, 52.
[563] Qur'ān, 6: 54.
[564] Tustarī, 35.
[565] Doğan, *Uṣūl al-Tafsīr*, 302.

Summary: Tustarī and His Work

1. Abū Muhammad Sahl ibn Abdullah at-Tustarī is one of the most important scholars of *ish'ārī tafsīr*.

2. Born in Iran in 818 C.E., he memorized the whole Qur'ān by age six or seven and was introduced to Sufism by his uncle, Muhammad ibn Sawwā.

3. He was educated by Abū Habib in 'Abbādān and later by the great Sufi Master Dhū'l-Nūn al-Miṣrī who he met in Mecca.

4. Following the death of Dhū'l-Nūn in 860 C.E., Tustarī began publicly teaching a large group of followers basing himself in Basra where he lived until his death in 896 C.E.

5. Tustarī was loyal to the Sunnah when establishing the principles of his teaching.

6. Tustarī was considered a moderate Sufi leader who defined *ma'rifa* (knowledge of God), *yaqin* (certainty in faith), soul and life based on the fundamentals of Islam.

7. Tustarī wrote many books few of which have survived until the present time.

His *Tafsīr*

8. Tustarī's *tafsīr* book is '*Tafsīr al-Qur'ān al-Aẓīm*'; a collection of his opinions delivered orally to his pupils and preserved and transmitted by them before being collated and written.

9. The *tafsīr* is composed of three layers: his actual comments on the verses; a number of his comprehensive maxims on mystical topics as well as illustrative material taken from the stories of the Prophets; further insertions by later scholars.

10. Rather than interpreting the whole Qur'ān, Tustarī's work includes comments on 1000 verses sourced from all the *surahs*, and includes exoteric interpretations as well as providing additional information about the context of the verses.

11. As well as explaining the literal meanings of the verses, Tustarī gives additional explanations that could be considered as ethical in nature.

Methodology in His *Tafsīr*

12. When discussing the process of revelation, Tustarī states that God sent down the Qur'ān in five parts at a time: five clear verses (*muḥkam*), five ambiguous verses (*mutashābih*), five verses concerning what is permis-

sible (*halal*), five verses concerning what is prohibited (*haram*), and five parabolic verses (*amthal*).

13. In his work, Tustarī also mentions knowledge of both the inner and outer levels of meaning in the Qur'ān.

14. Tustarī holds that every verse has four levels: an outward (*zāhir*) and an inward sense (*bātin*), a limit (*hadd*) and a level that enlightens the heart by understanding the purpose of the verse (*matla'*).

15. Tustarī warns against interpreting the Qur'ān according to one's own whims or desires.

16. The hidden or esoteric meanings of the Qur'ān are the unseen mysteries contained therein and are only exposed to special servants of God.

17. Tustarī holds that the secrets contained within the Qur'ān are infinite and cannot possibly be encompassed all together, for the Qur'ān represents the knowledge of God, which is unlimited.

18. Through his interpretations, Tustarī struggles to purify the hearts, discipline the desires and embellish the minds with good thoughts.

19. For Tustarī, practising Islam and its obligations are preconditions for understanding the inner meanings of the verses of the Qur'ān and is it only if one listens to the Qur'ān wholeheartedly and practices it in his life that God distinguishes him with the special ability to extract the inner meanings.

SURAH NASR (HELP)

بِسْمِ اللهِ الرَّحْمٰنِ الرَّحِيمِ

اِذَا جَاءَ نَصْرُ اللهِ وَالْفَتْحُ ۙ ﴿١﴾ وَرَاَيْتَ النَّاسَ يَدْخُلُونَ فِي دِينِ اللهِ اَفْوَاجاً ۙ ﴿٢﴾

فَسَبِّحْ بِحَمْدِ رَبِّكَ وَاسْتَغْفِرْهُ ؕ اِنَّهُ كَانَ تَوَّاباً ﴿٣﴾

Surah Nasr (Help)

In the Name of God, the All-Merciful, the All-Compassionate

1. When God's help comes and victory (which is a door to further victories),
2. And you see people entering God's Religion in throngs,
3. Then glorify your Lord with His praise, and ask Him for forgiveness, for He surely is One Who returns

Tafsīr

This three-verse *surah* was revealed in Medina just three months before the death of the Prophet (pbuh). It relates God's completion of His favor upon the Prophet (pbuh) conveying that his mission has been successful in the best way. The *surah* implies the Prophet's (pbuh) imminent death, as with the completion of his mission, there is no need for him to remain in this world. It also implies a warning to the believers to be extra alert against sins and following their carnal desires as their victories are the result of God's favors upon them.

First verse: إِذَا جَاءَ نَصْرُ اللهِ وَالْفَتْحُ *When God's help comes and victory (which is a door to further victories)*

Tustarī said; God's help and promise of victory for your religion is a result of His previous promise to you.[566] There were many occasions where God promised help and victory for the Prophet (pbuh) giving the news that Islam will prevail over polytheism. However, His help and victory were made dependent on the believers' struggle in His way. The believers are in a continuous state of trial in this world. This verse is one of the miracles of the Qur'ān and proves its Divine authorship as only God can speak so certainly about the future.

Second verse: وَرَأَيْتَ النَّاسَ يَدْخُلُونَ فِي دِينِ اللهِ أَفْوَاجًا *And you see people entering God's Religion in throngs*

Tustarī interprets this verse as telling the Prophet (pbuh) that he would see people entering Islam in throngs, the people of Yemen entering God's religion in throngs, the tribes and their families and all people.[567] Ibn Abbas reported that the revelation of this *surah* was the cause of great happiness among the Companions, but Abū Bakr wept profusely when he heard it. When the Prophet (pbuh) asked him why he was crying he said, 'The *surah* announced that your death is imminent.' Thereupon the Prophet (pbuh) told him, 'You have spoken the truth.' Then he said, 'O God! Grant him understanding of the religion, and teach him the science of interpretation.'[568] Tustarī understands this statement to mean the teaching of the religion and glorification for his nation. He does not examine the authenticity of this report according to hadith criteria and, in this regard, his work shares characteristics with *riwāyah tafsīr*.

Third verse: فَسَبِّحْ بِحَمْدِ رَبِّكَ وَاسْتَغْفِرْهُ إِنَّهُ كَانَ تَوَّابًا *Then glorify your Lord with His praise, and ask Him for forgiveness, for He surely is One Who returns*

---

566 Tustarī, *Tafsīr*, 110: 1.
567 Tustarī, *Tafsīr*, 110: 2.
568 Tustarī, ibid.

Tustarī interprets this verse to mean one's helping his own soul to fight against the lower self (*nafs*) by preparing it for the afterlife, because the soul originates from there.[569] The lower self (*nafs*) desires this world because it belongs to it. Tustarī attempts to understand the complexity of the human inner self, perceiving an opposition within human nature. One side is that which tends towards earth and the physical and sensory pleasure, the lower self or *nafs*. On the other side is that which yearns for heaven and the spiritual realm, the higher self or *rūḥ*. Tustarī often contrasts these two sides of the self, the natural self which inclines to darkness and the spiritual side which inclines to light. He uses the word *rūḥ* (spirit-soul) to represent the spiritual aspect of human nature and the term *nafs* to designate man's basic nature, or his physical appetites and instincts. In fact, this term on its own is frequently used by Tustarī to designate the darker, earth-bound side of the human being that is opposed to the spiritual self (or spirit).[570]

This verse commands the Prophet (pbuh) to gain ascendancy over the lower self and open the door to the afterlife by glorifying God and seeking forgiveness for his nation.[571] Following this revelation, the Prophet (pbuh) spent more time repenting and glorifying God. He asked forgiveness from God a hundred times in the morning and evening.[572] He would strive in worship day and night to the point where his feet swelled up, his eyes became red, and his cheeks became pale. He would smile little and weep and ponder a lot. Tustarī holds that the lower self can potentially be saved through the glorification of God. He maintains that the natural self can be nurtured into a coalition with the spiritual self through the remembrance of God. He states:

> The natural self and spiritual self will be joined together and will be mingled in their partaking of the bliss of Paradise inasmuch as they were allied in this world in keeping remembrance constantly and upholding a state of gratitude.[573]

The sustenance of the spiritual self is the remembrance of God whilst the sustenance of the natural self is food and drink. If a person cannot reconcile these two opposite selves, or *nafs*, according to Tustarī he cannot be considered a Sufi.[574]

---

[569] Tustarī, *Tafsīr*, 110: 3.
[570] al-Tustarī, *Great Commentaries on the Holy Qur'ān*, Introduction.
[571] Tustarī, *Tafsīr*, 110: 3.
[572] Tustarī, ibid.
[573] Tustarī, *Tafsīr*, 81: 7.
[574] Tustarī, *Tafsīr*, 39: 42.

Tustarī sometimes discusses the lower self in relation to the heart and emphasizes the latter:

> If the *nafs* prevails over the heart, it will drive the person to follow his desires. But if the heart maintains dominance over the *nafs* and the body it will gain the virtues which will lead them into worship, and embellish them with sincerity in servanthood.[575]

Tustarī relates the following tradition of the Prophet (pbuh) to emphasize the remembrance of God:

> Reduce your voice except in nine places; *tasbeeh* (glory be to God), *tahmeed* (praise be to God), *tawḥīd* (there is no god except God), *takbir* (God is great), when reciting the Qur'ān, commanding what is right, forbidding what is wrong, asking for goodness and seeking refuge from evil.[576]

Tustarī holds that the believers will see God in the afterlife but this vision will be the share of the intuition of the spiritual self, the understanding of the intellect and the discernment of the heart. The natural self will receive some pleasures in Paradise such as a fragrant breeze, due to its being fused with those lights.[577] The heart, intellect and spirit must work together to prevail over the lower self to be eligible to enter Paradise and enjoy the favors there.

"Ask Him for forgiveness, for He surely is One Who returns";

Tustarī interprets this verse to mean that God always accepts repentance. He states:

> He accepts repentance over and over again, each time the servant repents to Him. And know that our Lord is too generous not to be with you, assisting you against your evil commanding self.[578]

To emphasize repentance, Tustarī presents the verse: "Truly God loves those who repent."[579] True repentance to God requires one to oppose the evil-commanding self to be able to find God at his side. If one opposes the commandments and prohibitions of God, he is left alone and deprived of His Divine blessings. To obey God's commands in spite of one's own desires will result in success and salvation. But, being a slave to one's desires and ignoring God's commands will only bring about failure and destruction.

---

[575] Tustarī, *Tafsīr*, 48: 4.
[576] Tustarī, *Tafsīr*, 110: 3.
[577] Tustarī, *Tafsīr*, 42: 20.
[578] Tustarī, *Tafsīr*, 110: 3.
[579] Qur'ān 2: 222.

Tustarī strengthens his interpretation using logical arguments, holding that obedience of God's commandments is bitter whereas following one's desires is sweet, however, real success and happiness only lie in obedience to God. He supports this argument with an analogy: if a delicious food contains poison or any other harmful material, it should not be eaten. Medicine is taken despite its bitterness because of the benefits in it.

Tustarī's commentary on Surah Nasr concludes with a statement quoted from a righteous servant; "They pity, even if God forgives them! For among them, there is one who is wary of the withdrawal of forgiveness, and another who weeps out of shame, even if he is forgiven."[580] God is glorified and exalted so are His words.

SUMMARY: SURAH NASR *TAFSĪR*

1. This three-verse *surah* was revealed in Medina just three months before the death of the Prophet (pbuh).
2. It relates God's completion of his favor upon the Prophet (pbuh) conveying that his mission has been successful in the best way and also implies the Prophet's imminent death.
3. It also implies a warning to the believers to be extra alert against sins and following their carnal desires as their victories are the result of God's favors upon them.

First verse:

4. Tustarī said; God's help and promise of victory for your religion is a result of His previous promise to you.
5. This verse is one of the miracles of the Qur'ān and proves its Divine authorship as only God can speak so certainly about the future.

Second verse:

6. Tustarī interprets this verse as telling the Prophet (pbuh) that he would see people entering Islam in throngs, the people of Yemen entering God's religion in throngs, the tribes and their families and all people.
7. He relates a report from Ibn Abbas but does not examine its authenticity and, in this regard, his work shares characteristics with *riwāyah tafsīr*.

Third verse:

8. Tustarī interprets this verse to mean one's helping his own soul to fight against the lower self (*nafs*) by preparing it for the afterlife, because the soul originates from there.

---

[580] Tustarī, *Tafsīr*, 110: 3.

9. He attempts to understand the complexity of the human inner self, perceiving an opposition within human nature between inclinations towards darkness and light.

10. Tustarī often contrasts these two sides of the self, using the word *rūḥ* (spirit-soul) to represent the spiritual aspect of human nature and the term *nafs* to designate man's basic nature.

11. This verse commands the Prophet (pbuh) to gain ascendancy over the lower self and open the door to the afterlife by glorifying God and seeking forgiveness for his nation.

12. The sustenance of the spiritual self is the remembrance of God whilst the sustenance of the natural self is food and drink. If a person cannot reconcile these two opposite selves, or *nafs,* according to Tustarī he cannot be considered a Sufi.

13. Tustarī holds that the believers will see God in the afterlife but this vision will be the share of the intuition of the spiritual self, the understanding of the intellect and the discernment of the heart.

14. The natural self will receive some pleasures in Paradise such as a fragrant breeze, due to its being fused with those lights.

15. The heart, intellect and spirit must work together to prevail over the lower self to be eligible to enter Paradise and enjoy the favors there.

16. According to Tustarī, God always accepts repentance. True repentance requires one to oppose the evil-commanding self to be able to find God at his side. If one opposes the commandments and prohibitions of God, he is left alone and deprived of His Divine blessings.

17. Tustarī strengthens his interpretation using logical arguments, holding that obedience of God's commandments is bitter whereas following one's desires is sweet and uses analogy to support his view.

CHAPTER 11

Modern *Tafsīr*

Introduction

The Qur'ān is the primary source of knowledge for all Muslims and has been interpreted numerous times by scholars since its revelation. The conditions of the time and the needs of people have influenced the exegetical approach to the Qur'ān. In the modern age, scholars have tried to interpret it pragmatically and in harmony with modern sciences. Modern exegeses have attempted to answer theoretical questions posed by modernism through the implementation of universal principles to address practical concerns.

Although there is only a single religious text, the rich content of the Qur'ān has afforded multiple types of exegesis. These works are also affected by the capacity of each scholar, the conditions of the time and the mentality behind the approach. Other factors influencing the various opinions evident in Qur'ān interpretations are the multiple meanings of words, scholars' aptitude in comprehending the Sunnah and the development of external evidences.

The Qur'ān constitutes the foundations of religious life; therefore, to avoid the potential for relativism, the fundamental and unchangeable principles of Qur'anic exegesis must not be neglected. The Qur'anic text contains universal principles and benefits for all humanity. Despite the cultural situation at the time the Qur'ān was revealed, it is inappropriate to limit its meaning to a single perspective; doing so restricts its application and negates its universality. Although each modern scholar may demonstrate a distinctive style for interpreting the Qur'ān, they all share the same fundamental qualifications.

Modern Qur'anic scholars follow a reason-based method of interpretation that rejects many of the more mystical and spiritual approaches and practices in Islam. This method rejects classical interpretation and the wealth of knowledge that has been built up by scholars over the centuries and instead relies on the Qur'ān alone (even to the point of rejecting narrations) for interpretation. These scholars' interpretations tend to be more worldly and literal than classical interpretations, prioritizing worldly affairs and reducing the importance of the miracles and Qur'anic stories by explaining them rationally or scientifically.

Essentially, they accept the Qur'ān as the only source and disregard the traditions (hadith). They believe that the scholars have no special authority over the Qur'ān and that everyone has the right to contemplate it and as such all learned Muslims can interpret it.[581] They hold that the meaning of the Qur'ān is very clear and there is no ambiguity or real *mutashābih* in it. Some modernist scholars also reject Prophetic traditions, reasoning that the body of hadith was compiled at a later period subsequent to the death of Prophet (pbuh), as well as inferring that Qur'ān does not need hadith to be understood. However, many other modern scholars severely criticized this approach and emphasized the importance of the authentic Sunnah to comprehend the Qur'ān correctly.

Modern exegetes distinguish between legal and ethical rules asserting the former to be temporary and the latter as eternal. In this regard, they developed two types of understanding: the first is interpreting the Qur'ān in its totality in addition to the specific principles that are related to particular circumstances; the second is extracting general moral principles from specific situations in the light of the socio-historic background.[582]

Modern exegesis deals with many current issues such as social, political, economic, democracy, polygamy, interest, family planning, women, education, right of divorce, equality, justice and so forth, and incorporate these concepts into their commentary of the Qur'ān. These new topics and methods in Qur'anic commentary emerged largely in answer to new questions that arose from the political, social and cultural changes brought about in Muslim societies by the impact of western civilization. They reinterpreted the verses that regulate the legal status of women in view of modern aspirations towards equal rights for both sexes. The need to find practical solutions and theoretical justifications for their modern interpretation resulted in discounting the traditional interpretations and simultaneously denied the authority of the original text of the Qur'ān.

Sayyid Ahmad Khan (d. 1898 C.E.) and Muhammad Abduh (d. 1905 C.E.) emphasized the importance of the modern approach being compatible with the conditions of the modern world. They were greatly impressed by the political and economic success of modern Western civilization and so embraced a philosophy of Enlightenment and a rationalistic approach to Qur'anic exegesis. Sayyid Ahmad Khan determines there can be no contradiction between science and the Qur'ān and states that there is nothing which prevents Muslims from cooperat-

---

[581] Ismail Albayrak, Klasik Modernizmde Kur'an'a Yaklaşımlar/*Approaches to the Qur'an in Classic Modernism*, İstanbul: Ansār Publication 2004.

[582] Massimo Campanini, *The Quran: Modern Muslim Interpretation*, Taylor and Francis, p. 78.

ing with Western understanding. Abduh holds a similar view to Khan; he considers that the history of humankind is a process of development and humanity reached its final stage of maturity in the age of science. He maintains that Muslims can play a leading role in this progress for Islam is a reason-based religion. The Qur'ān emphasizes human reason and has an inherent understanding of the laws of nature and the laws that are effective in the historical development of nations and societies. The guidance and goals, which God asks human kind to attain, can only be achieved by using one's reason proportionately. Abduh started to lecture on the interpretation of the Qur'ān at Azhar University in Cairo, reaching up to *surah* 4, verse 124. His pupil, Muhammad Rashid Riza, took notes of these lectures and completed the rest of the work based on his methodology. Abduh's voluminous commentary is widely known as '*Tafsīr al-Manār*' and acts as an invaluable reference text for later scholars.

Modern exegetes try to interpret the Qur'ān in a meaningful way for modern Muslims. They tried to connect the believers to the religious text according to the socio-political environment. For example, Sayyid Qutb, Muhammad al-Ghazali and Hasan al-Turabi incorporated political analysis of the Qur'ān in light of the modern world. In terms of interpretation and understanding, their techniques vary, but they are in agreement that a correct understanding of the text necessitates knowledge of the aims of the Qur'ān (*maqāsid al-Qur'ān*).

Modern scholars attempted to rationalize religious concepts, explaining Qur'anic narratives and miracles from a rational perspective. They firmly believed that reason does not contradict revelation. For example, Tantawi Jawahiri (d. 1940 C.E.) wrote an encyclopedia named '*al-Jawāhir fī Tafsīr al-Qur'ān al-Karīm*' on scientific exegesis to reconcile the verses of the Qur'ān with scientific findings. Using this approach, modern scholars aimed to demonstrate that the Qur'ān predicted modern scientific achievements centuries ago. According to these scholars, the scientific findings mentioned in the Qur'ān range from cosmology to the properties of electricity, from the regularities of chemical reactions to the agents of infectious diseases. The notion of scientific Qur'anic exegesis is not completely new; early scholars such as Rāzī had already articulated these concepts some years earlier. However, modern scholars did not unanimously agree with this method, and some, such as Rashid Rizā and Amīn al-Khūlī, amongst others, strongly rejected it. They argued that the scientific meanings presented could not be supported from a linguistic perspective and additionally this method neglected the context of the words and verses in the Qur'anic text and the occasions behind the revelations. The other point raised was that its first addressees best comprehend the Qur'ān, so the interpretation should conform to the language and the intellectual horizon of the Companions. Scientific theories have remained incomplete and subject to change so it is not rational to try to reconcile such theories with the Qur'anic verses. Additionally the Qur'ān is not a book of science; rather it is a book of guidance for humanity that teaches the essentials of the Islamic faith and universal moral values.

The classical approach for the interpretation of the Qur'ān was a verse-by-verse explanation, starting from the beginning of the first *surah* until the last verse of the last *surah*. Some modern scholars dedicated their work to a single *surah* whiles others dealt only with a selection of *surahs* to demonstrate the usefulness of a new exegetical method. Aisha Abd al-Rahman and her work *'al-Tafsir al-Bayānī'* is an example of this type of modern exegesis.

A thematic approach is another characteristic of modern Qur'anic exegesis. Towards the end of the twentieth century, scholars produced works that emphasized key passages and main themes in the Qur'ān, with a particular focus on certain concepts and views. Amīn al-Khūlī (d. 1967 C.E.) was one of the scholars who considered concentrating on specific themes in Qur'ān commentary as most beneficial. Amin holds that the Qur'ān is the greatest book of Arab literature and that there are two important preconditions to understanding it; firstly, the historical background and the circumstances of its revelation must be well known. This precondition dictates the importance of a familiar knowledge of the culture, social conditions and religious traditions of the Companions as they were the original addressees. Secondly, it is essential to know the Arabic which the first addressee of the Qur'ān understood, since God used their language and adapted their modes of comprehension in His speech.

Fazlur Rahman, who was professor of Islamic Thought at the University of Chicago until 1988, tried to find a solution for the hermeneutical problem of the eternal message of the Qur'ān. He aimed to interpret the historical mission of the Prophet Muhammad (pbuh) for today's believers. He holds that the Qur'ān mainly deals with moral, religious and social pronouncements and in order to understand it better, three steps must be taken: firstly, the verses should be understood in their historical context; secondly, statements regarding general moral-social objectives should be extracted and; thirdly, these general principles must be embodied in the present concrete socio-historical context.

Muhammad Arkoun is another modern scholar who taught in Paris for many years. He holds that the Qur'ān is best understood by the knowledge of oral Prophetic speech, because it was revealed in a language which was tied to a specific historical situation. So, for every interpretation the final reference point must be this speech. As language is subjected to change over time, it is necessary to understand the Qur'ān according to the language at the time of the Prophet (pbuh). Sayyid Qutb holds a similar view in that the Qur'ān can be best understood by returning to the belief of the first Muslims and by actively struggling for the restoration of the pristine Islamic social order. He states in his *tafsīr* book '*Fī Żilāl al-Qur'ān*' that the Qur'ān in its entirety is God's message, and its instructions for social justice are indefinitely valid.

Summary: Modern *Tafsīr*

1. In the modern age, scholars have tried to interpret the Qur'ān pragmatically and in harmony with modern sciences.
2. Although each modern scholar may demonstrate a distinctive style for interpreting the Qur'ān, they all share the same fundamental qualifications.
3. Modern Qur'anic scholars follow a reason-based method of interpretation that rejects many of the more mystical and spiritual approaches and practices in Islam.
4. They accept the Qur'ān as the only source and disregard the traditions (hadith).
5. They believe that the scholars have no special authority over the Qur'ān and that everyone has the right to contemplate it and as such all learned Muslims can interpret it.
6. They hold that the meaning of the Qur'ān is very clear and there is no ambiguity or real *mutashābih* in it.
7. Modern exegetes distinguish between legal and ethical rules asserting the former to be temporary and the latter as eternal.
8. Modern exegesis deals with many current issues such as social, political, economic, democracy, polygamy, interest, family planning, women, education, right of divorce, equality, justice and so forth, and incorporate these concepts into their commentary of the Qur'ān.
9. Sayyid Ahmad Khan (d. 1898 C.E.) and Muhammad Abduh (d. 1905 C.E.) emphasized the importance of the modern approach being compatible with the conditions of the modern world.
10. Modern exegetes try to interpret the Qur'ān in a meaningful way for modern Muslims. They tried to connect the believers to the religious text according to the socio-political environment.

11. Modern scholars attempted to rationalize religious concepts, explaining Qur'anic narratives and miracles from a rational perspective. They firmly believed that reason does not contradict revelation.

12. Some modern scholars dedicated their work to a single *surah* whiles others dealt only with a selection of *surahs* to demonstrate the usefulness of a new exegetical method.

13. A thematic approach is another characteristic of modern Qur'anic exegesis.

Sayyid Qutb and His *Tafsīr*

His Life and Education

Sayyid Qutb was born in 1906 C.E. to a very religious family. Qutb was a keen student and his education continued throughout his life. He completed his elementary school education in Asyut, in southern Egypt memorizing the whole Qur'ān by the age of 10. Graduating from college in 1928 C.E., he went on the study at the university of Dar al-Ulūm in Cairo, graduating in 1933. Qutb began his teaching career and soon after became involved with the Ministry of Education in Egypt.

In 1948, Qutb migrated to the United States to research the educational system in Western countries. He remained there for two years, completing his MA in Education at University of Northern Colorado.[583] He observed the spiritual and moral corruption in the US and shared these views in his published works, 'The America I Have Seen,' which expressed his views on the negative and positive aspects of Western civilization. He stated that from an economic and scientific perspective the US was at the forefront in its leadership, however from a moral viewpoint it had collapsed.[584] Consequently, he also wrote a book entitled 'Social Justice in Islam' which espoused Islam as a superior system above all others. His experiences in the US resulted in an apparent antagonism towards Western countries.

Qutb's desire to contribute to society inspired him to join the Muslim Brotherhood, an Egyptian organization founded by Hasan al-Banna. The Egyptian government perceived this organization as a serious threat to the secular monarchy and prohibited their activities. During this turbulent political period Qutb became an editor for the Brotherhood's weekly paper and with their support, Abdul Nasser, the government opposition was able to successfully retire the monarchy in

---

[583] Kamal Abdel-Malik, *America in an Arab Mirror*, (New York 2000), 10.
[584] Sayyid Qutb, *The America I Have Seen*, (New York 2000), 11.

Egypt in 1952. Surprisingly, Abdul Nasser arrested Qutb and other leaders of the Brotherhood for plotting against him.[585] Qutb spent 10 years in prison and while in confinement wrote his famous *tafsīr*, '*In the Shade of the Qur'ān*.' This work is an extensive and comprehensive commentary on the Qur'ān and is inarguably one of the most read books of its kind today.[586]

Qutb was released from prison in 1964 and penned another famous work entitled '*Milestones*.' This book has four sections with the bulk of the information taken from his *tafsīr* book. It presents his political philosophy and concludes that all earthly sovereignty belongs to God alone. The textual content of his writings threatened the legitimacy of Nasser's government and so Qutb was arrested again in 1955 and sentenced to death by hanging.[587] Consequently, Qutb was martyred in 1966. Besides his *tafsīr* work, Qutb also wrote the following books;

- *Al-Adālah al-Ijtima'iyya in Islam*
- *Ma'rakah al-Islam wa'l-Ra'sumaliyya*
- *Al-Salam al-Alamiyya wa'l-Islam*
- *Nahwa Mujtama' Islamiyya*
- *Hasāis al-Tasawwir al-Islamiyya*
- *Al-Islam wa Mushkilat al-Khadariyya*
- *Dirasat al-Islamiyya*
- *Hadha'd-Din*
- *Al-Mustaqbal fi Hadha'd-Din*
- *Mealim al-Tariq*
- *Al-Tasawwur al-Fanniyya fi'l Qur'ān*
- *Al-Qasas al-Diniyya*

His *Tafsīr*

As mentioned earlier, Qutb wrote his *tafsīr* whilst in prison. The title of his work is '*In the Shade of the Qur'ān*' and the commentary reflects severe persecution and strong faith against such persecution. The book reflects Qutb's disappointment that a military government could mistreat so many members of the Brotherhood without having sound evidence against them.[588] Qutb concluded that the

---

[585] Hussain, *Global Islamic Politics*, 74.
[586] Sayyid Qutb, *Social Justice in Islam*, (New York 2000), 7.
[587] Hussain, *Global Islamic Politics*, 74.
[588] Luke Loboda, *The Thought of Sayyid Qutb*, Ashbrook Statesmanship Thesis, 2.

common Muslim had adopted a Western conception of faith, an abstract theory that proved quite impractical.[589]

Qutb's work is a socio-political *dirāyah* style interpretation. Qutb tries to interpret the Qur'ān in a meaningful way for modern Muslims. He tries to connect the audience to the religious text through a socio-political awareness seeking refuge in the shade of the Qur'ān against the intense turmoil of his time and expressing his feelings in his work. He emphasizes the Qur'ān as being the source of life and guidance and according to him, a life which is far from the Qur'ān is a life of *jahiliyyah* (ignorance).

Qutb's superior style and method depicts the verses of the Qur'ān most eloquently. He connects the verses to the present time and analyses them in the light of modern day problems, successfully illustrating the social and political events of his time in the shade of the Qur'ān. Beginning with the preface, he goes on to interpret Surah Fatiha and continues until he has interpreted all the *surahs.* In his interpretation, he analyses the verses in certain groups, which are labeled according to their content, thus aiding the fluency and appeal of his work.

Qutb explains the meanings of the verses eloquently and analyses the interrelationship between the Qur'ān and social laws. Importantly, he approaches the Qur'ān as guidance for all humanity that must be constantly reviewed according to the time and conditions. So, contemporary problems must be examined in the light of Qur'anic verses. The main themes in this *tafsīr* are human beings, social justice, social problems, strong faith, the notion of resurrection, the essentials of the Islamic faith, the oneness of God, education and the foundations of just government. He holds that any interpretation must be related to real-life issues, because the purpose of the Qur'anic revelation is to regulate human relations at the individual, family, social and governmental levels. In fact, the Qur'ān deals with many social issues such as family affairs, the rules of marriage and divorce, helping the needy, inheritance and property rights, the national and international relationships, governmental rules, war and peace rules and many more.

Qutb labels all ways of life that do not accept Islam as *jahiliyyah* (ignorance). He uses this term to describe all human beings who disobey God's authority by ignoring His revelation. He notes the continuous fight between evil and humankind since the latter became God's vicegerent on Earth.[590] Mankind and *Iblis* (Satan) descended from Paradise to Earth according to Divine destiny. God firmly com-

---

[589] Sayyid, Qutb, *In the Shade of the Qur'ān*, (The Islamic Foundation 2003) 1/13.
[590] Qutb, *In the Shade of Qur'ān*, 1/61.

manded human beings to follow His Divine guidance; otherwise, they would lose their vicegerent authority in this world.[591]

Qutb believes that the last Messenger is Muhammad (pbuh) and the Qur'ān is the final Divine Message for humankind. Whoever ignores the message falls into a state of *jahiliyyah* (ignorance) as Adam did by eating the forbidden fruit. Throughout history, God has always supported human beings by sending Prophets to them, but only some of them followed the truth.[592] Qutb offers chapter 7 in the Qur'ān as a detailed illustration of the fight between good and evil, or truth and falsehood, which has been played out throughout human history. He purports that the purpose of the Prophets was to rescue humankind from deviance[593] however despite this; human beings have often used their free will to reject the invitation to guidance.

Qutb holds that the stories in the Qur'ān remind us of the consequences of *jahiliyyah* in human history. Every Prophet came with the same message but ignorant people denied them. God's final address to humanity was through Muhammad (pbuh);

> Say (O Messenger to all humankind): 'O humankind! Surely I am to you all the Messenger of God, of Him to Whom belongs the sovereignty of the heavens and the earth. There is no deity but He. He gives life and causes to die.' Believe, then, in God and His Messenger, the Prophet (pbuh) who neither writes nor reads, who believes in God and His words (all His Books, commandments, and deeds); and follow him so that you may be rightly-guided.[594]

Qutb holds that Western civilization fell into *jahiliyyah* due to their denial of Muhammad (pbuh) and asserts that true faith is related to an unconditional submission to God, since all in the universe submits to the Will of God.[595] Through their submission, humans should implement the way of life prescribed by the Qur'ān. In this regard, God has provided human beings the Divine Guidance, which includes faith, morals, values, standards, systems, and laws.[596] Submission is obedience and in turn, obedience is worshipping God; obeying someone other than God would be worshipping another deity, therefore a true believer worships

[591] Qutb, ibid, 1/59–66.
[592] Qutb, ibid, 6/122–123.
[593] Qutb, ibid, 6/122.
[594] Qur'ān 7: 158.
[595] Qutb, ibid, 2/135.
[596] Qutb, ibid, 5/207.

only God. Mawdudi, a contemporary Muslim thinker, was very influential in shaping Qutb's beliefs regarding government. He states:

> The whole question of human well-being depends entirely on who exercises control over human affairs. A train runs only to the destination determined by its driver. All passengers can travel only to the same destination, whether they like it or not. In the same way, the train of human civilization travels where those who exercise power dictate.[597]

Qutb maintains that religion is intended to be a full system of life, supporting his argument with the verse:

> Humankind were (in the beginning) one community (following one way of life without disputing over provision and other similar concerns. Later on differences arose and) God sent Prophets as bearers of glad tidings (of prosperity in return for faith and righteousness) and warners (against the consequences of straying and transgression), and He sent down with them the Book with the truth (containing nothing false in it) so that it might judge between the people concerning that on which they were differing. And only those who were given it differed concerning it, after the most manifest truths came to them, because of envious rivalry and insolence among themselves. God has guided by His leave those who have believed (in the Book and the Prophets, those who now believe in the Qur'ān and Muhammad) to the truth about that on which they were differing. God guides whomever He wills to a straight path.[598]

He believes that this verse proved the common origin of humanity at the beginning of time, but that humans later diverged by developing differing customs and practices. To restore unity amongst humankind, whose nature is to disagree, God sent the Prophets and lastly the Qur'ān to put forth the universal system of life and eliminate disputes so humans could return to their original unity.

In order to understand Qutb's methodology in *tafsīr*, Surah Tabbat (Ruin) is quoted and the characteristics of his approach are analyzed.

SUMMARY: SAYYID QUTB AND HIS *TAFSĪR*

1. Sayyid Qutb was born in 1906 C.E. in Egypt, he was a keen student and memorized the Qur'ān by the age of 10.

---

[597] Qutb, ibid, 6/149–150.
[598] Qur'ān 2: 213.

2. He graduated from Dar al-Ulūm University in Cairo in 1933, becoming a teacher and soon after became involved with the Ministry of Education.

3. In 1948, he migrated to the United States and completed his MA in Education at University of Northern Colorado.

4. His work, '*The America I Have Seen*,' expressed his views on the negative and positive aspects of Western civilization, which he had observed whilst in the USA.

5. His later work, '*Social Justice in Islam*' espoused Islam as a superior system above all others.

6. Qutb joined the Muslim Brotherhood, becoming the editor for the Brotherhood's weekly paper.

7. He was arrested in 1952 and spent 10 years in prison using this time to write his famous *tafsīr*, '*In the Shade of the Qur'ān*.'

8. On release from prison in 1964 he wrote '*Milestones*' which presents his political philosophy.

9. His views threatened the legitimacy of Nasser's government resulting in his arrest in 1955 and subsequent death sentence, which was carried out in 1966.

His *Tafsīr*

10. The commentary of his work reflects severe persecution and strong faith against such persecution.

11. Qutb's work is a socio-political *dirāyah* style interpretation. Qutb tries to interpret the Qur'ān in a meaningful way for modern Muslims.

12. He analyses the verses in certain groups, which are labeled according to their content, thus aiding the fluency and appeal of his work.

13. Importantly, he approaches the Qur'ān as guidance for all humanity that must be constantly reviewed according to the time and conditions. So, contemporary problems must be examined in the light of Qur'anic verses.

14. The main themes in this *tafsīr* are human beings, social justice, social problems, strong faith, the notion of resurrection, the essentials of the Islamic faith, the oneness of God, education and the foundations of just government.

15. Qutb labels all systems of life that do not conform to Islam as *jahiliyyah* (ignorance).

16. Qutb holds that Western civilization fell into *jahiliyyah* due to their denial of Muhammad (pbuh) and asserts that true faith is related to an unconditional submission to God.

17. Qutb maintains that religion is intended to be a full system of life - God sent the Prophets and lastly the Qur'ān to put forth the universal system of life and eliminate disputes so humans could return to their original unity.

Surah Tabbat (Ruin)

بِسْمِ اللهِ الرَّحْمٰنِ الرَّحِيم

تَبَّتْ يَدَا اَبِي لَهَبٍ وَتَبَّ ﴿١﴾ مَا اَغْنٰى عَنْهُ مَالُهُ وَمَا كَسَبَ ﴿٢﴾ سَيَصْلٰى نَاراً ذَاتَ لَهَبٍ ﴿٣﴾ وَامْرَاَتُهُ حَمَّالَةَ الْحَطَبِ ﴿٤﴾ فِي جِيدِهَا حَبْلٌ مِنْ مَسَدٍ ﴿٥﴾

Surah Tabbat (Ruin)

1. May both hands of Abū Lahab be ruined, and are ruined are they!
2. His wealth has not availed him, nor his gains.
3. He will enter a flaming Fire to roast;
4. And (with him) his wife, carrier of firewood (and of evil tales and slander),
5. Around her neck will be a halter of strongly twisted rope.

Tafsīr

This five-verse *surah* was revealed in Mecca in the early period of the Prophet's (pbuh) mission and takes its name from the Arabic verb 'tab-ba' (be ruined), in the first verse. It is also called *al-Masad* which means flames. The verse predicts the final end of Abū Lahab, the Prophet's (pbuh) uncle and his wife, Umm Jamil. He was an uncle of the Prophet (pbuh) but at the same time, one of his most fervent enemies. Despite knowing Muhammad (pbuh) from his childhood, he opposed, denied and cursed him saying 'may your hands be ruined.' He was the fiercest enemy of the Prophet (pbuh) and so God appropriately named him the 'Father of the Flame' (Abū Lahab).

This *surah* foretells the final destination of Abū Lahab to Hell and portends that he will perish without accepting Islam. His end was just as predicted in the

Qur'ān; on learning of the Muslim victory over the Quraysh at Badr, he was inconsolable and died in great sorrow. Abū Lahab's illness was so contagious no one wanted to touch his body, so to bury him they dug a pit and pushed his body into it using long cudgels before throwing stones from a distance to cover it.

Abū Lahab's wife, Umm Jamil, equaled her husband in her enmity towards the Prophet (pbuh) scattering thorns on the path in front of his house and frequently slandering him and the holy Qur'ān. The Qur'ān also predicted her final destination to be Hell.

Background

Qutb's interpretation begins with an extensive historical background of the people mentioned in the *surah*. To do this he benefits from *sīrah* books such as Ibn Isḥāq and Ibn Hishām. He notes that Abū Lahab's real name was 'Abd al-'Uzzā ibn 'Abd al-Muttalib and he was one of the uncles of the Prophet (pbuh). He was nicknamed due to the radiant look on his face. Along with his wife Umm Jamil, Abū Lahab was one of the fiercest enemies of the Prophet and his message.[599]

Qutb quotes from Ibn Isḥāq the following report by the narration of Rabia ibn Abbād al-Daylī:

> Once, when I was young, I was with my father when God's Messenger was preaching about Islam to the Arab tribes. He said, 'O sons of... (calling their respective tribal names), I am the Messenger of God. I have been sent to command you to submit to God and worship Him alone, invoking nothing else beside Him, and to believe in me and protect me until I carry out what God has entrusted to me.' Behind him sat a cross-eyed, bright-faced man. When God's Messenger finished speaking he said, 'O sons of... This man wants you to forsake al-Lāt and al-'Uzzā [two prominent idols worshipped by the pagan Arabs] and your allies of the jinn, the children of Mālik ibn Aqmas and to substitute them with these innovations and nonsense he has invented. Don't listen to him and don't follow what he preaches.' I asked my father about that man and he told me it was Abū Lahab, the Prophet's uncle.[600]

This report is found in the hadith books of Ahmad ibn Hanbal and Tabaranī. Without examining the report according to the principles of hadith methodology, Qutb quoted it from the historian Abū Isḥāq. He continues to give background

---

[599] Qutb, *In the Shade of the Qur'ān*, 18/284.
[600] Qutb, ibid, 18/285.

information about the people who are mentioned in the *surah*. He explains that this hadith illustrates just one of many incidents in which Abū Lahab treated the Prophet (pbuh) and his message badly. His wife, Arwā b Harb ibn Umayyah, Abū Sufyān's sister, continuously supported him in his propaganda war against the Prophet (pbuh). This was their usual attitude towards him from the very start of his Divine mission.[601] Qutb relates from the prominent hadith scholar, Bukhari, the following incident as an occasion behind the revelation of this *surah*.

Ibn Abbās reports:

> One day the Prophet (pbuh) went out to al-Batha, a large square in Mecca, climbed a hill and summoned the people of the Quraysh. When they came to him, he addressed them; 'Were I to tell you that an enemy is drawing near and will attack you tomorrow morning or evening, would you believe me?' 'Yes' they replied. He continued; 'O Quraysh! Listen to me; I am warning you of God's severe punishment.' Abū Lahab was there and became very angry upon hearing the words of the Prophet (pbuh) and said; 'Damn you! For this have you called us? Then this *surah* was revealed.[602]

To illustrate why God called him the 'Father of the Flame,' Qutb mentions another evil act of Abū Lahab:

> When the Hashemite clan [i.e. the Prophet's own clan], under Abū Tālib's leadership, decided on grounds of tribal loyalty to protect the Prophet (pbuh) despite their rejection of the religion he preached. Abū Lahab was the only one to take a different stand. He joined with the Quraysh instead and was with them in signing the document imposing a complete social and business boycott on the Hashemite, so as to starve them out unless they delivered the Prophet (pbuh) to them. Abū Lahab also ordered his two sons to renounce Muhammad's (pbuh) two daughters to whom they had been engaged before Muhammad's Prophetic assignment. His aim was to burden the Prophet (pbuh) with their living and welfare expenses. Thus, Abū Lahab and his wife, Arwā, who was also called Umm Jamīl, continued with their persistent onslaught against the Prophet (pbuh) and his message. The fact that they were close neighbors of the Prophet (pbuh) made the situation even worse. Umm Jamīl used to carry thorns and sharp pieces of wood and place them along the Prophet's (pbuh) path.

---

[601] Qutb, ibid, 18/285.
[602] Bukhari, *Saḥīḥ*, Prophetic Commentary on the Qur'an, 496.

The Final Word[603]

Qutb holds that this *surah* was revealed as a counterattack against Abū Lahab and his wife's hostile campaign. God took it upon Himself to say the final word on behalf of His Messenger.[604]

First verse: تَبَّتْ يَدَا أَبِي لَهَبٍ وَتَبَّ *May both hands of Abū Lahab be ruined, and ruined are they!*

The Arabic verb '*tab-ba*,' rendered here as 'ruined,' signifies the failure of Abū Lahab. This word is used twice in two different senses; firstly, as a prayer and secondly as a prayer that has already been answered. So, in one short verse, an action is realized which opens the curtains upon a battle scene followed by a remark that is merely a description of what took place.[605]

Second verse: مَا أَغْنَى عَنْهُ مَالُهُ وَمَا كَسَبَ *His wealth has not availed him, nor his gains.*

Qutb interpreted this verse to mean that Abū Lahab could not escape and therefore he was defeated, vanquished and damned.[606] This was not his fate in this world, but in the afterlife.

Third verse: سَيَصْلَى نَارًا ذَاتَ لَهَبٍ *He will enter a flaming Fire to roast;*

Qutb stated that the fire is described as having flames in order to emphasize that it is raging.

Fourth verse: وَامْرَأَتُهُ حَمَّالَةَ الْحَطَبِ *And (with him) his wife, carrier of firewood (and of evil tales and slander),*

Abū Lahab's wife will reside in Hell with him.

Fifth verse: فِي جِيدِهَا حَبْلٌ مِنْ مَسَدٍ *Around her neck will be a halter of strongly twisted rope.*

Qutb gives the literal and metaphoric meaning of this verse. The meaning for the wife being dragged into Hell by a strongly twisted rope is related to her evil acts in the world. So, the verse depicted her miserable end with a dramatic scene.

Having given a brief explanation of the verses, Qutb concentrates on analyzing them linguistically paying attention to the articulacy. He highlights the choice of words and their intended meanings, aiming to show the eloquence and artistic style in the expressions of the Qur'ān.

---

[603] Qutb, ibid, 18/285.

[604] Qutb, ibid, 18/286.

[605] Qutb, ibid, 18/286.

[606] Qutb, ibid, 18/286.

Qutb describes how the language of this *surah* achieves a remarkable harmony between the subject matter and the atmosphere that is developed around it. The Father of Fire (Abū Lahab) will be plunged into Hell with flames of fire and his wife who carries the wood as fuel, will be met with the same fire with a palm-fiber rope around her neck.[607] Hell, with its fiercely burning flames, will be inhabited by Abū Lahab along with his wife, who used to collect thorns and sharp woods to put them in the Prophet's (pbuh) way. She will increase the blaze of the fire with the firewood she carries and will in time, be dragged into Hell with a rope tied round her neck, bundled like firewood.

Qutb notes how the words of the *surah* work collectively to present a powerful conceptual image in the mind of readers. The punishment is presented as being of the same nature as the deed: wood, ropes, fire and flames![608] Phonetically, the words are arranged in such a way as to compose a wonderful harmony between the sounds made by the tying of wood into bundles and pulling the neck by ropes.[609] When reading the first verse in Arabic, the words sound like a hard, sharp tug, analogous to that of bundles of wood or an unwilling person being dragged by the neck into a wild fire; all is consistent with the furious, violent and hostile tone attributed to the theme of the *surah*.[610] Thus, in five short verses, the vocal melodies syncopate skillfully with the actual movement of the scene portrayed.[611]

Qutb describes Umm Jamil's character as follows:

> The extremely rich and powerful style of the Qur'ān verses led Umm Jamīl to claim that the Prophet (pbuh) was in fact satirizing her husband and herself. This arrogant and vain woman could not endure being referred to by such a humiliating phrase as 'the carrier of firewood,' who 'shall have a rope of palm fiber round her neck.' Her rage grew wilder when the surah became popular among the Arab tribes who greatly appreciated such a fine literary style![612]

After this analysis, Qutb quotes from Ibn Isḥāq to provide further insight into the content of the *surah*:

---

[607] Qutb, ibid, 18/287.
[608] Qutb, ibid, 18/287.
[609] Qutb, ibid, 18/287.
[610] Qutb, ibid, 18/286.
[611] Qutb, ibid, 18/287.
[612] Qutb, ibid, 18/287.

Umm Jamīl having heard what the Qur'ān said about her and her husband came to the Prophet (pbuh) who was with Abū Bakr at the Ka'ba. She was carrying a handful of stones. God momentarily took her sight away from the Prophet (pbuh) and she could only see Abū Bakr to whom she questioned, 'Where is your comrade? I have heard that he has been satirizing me. Were I to find him, I would throw these stones right into his face. I, too, am gifted in poetry.' Then she chanted before leaving: The contemptible we obey not! Nor what he says shall we accept! Abū Bakr turned around to the Prophet (pbuh) and said, 'Do you think that she saw you?' the Prophet said; 'No, God made her unable to see me.'[613]

Qutb quotes another report from Al-Bazzār who is a famous hadith scholar in the narration of Ibn Abbas:

When this surah was revealed Abū Lahab's wife sought the Prophet (pbuh). While he was with Abū Bakr she appeared and Abū Bakr suggested to the Prophet (pbuh): 'She will not harm you if you hide from her.' The Prophet (pbuh) said; 'Do not worry, she will not see me.' She came to Abū Bakr and said: 'Your friend has satirized us!' Abū Bakr said; 'By the Lord of this Ka'ba, he has not, he is not a poet and what he says is not poetry.' She left saying 'I believe you.' Abū Bakr then enquired from the Prophet (pbuh) whether she had seen him and the Prophet (pbuh) said; 'No, an angel was shielding me the whole time she was here.'[614]

Qutb concludes Abū Lahab and his wife have been humiliated forever with their deeds recorded in this eternal book, the Qur'ān; a reflection of God's anger with them for their animosity towards His Messenger (pbuh) and His Message.[615] This is a warning to all those who choose to take a similar attitude towards Islam; they will meet with the same disgrace, humiliation and frustration, both in this life and in the life to come.[616]

Summary: Surah Tabbat (Ruin)

1. This five-verse *surah* was revealed in Mecca in the early period of the Prophet's (pbuh) mission and takes its name from the Arabic verb '*tab-ba*' (be ruined), in the first verse.

2. The verse predicts the final end of Abū Lahab, the Prophet's (pbuh) uncle and his wife, Umm Jamil who were the fiercest enemies of the Prophet (pbuh).

---

[613] Qutb, ibid, 18/287.
[614] Qutb, ibid, 18/287.
[615] Qutb, ibid, 18/287.
[616] Qutb, ibid, 18/287.

3. Abū Lahab's end was just as predicted in the Qur'ān.

Background

4. Qutb's interpretation begins with an extensive historical background of the people mentioned in the *surah* for which he benefits from Ibn Isḥāq and Ibn Hishām quoting hadith from their works.

5. To illustrate why God called him the 'Father of the Flame,' Qutb mentions another evil act of Abū Lahab.

6. Qutb holds that this *surah* was revealed as a counterattack against Abū Lahab and his wife's hostile campaign.

7. **First verse:** The Arabic verb '*tab-ba*,' rendered here as 'ruined,' signifies the failure of Abū Lahab. The verse both sets the scene of the battle and informs of its conclusion.

8. **Second verse:** Qutb interpreted this verse to mean that Abū Lahab could not escape and therefore he was defeated, vanquished and damned.

9. **Third verse:** Qutb stated that the fire is described as having flames in order to emphasize that it is raging.

10. **Fourth verse:** Abū Lahab's wife will reside in Hell with him.

11. **Fifth verse:** Qutb gives the literal and metaphoric meaning of this verse as the wife being dragged into Hell by the rope that she used for fastening wood bundles together.

12. Qutb then analyzes the verses linguistically illustrating the remarkable eloquence of the style.

13. Qutb notes how the words of the *surah* work collectively to present a powerful conceptual image within the readers mind.

14. Qutb describes Umm Jamil's character and then quotes from Ibn Isḥāq to provide further insight into the content of the *surah*.

15. He concludes Abū Lahab and his wife have been humiliated forever in the Qur'ān which is an eternal warning to all those with the same attitude towards Islam.

Elmalılı Hamdi Yazır and His *Tafsīr*

His Life and Education

Elmalılı Muhammad Hamdi Yazır was born in Elmalı, Antalya in southern Turkey in 1878. A descendant of a pious scholarly family, he completed his primary and middle school education in his town, memorizing the whole Qur'ān at an early age, before continuing his education in Ayasofya (Hagia Sophia) Madrasa

(Islamic school) in Istanbul. He attended lectures in Beyazıt Mosque and received his *ijāzah* (teaching license) from Mahmut Hamdi Efendi. From then on, he was known as the younger Hamdi, while his teacher was referred to as the older Hamdi. He learned the art of calligraphy, receiving an *ijāzah* in this field as well. He finished his university education while learning philosophy, literature and music through self-study.

Hamdi supported the new constitutional movement in Turkey with the purpose of promoting a superior modern educational system. He became a member of the organization Ittihad and Terakki, which advocated the tenets of the new constitution, working hard to develop the ideology of a democratic government compatible with Islamic values. He gave lectures in Beyazıt Mosque for two years as chief lecturer and represented the city of Antalya as a member of the Grand National Assembly of Turkey. Hamdi focused his efforts on being at the forefront of religious of affairs in Turkey.

Hamdi taught *Fiqh* (Islamic Law), *Uṣūl al-Fiqh* (Methodology of Islamic Jurisprudence) and *Mantıg* (Logic) in various madrasas (Islamic schools). He was promoted to the esteemed status of lecturer at Süleymaniye Madrasa. He was a member of Dar al-Hikmah al-Islamiyya (an official religious institution) and later became the head of this institution. With the collapse of the Ottoman Empire and establishment of the new Turkish Republican Government Hamdi lost all his titles and positions. He was arrested by the new government but released 40 days later. Following this incident, he spent the majority of his remaining time between his home and the mosque. In the interim, the Turkish Religious Affairs Directorate decided to prepare a Turkish commentary on the Qur'ān, offering the opportunity Muhammad Hamdi, who accepted. He commenced writing his famous *tafsīr* '*Hak Dini Kur'an Dili*' and died in the same year of its completion, 1942.

A profound scholar, Muhammad Hamdi's broad encompassing knowledge spanned numerous Islamic sciences as well as the creative arts. He authored poems in Turkish, Arabic and Persian, selecting simple vernacular for his poetry in contrast with his sophisticated style of language when discussing religious affairs. He expressed certain anxieties about the infiltration of European culture and its negative impact on Turkish society. He strongly believed that only science and technology should be adopted from Western civilization and that the culture should be discarded, as it would introduce moral corruption into the Islamic society. He maintained that people could be happy as long as they remained loyal to fundamental Islamic values. He even believed that all humanity would eventually have to accept Islam in order survive.

As well as having a deep knowledge of many Islamic disciplines, Hamdi's knowledge also encompassed philosophy and the modern sciences. He believed that as science and religion are related and complementary, the positive sciences should not be prevented for religious reasons. He also considered that Islam promised real freedom for humankind through education and the encouragement of free will in the right path.

His books;
- 'Hak Dini Kur'an Dili'—his famous *tafsīr* book.
- 'Irshād al-Ahlaf fi Aḥkām al-Awqāt'—a book covering the rules of charity that was employed as a university textbook.
- 'Hz. Muhammad'in Dini Islam'—a book containing the answers that are given for the questions of the Anglo-Saxon church.
- 'Metalib ve Mezahib'—a translation from French dealing with philosophical topics
- 'İstintaci ve İstikradi Mantık'—a translation dealing with the topics of logic.

His *Tafsīr*

Muhammad Hamdi acquired his fame through his *tafsīr*, 'Hak Dini Kur'an Dili.' He held the view that Qur'ān cannot be correctly translated into any language other than Arabic. Hamdi asserts that although it is difficult to discover the true meaning of the Qur'anic words, the science of Arabic philology aids significantly in this endeavour. He holds that the literal and metaphorical meanings of the words, the interrelationships between them, the context of the verses and the general principles of the Qur'ān must be known in detail to be able to comprehend the true meanings.[617] He maintains that the text of the Qur'ān should not be interpreted according to valid scientific theories of the present time alone, for they will undoubtedly be proved false in the future.

Hamdi employed both the *riwāyah* and *dirāyah* techniques in his work with *dirāyah* being the prominent method. When interpreting the Qur'ān, he benefitted from a variety of early scholars' works such as Tabarī, Zamakhsharī, Rāghib al-Isfahānī, Rāzī, Abu Hayyan and Ālūsī. Hamdi was strongly influenced by the works of Muhyiddin ibn al-Arābī in Sufi-related matters however, he was selective in his agreement with his views, accepting some whilst rejecting others. Hamdi was a Ḥanafī jurist and generally benefited from the resources of this school in juristic matters.

---

[617] Elmalılı Muhammad Hamdi Yazır, *Hak Dini Kur'an Dili*, 1/122.

Hamdi occasionally delved into the socio-political discussions of his time and indicated the ideal opinions according to the Qur'ān and Sunnah. He insisted that Qur'anic verses must always be understood according to their literal meanings unless there is a logical reason to resort to the metaphorical usage. For example, he rejected the interpretation of Muhammad Abduh in Surah Elephant who contended that the stones, which were thrown by the birds at the army of Abraha, were the viruses of measles or smallpox. Muhammad Hamdi deems this type of interpretation as a distortion of the Qur'ān.[618]

He only accepted a scientific interpretation of the verses if the text material was related to such matters, for example:

> And We sent the winds to fertilize, and so We sent down water from the sky, and gave it to you to drink (and use in other ways); it is not you who are the keepers of its stores (under earth).[619]

When interpreting this verse, he states that winds fertilize plants by carrying and spreading pollen; this indicates that plants have male and female counterparts. He accepts these types of verses as the miracles that prove the Divine authorship of the Qur'ān.[620] In order to truly appreciate Hamdi's *tafsīr* methodology, his commentary and analysis on Surah Falaq has been provided below.

SUMMARY: ELMALI HAMDI YAZIR AND HIS *TAFSĪR*

1. Born in Elmalı, Antalya in southern Turkey in 1878 C.E. (d. 1942 C.E.), he memorized the whole Qur'ān at an early age, before continuing his education in Ayasofya Madrasa in Istanbul.

2. He received his *ijāzah* from Mahmut Hamdi Efendi then learned the art of calligraphy, receiving an *ijāzah* in this field as well.

3. He finished his university education while learning philosophy, literature and music through self-study.

4. Hamdi supported the new constitutional movement in Turkey with the purpose of promoting a superior modern educational system. He focused his efforts on being at the forefront of religious of affairs in Turkey.

5. Hamdi taught *Fiqh*, *Uṣūl al-Fiqh* and *Mantıg* and was promoted to lecturer at Süleymaniye Madrasa.

---

[618] Hamdi Yazır, *Hak Dini Kur'an Dili*, 5/3731.
[619] Qur'ān 15: 22.
[620] Hamdi Yazır, *Hak Dini Kur'an Dili*, 4/2957.

6. Hamdi was well versed in Islamic sciences and creative arts, and even authored poems in Arabic, Persian and Turkish.

7. He was concerned about the impact of European culture, which he saw as immoral on Turkish society and believed people should be loyal to Islamic values.

8. Hamdi believed religion and science complemented each other.

His *Tafsīr*

9. Hamdi held that the Qur'ān cannot be correctly translated into any language other than Arabic but that Arabic philology aids significantly in discovering the meaning of words.

10. He maintains that the text of the Qur'ān should not be interpreted according to valid scientific theories of the present time alone.

11. He used *riwāyah* and *dirāyah* techniques in his work with *dirāyah* being the prominent method.

12. When interpreting the Qur'ān he benefitted from a variety of early scholars' works.

13. Hamdi occasionally delved into the socio-political discussions of his time and indicated the ideal opinions according to the Qur'ān and Sunnah.

14. He only accepted a scientific interpretation of the verses if the text material was related to such matters.

SURAH FALAQ (THE DAYBREAK)

بِسْمِ اللهِ الرَّحْمٰنِ الرَّحِيمِ

قُلْ اَعُوذُ بِرَبِّ الْفَلَقِ ﴿١﴾ مِنْ شَرِّ مَا خَلَقَ ﴿٢﴾ وَمِنْ شَرِّ غَاسِقٍ اِذَا وَقَبَ ﴿٣﴾
وَمِنْ شَرِّ النَّفَّاثَاتِ فِي الْعُقَدِ ﴿٤﴾ وَمِنْ شَرِّ حَاسِدٍ اِذَا حَسَدَ ﴿٥﴾

Surah Falaq (The Daybreak)

In the Name of God, the All-Merciful, the All-Compassionate

1. Say: 'I seek refuge in the Lord of the daybreak

2. From the evil of what He has created,

3. And from the evil of the darkness (of night) when it overspreads,

4. And from the evil of the witches who blow on knots (to cast a spell),

5. And from the evil of the envious one when he envies.'

Tafsīr

This five-verse *surah* was revealed in Medina and derives its name from the word *al-falaq* (the daybreak) in the first verse. It teaches us how to seek refuge in God from every evil to which we may be exposed.

First verse: قُلْ أَعُوذُ بِرَبِّ الْفَلَقِ *Say: 'I seek refuge in the Lord of the daybreak'*

Hamdi begins his interpretation by analyzing the expression 'say,' giving the intended meaning of such a command. He relates different opinions regarding the permissibility of removing the expression 'say.' Some scholars hold that it is permissible to remove it, since the intended command from this expression is alluded to right after it, and so voids the necessity of repeating this command during supplication. Other scholars, however, hold that it is not permissible to remove any word of the Qur'ān, neither during supplication nor in recitation. Hamdi maintains that the command can be removed during supplication but cannot be removed during the recitation of the Qur'ān as this is the official writing in the *Muṣḥāfs*.[621] He supports his view by relating from Imam Māturīdī; the addressee for the command 'say' is not only the Prophet (pbuh) but also all Muslims until the end of days, so it is kept in the *Muṣḥāfs* to remind them of their duty.[622]As a matter of fact, the duty falls upon every reciter whenever they read the expression 'say.'

Hamdi begins with a linguistic analysis of the words continuing with an explanation of the meaning. The Arabic expression أَعُوذُ (I seek refuge) is derived from 'a-w-dh' meaning 'to seek refuge in someone to be protected against evil things,' or 'asking for his protection.' Therefore, the meaning of this verse is 'I seek refuge in the Lord of the daybreak.'

The Arabic word '*falaq*' (the daybreak) has multiple meanings such as 'split,' 'crack open' and 'bulges out.' Hamdi analyses different derivations of this word and its various forms to indicate its broad concept. He mentioned the following verse to explain this word further:

> God is He Who *splits* the grain and the fruit-stone (so that they germinate by His command). He brings forth the living from the dead, and He is One Who brings forth the dead from the living; Such is God: how then are you turned away from the truth and make false claims?[623]

God is the One who splits the grain and the fruit stone to enable germination, bringing forth what is alive from what appears to be dead, and vice versa.

---

[621] Yazır, *Hak Dini Kur'an Dili*, see the interpretation of Surah Falaq.

[622] Māturīdī, *Ta'wilāt*, see the interpretation of Surah Falaq.

[623] Qur'ān 6: 95.

He is the One who splits the darkness and opens the daylight. He brings forth creation from non-existence and sets the laws for it. So, the creation can reproduce, be sustained and trained by God to mature in accordance with His laws. However, He is not in need of anything, because He is the eternally besought of all. He begets not, nor is He begotten and therefore is none comparable to Him.[624]

The Arabic word 'falaq' also means 'speed,' 'charming beauty,' 'pressure' and 'oppression.' After giving all the linguistic meanings, Hamdi mentions some other possible meanings of *falaq* when it is used as a name:

- God is eternally besought by all, therefore He is not split from anything. In contrast, all creation is in need, incomplete and can be split. Fountains come forth by splitting the mountains, rain from the clouds, plants from the soil and babies from the womb.
- In Islamic terminology, the early light of the day, specifically the horizontal light, is named as the daybreak.
- The lower and flat space between two hills.
- A cane used to strike the feet of prisoners as a punishment.
- The remnant of milk in the bottom of a pot.
- One of the names of Hell or a pit in Hell.

Hamdi benefits considerably from the early scholars and relates their opinions to provide a sound insight into the meanings of the verses, as illustrated with the term 'falaq.' Ibn Sīnā holds that *falaq* is the darkness of non-existence that is split by the light of creation.[625] This word implies that light follows the darkness and ease comes after difficulty. So, the servants of God should worship the Lord of the *falaq* in a state between hope and fear and they should seek refuge in His Lordship. Since *falaq* is ascribed to the Lord, it implies that God always protects His servants by preventing evils from befalling them and providing benefits to them. God continuously bestows His favors and blessings upon His servants but only those who are awake and aware of Him benefit from these blessings at the highest level. As a matter of fact, the Prophet (pbuh) emphasized the significance of this meaning when he said; 'The days of your time contain the breezes of your Lord's Mercy, so wake up and offer yourself to them.'[626]

Hamdi mentions additional hadiths related by Ibn Mardūya and Daylamī to further explain the term 'falaq'; Abdullah ibn 'Amr ibn As asked the Prophet (pbuh)

---

[624] Qur'ān 112: 1–3.
[625] Yazır, *Hak Dini Kur'an Dili*, see the interpretation of Surah Falaq.
[626] Yazır, ibid.

about the meaning of *falaq* and the Prophet (pbuh) answered, 'it is a dungeon and the tyrants and arrogant are imprisoned there. Hell seeks refuge in God from its evils.'[627]

Ibn Mardūya also relates from Amr ibn Anbasa the following incident:

> The Prophet (pbuh) led us in the prayer and recited Surah Falaq. After the prayer he asked; 'O Ibn Anbasa! Do you know what *falaq* means?' I said; 'God and His Messenger know best.' Upon this, he said; 'It is a pit in Hell. When that pit is heated, it heats Hell. Just as human beings suffer from the heat of Hell, so does Hell suffer from the heat of that pit.'"[628]

Ibn Abī Hātim relates from Ka'b; '*falaq* is a house in Hell, when its door is opened the people of Hell scream due to the intensity of the heat.'[629]

Second verse: مِنْ شَرِّ مَا خَلَقَ *From the evil of what He has created*

This verse conveys that humankind should seek protection from God against anything in the creation that could cause them harm. The evil can be physical or metaphysical, worldly or otherworldly, objective or subjective, natural and optional. Human beings should seek refuge in God from the evils of humans, demons, predatory animals, harmful pests, viruses, poisons, fire, and from capricious and sins. Therefore, it is possible to seek refuge in God from anything in creation.

It is clear that this verse refers to anything that is evil and harm human beings, but not the creation itself. Evil can come from outside, or from a person's own actions such as wrong decisions and wrongful use of their own free will. God states in the Qur'ān:

> (O human being!) Whatever good happens to you, it is from God; and whatever evil befalls you, it is from yourself. We have sent you (O Messenger) to humankind as a Messenger, and God suffices for a witness.[630]

The verse clearly states that evils do not only emanate from external forces but from the human self as well. The Prophet (pbuh) said; "your most vicious enemy is your *nafs* (carnal desires) which is in your nature."[631] As exemplified, Hamdi expounded the meaning of this verse by means of another verse as well as statements of the Prophet (pbuh), displaying application of both *riwāyah* and *dirāyah* methods.

---

[627] Yazır, ibid.
[628] Yazır, ibid.
[629] Yazır, ibid.
[630] Qur'ān 4: 79.
[631] Yazır, ibid.

The first two verses of this *surah* illustrate its implications whilst the following verses serve to elaborate the most commonly occurring evils.

Third verse: وَمِنْ شَرِّ غَاسِقٍ إِذَا وَقَبَ *And from the evil of the darkness (of night) when it overspreads,*

Hamdi begins by linguistically analyzing the words in the verse then goes on to relate the opinions of the early scholars and utilizes specific dictionaries to elaborate the meanings. He maintains that the Arabic word غَاسِق *'ghā-siq'* translated as 'the darkness' has multiple meanings and is a broad concept.

This word is derived from *'ghasaq'* which means 'intensive darkness,' 'fullness,' 'to flow,' 'to fall down,' 'coldness' and 'smell.' Three of these meanings are essential; 'to be filled,' 'to flow' and 'to fall down.' When the darkness of night falls, it overspreads and this is expressed with the Arabic word *'ghasaq.'* This word is the exact opposite of *'falaq'* (daylight) and covers the time from evening to dawn.

The word وَقَبَ which is translated as 'overspreads' is derived from *'waqb'* which means a pit. *'Waqb'* has multiple meanings including 'a cavity in the rocks,' 'a pit in mountains,' 'the cavity of the eyes on the human face' and 'an idiot.' *'Wuqub'* is another infinitive form deriving from the same root, which also has multiple meanings, such as 'to enter into a pit,' 'to disappear,' 'to come,' 'to return,' 'the darkness overspread,' 'the sunset' and 'the eclipse of the moon.' Having mentioned all the linguistic possibilities of *'waqab,'* Hamdi continues in a contextual order by discussing the possible meaning of *ghasaq*:

- The word *ghasaq* is well understood to mean darkness, being the opposite of *falaq* (daylight). The majority of Qur'anic exegetes assign darkness as the meaning of *ghasaq* whereas they explain *waqab* as the darkness that overspreads it all. The meaning of this verse is 'to seek refuge in God from the evil of the darkness of night when it overspreads.' Evil is ascribed to the night for that is the time when evil transpires though it is not the actual cause of evil. Evil usually spreads or occurs during the night, so it is recommended to seek refuge in God before darkness falls. Hamdi mentions that Tabarī, ibn Mundhir, Ibn Abbas, Mujāhid and Dahhaq hold this view and interpreted the verse as explained above.[632] Rāghib holds that *ghasaq* is extreme darkness and its evil is the calamities and unfortunate events that strike unexpectedly.
- *Ghāsiq* means the moon and *waqab* means the eclipse of the moon or the last three days of the month. A hadith, reported on the authority of A'isha,

---

[632] Yazır, ibid.

is given to support this explanation; "One day the Prophet (pbuh) looked at the moon and said; 'O A'isha! Seek refuge in God from the evil of this (the moon), because it is a night when darkness overspreads.'"[633] Tirmidhi deems this hadith as *hasan,* which is a mid-category between authentic and weak. Hamdi analyses this report in accordance with the principles of *uṣūl hadith,* which illustrates the *dirāyah* aspect of his *tafsīr.*

- It is the sun when it sets, based on the report on the authority of Ibn Shihab al-Zuhrī. So here, the overspreading of night is taken to mean sunset.
- *Ghāsiq* is a specific star and its disappearance in darkness. The Arabs believed that the plague and other diseases increase when this star disappears in the dark.
- Zamakhsharī understands *ghāsiq* as the bite of a black snake.
- Firuzābādī relates an opinion about *ghāsiq* in his dictionary (*Qāmus*); it is an increasing of desire that affects a person's mind negatively. Hamdi holds that this is not a reliable view but may be accepted in the metaphoric sense, since desires are a source of all kinds of evil deeds.
- *Ghāsiq* is any kind of calamity that inflicts human beings and prevents them from achieving their desires. It causes sadness and leaves despair in the human conscience. Sadness and grief are evils that can be physical or metaphysical and they are described as darkness in the verse.

Fourth verse: وَمِنْ شَرِّ النَّفَّاثَاتِ فِي الْعُقَد *And from the evil of the witches who blow on knots (to cast a spell)*

It is essential to seek refuge in God from the evil of witches who blow on knots, threads and hearts to establish sovereignty over them. Therefore, God recommended His servants to seek His protection against them. Witches enact black magic by blowing on knots. Ibn Qayyim notes that witches blow their breath when they cast a spell to increase its effect, and sorcerers blow onto knots to cast a spell just as snakes blow their poison from their teeth. Hamdi analysed the essence of blowing in this verse from a linguistic perspective and distinguished the differences in meaning and practice from other synonymous words. He highlighted that rather than always being used for evil purposes, blowing can sometimes be beneficial such as when Archangel Gabriel blew spiritual meanings into the heart of the Prophet Muhammad (pbuh).

In order to understand the meaning of this verse it is necessary to analyse the Arabic word 'uqad' (knots). This word is plural; its singular form is 'uqda' which

---

633 Yazır, ibid.

means 'to tie,' 'to knot' and 'to unite two things firmly.' The term *'uqda'* has multiple meanings as determined by Hamdi through the use of well-known Arabic dictionaries; *Qāmus, Nihāya* and *Mufradaat*. Some of the other important meanings of *'uqda'* are:

- A knot and its place
- Governorship over cities, because the standards are knotted for the governors
- An agreement of governors, which is solemnly bound
- The property, which its owner assumes as his/her own
- It is a place, which has an abundance of trees
- Pasture which has sufficient grass for camels
- Fertile land
- Animals which have to eat from the trees
- The absolute necessity of something. Marriage and business contracts fall into this group
- Hatred and fury
- Tongue tied

Sorcerers blow on knots with the resolve of affecting another's will with their black magic. The intentions of sorcery are wicked. Its purpose is to cause harm to someone, therefore, only those with wicked hearts engage in these activities. Acts of sorcery cause their victims to act in uncharacteristic ways, often becoming nervous or excited. Any act of sorcery, such as blowing on knots, black magic and anything to bring about turmoil or cause unrest between people, is an act of disbelief.

There are three views regarding why witches are mentioned as female in the verse. Firstly, females are the major perpetrators of this type of sorcery, as well as having a greater effect on men. Women have been known to use their magic and beauty to tempt men into deviation. The second view includes male and female witches whereas the third view refers to social groups. After making these explanations of the verses, Hamdi relates the opinions of the interpreters.

The interpreters usually explained this verse in three ways:

1) God commanded the believers to seek refuge in Him from the evils of sorcery, especially the females who blow on knots; this is the general scholastic understanding of this verse. Scholars dispute about the permissibility of reading the Qur'ān then blowing over the body with the intent of requesting a cure to an illness, even though Muslims are commanded to read the Qur'ān and seek God's protection through prayer. Some scholars claim that it is not permissible to write out

amulets to cure people and hadiths are provided below as evidentiary support for their claim. Ibn Abbas reports:

> God's Apostle said: "Nations were displayed before me; one or two Prophets would pass by along with a few followers. A Prophet would pass by accompanied by nobody. Then a big crowd of people passed in front of me and I asked; 'Who are they? Are they my followers?' It was said; 'No, it is Moses and his followers.' It was said to me; 'Look at the horizon.' Behold! There was a multitude of people filling the horizon. Then it was said to me; 'Look there and there as far as the stretching sky!' Behold! There was a multitude filling the horizon. It was said to me; 'This is your nation out of whom seventy thousand shall enter Paradise without reckoning.' Then the Prophet (pbuh) entered his house without telling his Companions who they (the 70,000) were. So, the people started talking about the issue and said; 'It is we who have believed in God and followed His Apostle; therefore those people are either ourselves or our children who are born in the Islamic era, for we were born in the time of ignorance (*jahiliyyah*).' When the Prophet (pbuh) heard that, he came out and said; 'Those people are those who do not treat themselves with *ruqya* (amulets), nor do they believe in bad or good omens (from birds etc.), nor do they get themselves branded (cauterized), but they put their trust (only) in their Lord."[634]

This tradition of the Prophet (pbuh) is authentic according to hadith criteria. In Hamdi's opinion, this is not a general reference but a specific one related to very pious people who achieved the highest degree in servanthood, therefore it is incorrect to apply a prohibition of *ruqya* (amulet) for everyone.[635] As a matter of fact, there are other authentic Prophetic traditions allowing *ruqya* and one of them is as follows:

> Some of the Companions of the Prophet (pbuh) went on a journey till they reached some of the Arab tribes at night. They asked the latter to treat them as their guests but they refused. The chief of that tribe was then bitten by a snake (or stung by a scorpion) and they tried their best to cure him but in vain. Some of them said (to the others); 'Nothing has benefited him, will you go to the people who resided here at night, it may be that some of them might possess something (as treatment).' They went to the group of the Companions of the Prophet (pbuh) and said; 'Our chief has been bitten by a snake (or stung by a scorpion) and we have tried everything but he has not improved. Have you got anything (useful)?' One

---

[634] Bukhari, *Saḥīḥ*, Medicine, 606.
[635] Yazır, ibid.

of them replied; 'Yes, by God! I can recite a *ruqya* (amulet), but as you have refused to accept us as your guests, I will not recite the *ruqya* for you unless you fix for us some wages for it.' They agreed to pay them a flock of sheep. One of them then went and recited Surah Fatiha and blew over the chief. He became immediately better as though he was released from a chain, and got up and started walking, showing no signs of sickness. They paid them what they agreed to pay. Some of them (i.e. the Companions) suggested dividing their earnings among themselves, but the one who performed the recitation said; 'Do not divide them till we go to the Prophet (pbuh) and narrate the whole story to him, and wait for his order.' So, they went to God's Apostle and narrated the story. God's Apostle asked; 'How did you come to know that Surah Fatiha is recited as *ruqya*?' Then he added; 'You have done the right thing. Divide (what you have earned) and assign a share for me as well.' The Prophet (pbuh) smiled thereupon."[636]

This hadith indicates that the prohibited amulets are the ones whose meanings are unknown and are used as black magic.

Blowing as an act of sorcery is prohibited, but reciting verses of the Qur'ān and then blowing over the patient is not. Denying every form of blowing is not logical as there is spiritual blowing to counteract evil blowing and its use is permissible as it is seeking a cure from God. However, it is not permissible to attribute the cure to anything other than God, as He creates everything and nothing happens without His permission. According to the Prophetic tradition 'there is a cure for everything' meaning that every illness has a cure in its kind; if the illness is spiritual or psychological the cure is spiritual or psychological and if the illness is physical the cure is also physical. If the illness is mixed the medicine should be mixed as well. However, the results come from God and truly, He cures all kind of illnesses without needing any cause. However, it is necessary for us to use ways or reasons to seek His cure without attributing any creative effect to them.

The act of reciting the Qur'ān or saying some prayers with the sincere intention of seeking the cure to an illness cannot be considered as an act of sorcery. For this reason, the scholars who permit *ruqya* present evidence from the most authentic hadith books. Muhammad Hamdi relates these evidences from Rāzī:

- The Prophet Muhammad (pbuh) was sick and Archangel Gabriel recited, 'I recite in the Name of God and make *ruqya* against whatever hurt you. May God give you a cure' and then he (Gabriel) blew on the Prophet (pbuh).

---

[636] Bukhari, *Ṣaḥīḥ*, Hiring, 476.

- Ibn Abbas reports; 'The Prophet (pbuh) taught us the following prayer to protect ourselves against all kind of pain and fever; 'in the Name of God who is Gracious, I seek refuge in God Almighty from every vessel in which blood flows and from the evil of the fire of Hell'.'
- The Prophet (pbuh) said; 'If one visits a patient whose death is not yet decreed and utters seven times 'I implore to God Almighty who is the Owner of the supreme throne,' God gives him a cure.'
- The Prophet (pbuh) prayed when he visited a patient by saying; 'O Lord of People! Remove the pain and give him a cure which does not leave any illness, for You are the only One who can cure.'
- The Prophet (pbuh) recited *surahs* Ikhlas, Falaq and Nās every night before sleeping and blew into his palms and then wiped over his face and whole body. Similarly, he read these *surahs* and then blew over his family when they were sick.

There is much more evidence proving the permissibility of reciting Qur'anic verses or prayers and lowing over a patient to request a cure from God. God recommended that believers petition Him in many verses:

Your Lord has said: 'Pray to Me, (and) I will answer you.'[637]

And when (O Messenger) My servants ask you about Me, then surely I am near: I answer the prayer of the suppliant when he prays to Me.[638]

Say: 'My Lord would not care for you were it not for your prayer.'[639]

Moreover, through the Qur'ān and the speech of the Prophet (pbuh), God taught us the best way to beseech Him. For this reason, it is necessary for people to petition God directly, without finding an intercessor, as this is not an Islamic custom; rather it originates from the time of *jahiliyyah* (ignorance).

2) The women who blow on knots are deceitful and lure men into corruption by presenting their beauty to them. It is recommended to seek refuge in God from the evil of these women. They make men as excited as if they had cast a spell and blown on their heart. They can affect the decisions of men and cause them to fall into evil acts, therefore God advised believers to seek refuge in Him against them.

---

[637] Qur'ān 40: 60.
[638] Qur'ān 2: 186.
[639] Qur'ān 25: 77.

3) Ibn Sīnā holds that everything contains within it a motivating force enabling it to grow and reproduce. The human body contains desires that motivate it to eat, drink and marry. For Ibn Sīnā, *ghāsiq* is the carnal desires and it is a dark power. The human soul is pure and clean, but it can be polluted by carnal desires. So, God advised believers to seek refuge in Him against the carnal desires.

In conclusion, blowing on knots to cast a spell is used to cause divergence.

Fifth verse: وَمِنْ شَرِّ حَاسِدٍ إِذَا حَسَدَ *And from the evil of the envious one when he envies.*

This verse means to seek refuge in God from the evil of one who becomes envious when he sees a favor granted to one whom he envies, and wishes the favor to be taken from that person. Or, to put it another way, when someone who is envious starts to act out the envy either verbally or practically, with the intention of harming the one he envies, it is necessary to seek God's protection against him. Envy is a destructive force that harms the envier as long as he harbours those feelings. It usually causes people to feel enmity and hatred for the one who is envied. The effect of the evil eye occurs in these moments; therefore, envy is associated with the evil eye and the two are inseparable.

At the moment of envy, the envious self becomes malevolent and capable of inflicting great harm upon the one who is envied, especially if the recipient is spiritually weak or exposed, the evil eye may strike him like a thunderbolt. The envious are more harmful in their envy than a venomous snake. When the feeling of envy enters and consumes one's heart, one is inclined to use every means at his disposal to harm the envied one. Perdition of the envied is his only consolation. This type of person harms himself with the constant feeling of envy in his heart, however, if a person struggles against this feeling and tries to supress it, he will be rewarded for his efforts and will not harm others. For this reason, seeking refuge is limited when a person envies. God is the best protector and He always protects His servants who seek refuge in Him sincerely; "God is the Best of protectors and He is the Most Merciful of the merciful."[640]

Hamdi discusses the meaning of envy (*hasad*) and relates from linguists to explain the term. He reports from Rāghib that envy is to wish someone to be deprived of a favor, or wishing every favor to be removed from its legitimate owner. It is reported that a believer admires but a hypocrite envies. The essential meaning in envy is that the envious wants the envied to lose the favors that he possesses and will not be happy even if he is offered similar favors. If the

---

[640] Qur'ān 12: 64.

favors are related to moral values and good character the envious one becomes a clear enemy of those values as he will never achieve them.

Sometimes, envy may be perceived as a form of emulation, as is the case in the following hadith:

> Envy is not justified except in two cases: a person who, having been given (knowledge of) the Qur'ān by God, recites it during the night and day (and also acts upon it) and a man who, having been given wealth by God, spends it during the night and the day (for the welfare of others seeking the pleasure of the Lord).[641]

In short, the envious one does not wish goodness for others, only harm. However, if he does not want others to lose their favors but wants to a share in the favor for himself, it is not considered envy (*hasad*), but known as *ghibta* (emulation or admiration). Sometimes the envious may want others to lose their favors and in other instances, they may desire for them to continue with their inferior situation. In both cases, such feelings are condemned and considered a major sin. It is necessary to fight against the feeling of envy and suppress it in order to prevent any kind of harm coming to others.

Envy is different from jealousy. For example, a man is jealous about his wife and similarly a wife is jealous about her husband. Jealousy is not prohibited; it is a form of protection. However, if a person is jealous about someone else's wife, property or children this is called envy and is therefore prohibited. The feeling of jealousy is given to protect one's own honor and chastity, but if it is used in the wrong circumstances than it becomes envy and is therefore a sin.

Summary: Surah Falaq (The Daybreak) *Tafsīr*

1. This five-verse *surah* was revealed in Medina and derives its name from the word *al-falaq* (the daybreak) in the first verse.
2. It teaches us how to seek refuge in God from every evil to which we may be exposed.
3. **First verse:** Hamdi analyses the expression 'say' and relates different opinions regarding the permissibility of removing it supporting his view by relating from Imam Māturidī.
4. Hamdi begins with a linguistic analysis of the words continuing with an explanation of the meaning. The Arabic word '*falaq*' (the daybreak) has

---

[641] Muslim, *Saḥīḥ, The Book of Prayers*, 1777.

multiple meanings. He analyses different derivations of this word and its various forms to indicate its broad concept using verses to explain it.

5. After giving all the linguistic meanings, Hamdi mentions some other possible meanings of *falaq* when it is used as a name.

6. Hamdi benefits considerably from the early scholars and relates their opinions to provide a sound insight into the meanings of the verses.

7. Second verse: This verse means to seek refuge in God from anything in creation or any creature that causes harm. This type of evil can be physical or metaphysical, worldly or otherworldly, objective or subjective, natural and optional.

8. It is clear that this verse refers to anything that is evil that may harm human beings, including that which comes from within, but not the creation itself.

9. Hamdi expounded the meaning of this verse by means of another verse as well as statements of the Prophet (pbuh), displaying application of both *riwāyah* and *dirāyah* methods.

10. Third verse: Hamdi begins by linguistically analyzing the words in the verse then goes on to relate the opinions of the early scholars and utilizes specific dictionaries to elaborate the meanings.

11. Having mentioned all the linguistic possibilities, Hamdi continues in a contextual order by discussing the possible meanings.

12. Fourth verse: It is essential to seek refuge in God from the evil of witches who blow on knots, threads and hearts to establish sovereignty over them. Therefore, God recommended His servants to seek His protection against them.

13. Hamdi analysed the essence of blowing in this verse from a linguistic perspective and distinguished the differences in meaning and practice from other synonymous words.

14. The intentions behind sorcery are wicked and intended to cause harm to someone; only those with evil hearts can perform these acts.

15. Hamdi relates three views of the interpreters about this verse: 1) God commanded the believers to seek refuge in Him from the evils of sorcery, especially the females who blow on knots; this is the general scholastic understanding of this verse. 2) The women who blow on knots are deceitful and lure men into corruption by presenting their beauty to them. 3) Ibn Sīnā holds that everything contains within it a desire to

grow and produce, so, God advised believers to seek refuge in Him against the carnal desires.

16. Fifth verse: This verse means to seek refuge in God from the evil of one who becomes envious when he sees a favor granted to one whom he envies, and wishes the favor to be taken from that person.

17. Hamdi discusses the meaning of envy (*hasad*) and relates from linguists to explain the term.

CHAPTER 12

Modern *Tafsīr*, Said Nursi, Fethullah Gülen and Their Works

Said Nursi and His Exegetical Work

His Life and Education

Said Nursi[642] (1877–1960 C.E.) was a prominent Turkish Islamic scholar who lived through the last decades of the Ottoman Empire, observing its collapse at the end of the First World War and the subsequent establishment of the Turkish Republic. The following twenty-five years of the republican government saw the oppression of anything associated with Islam including its devotees. Nursi introduced many innovative solutions for Muslims who had been suffering from a lack of education, poverty and disunity. He successfully combined a scientific view within the Qur'anic framework and interpreted Qur'anic verses in light of the troubles of his time. He reasoned that, as a Divine work, the Qur'ān contained the principles that would help human kind to progress and their civilization to flourish rather than philosophies of human origin.

Said Nursi was born 1877 C.E. in the village of Nursi, in the Bitlis province of eastern Anatolia. He was the fourth child of parents Mirza and Nuriye. His father, Mirza, belonged to the Sayyids (related to the Prophet Muhammad (pbuh)) lineage and was renowned for his virtue and sensitivity in only living by lawful (*halal*) means. He was educated at home until he reached nine years old, after which he spent a brief amount of time at the local madrasas (religious schools). His extraordinary memory and ability to absorb knowledge led to his early graduation at the age of fifteen. He gained the illustrious title Bediüzzaman, which can be translated as 'the wonder of the time,' due to his extraordinary intelligence and ability to answer difficult questions on various topics. He was famous for his unbeaten record in debating with other scholars.

Said Nursi studied many modern sciences, which were divergent to the practices of religious scholars of that time and combined religion and science in his

---

[642] To learn more about his life, education and methodology please refer to Bediüzzaman Said Nursi, *The Words* [Eng.tr.] (Istanbul: Sözler Publications, 2004); *The Rays* [Eng. tr.] (Istanbul: Sözler Publications, 2002); *The Flashes* [Eng.tr.] (Istanbul: Sözler Publications, 2000); Letters 1928–1932 [Eng.tr.] (Istanbul: Sözler Publications, 2001); Şükran Vahide, Islam in Modern Turkey: An Intellectual Biography of Bediüzzaman Said Nursi (Albany: SUNY Press, 2005).

Qur'anic interpretations. His studies included philosophy, so theology could be renewed and successfully answer the questions of the modern age. He criticized the existing education system in the Islamic world and made comprehensive proposals for a radical reform. The core idea of his proposal was combining the traditional religious sciences with modern sciences. He, in fact, initiated a project to establish a university in the Eastern Provinces of the Empire, the Medresetü'z-Zehra, to actualize his proposals through a systematic application. He received substantial funds for the construction of the university and its foundations were laid in 1913. However, due to political conflict and other difficulties it was never completed. He predicted that Islamic civilization would dominate the future and people from all around the world would embrace the message of the Qur'ān. For this purpose, he offered a number of remedies from the pharmacy of the Qur'ān, which could cure the spiritual illnesses that afflicted modern society.

Just before the First World War, Nursi had a dream in which the Prophet (pbuh) ordered him to explain the miraculous aspects of the Qur'ān and he came to realize that he had been tasked with an important mission. As a way of fulfilling this mission, he started to write *Ishārāt al-I'jāz* (Signs of Miracles). He continued his writing even as he took an active fighting role in the defense of his country against the Russian invasion of eastern Anatolia in 1914.

Nursi was greatly affected by the collapse of the Ottoman Empire but never lost hope and continued to resist the occupying forces with his pen. After the war, he was appointed to Darü'l-Hikmeti'l-İslamiye (the Institute of Religious Affairs). Sometime later, he was moved by his profound mental and spiritual transformation to withdraw from public office in favor of leading a solitary live and devoting himself to the Qur'ān alone. He later termed this momentous change in his life as 'the new Said.'

During this new phase of his life, Nursi developed a unique method to interpret the Qur'ān according to the needs of the modern time. His aim was to illustrate an effective way for Muslims to strengthen their faith in the face of challenging conditions and protect their identity in spite of the persecutions of the new Turkish regime. Nursi was offered various posts in the first republican government but refused them in order to serve Islam freely and without influence. Consequently, he was sent to exile in western Anatolia and spent twenty-five years of his life in seclusion. During those years, he was poisoned 19 times by his guarding officers but God miraculously protected him. The new government hoped that with his disappearance from public life, Said Nursi would be forgotten. However, this proved to be the most productive period of his life. He produced the greater part of his collective words, the *Risale-i Nur* in this period and attracted many students, despite the severe conditions and surveillance under which he was held.

His Methodology in *Tafsīr*

The *Risale-i Nur* is a collection of modern *tafsīr* writings arranged in volumes. With his work, Nursi aimed to provide conclusive proofs from the teachings of the Qur'ān related to faith and worship. He also tried to refute the basic assumptions and concepts of materialistic philosophy. He applied a unique methodology when interpreting the Qur'ān utilizing both traditional Islamic sciences and modern sciences and combining them successfully in his exegetical work. He believed that science and religion are the two faces of one truth and one complements the other. Nursi holds that there is no contradiction between them and affirms that one cannot be understood without the support of the other.

The foundation of his method was reasoning on nature, for nature itself is a book that needs to be read and understood. The letters and words of nature teach us about their inscriber. In order to elaborate this method, he expounded many Qur'anic verses which describe the Divine acts in the universe and invited people to ponder them deeply. He declared that there is a strong relationship between the Qur'ān as God's Word and the universe as His creation. The Qur'ān interprets the book of the universe and instructs humankind on how to read its words and, in turn, the universe helps the reader to understand the Qur'ān better by presenting its physical form. In other words, the realities in the Qur'ān are presented by the Divine creation in the universe and therefore reading and comprehending the universe leads to a deeper understanding of the written Qur'ān.

Observing the universe with this method, Nursi extracted many truths and established the essentials of the Islamic faith based on these proofs and arguments. These proofs are very logical and are deduced from the Qur'anic view on the universe. Therefore, there is no contradiction between human reason and the Islamic faith, because the tenets of Islam are the facts that are extracted from life and reality. By employing this method, Nursi aimed readers to gain sincere faith as he believed that only such faith could survive the assaults of modernity and materialism. With these works, Nursi introduced a new way of realizing and knowing God. He described this way as the Qur'anic path and the path of the Companions. He maintained that whoever follows the path of the Prophet (pbuh) would gain true belief.

Rather than producing a comprehensive interpretation of the whole Qur'ān, Nursi focused on verses that deal with matters of faith such as; the Names and Attributes of God, Divine existence and unity, resurrection, Prophethood, destiny and worship. When interpreting the Qur'ān, Nursi does not expound the verses by giving the immediate reasons for their revelation and the apparent meanings of the words, as is the case in the classical *tafsīr* works. He adopts a particular method of explicating the truths according to his time. With this approach, he aims to prove that the Qur'ān addresses all human beings of every age in accordance with the varied degree of their understanding and development. The miraculous nature of the Qur'ān facilitates its comprehension by laymen and scholars alike.

Under the title '*Risale-i Nur*' Nursi produced the following collection of works:

- *The Words*
- *The Flashes*
- *Letters*
- *The Rays*
- *The Staff of Moses*
- *Signs of Miracles*
- *The Gleams*
- *The Reasoning*

SUMMARY: SAID NURSI AND HIS EXEGETICAL WORK

1. Said Nursi was a prominent Turkish Islamic scholar (1877–1960).
2. He witnessed the collapse of the Ottoman Empire, the founding of the Turkish Republic and the first 25 years of republican rule.
3. He introduced innovative for oppressed Muslims.
4. He interpreted the Qur'ān within a scientific framework addressing the problems of his time.
5. His father descended from the Sayyid lineage of Prophet Muhammad (pbuh).
6. Nursi was renowned for his virtue, living by *halal* means, his extraordinary intelligence and memory and was given the title, Bediüzzaman, 'wonder of the time.'
7. He studied modern sciences and philosophy as well as religion, believing that science and religion complemented each other and that religion had the answer to many questions of the modern age.

8. He was critical of modern education and made proposals for reform, with the idea that religious and modern sciences should be combined.

9. Nursi was inspired by a dream to prove the miraculous nature of the Qur'ān and wrote *Ishārāt al-I'jāz* (Signs of Miracles) as a response.

10. After the First World War, he took a post in the Darü'l-Hikmeti'l-İslamiye (the Institute of Religious Affairs) but later withdrew into seclusion to focus on the Qur'ān.

11. He developed a new method for interpreting the Qur'ān according to the needs of the modern time and was perceived as a threat to the republican government that resulted in him being sent to exile.

12. In exile, he wrote the *Risale-i Nur* and attracted a large following of students.

Tafsīr

13. The *Risale-i Nur* is a collection of modern *tafsīr* writings arranged in volumes.

14. Nursi aimed to provide conclusive proofs from the teachings of the Qur'ān related to faith and worship and to refute the basic assumptions and concepts of materialistic philosophy.

15. He combined traditional Islamic and modern sciences in his work.

16. The foundation of his method was reasoning on nature for nature itself is a book that needs to be read and understood.

17. With this method, Nursi extracted many truths and established the essentials of the Islamic faith based on these proofs and arguments.

18. Nursi did not interpret the whole Qur'ān but focused on verses that focus on matters of faith such as the Names and Attributes of God, Divine existence and unity, resurrection, Prophethood, destiny and worship.

19. He does not expound the verses by giving the immediate reasons for their revelation and the apparent meanings of the words, as is the case in the classical *tafsīr* works.

20. He adopts a particular method of explicating the truths according to his time.

Commentary on Various Verses

Said Nursi did not produce a classical *tafsīr* work, he concentrated his efforts on *dirāyah* style commentaries of selected verses from the Qur'ān. Nursi maintains that there is an extraordinary eloquence and stylistic purity in the Qur'ān's words, order and composition.

First example;[643]

> Say: He is God, (He is) One. God is the Eternally- Besought-of-All. He did not beget, nor was He begotten. There is none comparable to Him.[644]

Said Nursi explains that this short *surah* is formed of six sentences, three of which are positive and three of which are negative. They prove and establish six aspects of Divine Unity and reject and negate six ways of associating partners with God. Each sentence has two meanings: one a priori (functioning as a cause or proof) and the other a posteriori (functioning as an effect or result). That means that the *surah* actually contains 66 *surahs*, each made up of six sentences. One is either a premise or a proposition, and the others are arguments for it.

Say: He is God, because He is One, because He is the Eternally-Besought-of-All, because He did not beget, because He was not begotten, because there is none comparable to Him.

Say: There is none comparable to Him, because He was not begotten, because He did not beget, because He is the Eternally-Besought-of-All, because He is One, because He is God.

He is God, therefore He is One, therefore He is the Eternally-Besought-of-All, therefore He did not beget, therefore He was not begotten, therefore there is none comparable unto Him.

Second example;[645]

> Alif Lam Mim. That is the Book, there is no doubt in it; it is a guidance for the God-revering pious people.[646]

Nursi's explanation of this verse is that the Qur'ān's inimitability arises from the possibilities of the disjointed letters, for it is a light manifested from the blending of the brilliant subtleties of eloquence. A number of *surah* in the Qur'ān, as this one, begin with disjointed letters, the meaning of which is hidden. Together with the other disjointed letters at the start of some *surahs*, they consist of half the letters in the Arabic alphabet, the basic elements of all words. That is, the Qur'ān uses half the twenty-eight letters as disjointed letters, and disregards the other half. The half it takes are those that are more commonly used than those it leaves. Of the letters it takes, the Qur'ān repeats those easiest on the tongue.

---

[643] Please see for details, Said Nursi, *The Words, The Twenty-fifth Word.*

[644] Qur'ān 112: 1–5.

[645] Please see for details, Said Nursi, *Ishārāt al-I'jāz,* 2:1–2.

[646] Qur'ān 2: 1–2.

The disjointed letters at the start of twenty-nine *surahs* correspond to the number of letters in the alphabet. The method the Qur'ān has chosen for the disjointed letters is one out of a possible five hundred and four different varieties, and this is the only possible way of halving the letters of the alphabet with their particular characters; for the division of the letters into different groups are interwoven with each other at the same time as being dissimilar. Each of these divisions is truly remarkable and unique.

These letters are each like the rap of a knocker; they rouse the listener, alerting him through their singularity that they are the harbingers of something strange and remarkable. Their disjointedness indicates that what they signify is assumedly one and not compound. The spelling out of the letters singularly is an indication that it is alluding to the material of the art of writing, or eloquence, as though providing pen and paper for those wanting to dispute them by writing. It is as if the Qur'ān is saying; "hey you obstinate rivals, you're the masters of fine speech! You have at your disposal the materials I had when I devised these. You do likewise if you can!" Calling the letters by their names is the custom of scholars and writers. But, both the one uttering this speech, the Prophet (pbuh), and those listening to him were unlettered. Therefore, considering its character, the unexpected form of these letters infers that "this speech is not his but was imparted to him." Spelling out the letters, syllable by syllable, is particular to those learning to read and write. It can be understood from this that the Qur'ān was establishing a new way and was teaching illiterate people.

The disjointed letters indicate the ultimate conciseness. For sometimes, the ordinances laid down in the whole Qur'ān are set out in summary in a single long *surah*; and sometimes a long *surah* is represented allusively in a short one; and sometimes a short *surah* is included symbolically in a single verse; and sometimes a verse is indicated in a single sentence; and sometimes a sentence is hinted at in a single word; and sometimes too such a comprehensive word may be discerned in the disjointed letters. The disjointed letters are Divine cyphers communicated by God to His Messenger (pbuh), with whom is the key, to which the human mind has not yet attained. These letters show the acute intelligence of the one to whom they were revealed, for he understood what was only allusive, symbolic, and obscure as though it were explicit and clear.

Third example;[647]

> (Having brought him into existence, God) taught Adam the names, all of them. He then presented them to the angels, and said, 'Now tell Me the

---

[647] Please see for details, Said Nursi, *Ishārāt al-I'jāz*, 2:31–33.

names of these, if you are truthful.' (The angels) said: 'All-Glorified You are. We have no knowledge save what You have taught us. Surely You are the All-Knowing, the All-Wise.' (God) said: 'O Adam, inform them of these things and beings with their names.' When he (Adam) informed them with their names, He said (to the angels), 'Did I not tell you that I know the unseen of the heavens and the earth, and I know all that you reveal and all that you have been concealing?'[648]

Said Nursi interpreted this verse as follows; the teaching of the names (the Names of God) to Adam is a miracle of humanity related to the question of the vicegerency. He maintains that the Qur'ān offers both clear statements and evidences. It teaches humanity through signs and indications in the stories of the Prophets and their miracles. It also encourages mankind to attain similar achievements. The main lines and final results in the future of mankind's efforts to progress, are explained in these stories. The future is built on the foundations of the past, while the past is the mirror of the future and therefore the Qur'ān encourages humanity to actively strive to achieve some of these wonders. Nursi believes that the production of human thought is related to manifestation of this verse; "and He taught Adam all of the names."

By means of smelting iron and forging copper and building railways or other industrial products humankind actualized the miracle of Prophet David for whom iron was softened. By building airplanes, they actualized the miracle of Prophet Solomon who travelled the distance of two month's journey in a day. By progressing in science and inventing technological tools, humankind caused the springs to gush forth in the deserts and transformed the sandy wastes into gardens. With this achievement, they actualized the miracle of Prophet Moses who strikes the rock with his staff and a spring gushed forth. The Prophet Jesus miraculously healed the blind, lepers and the chronically sick. The developments in the science of medicine indicate the actualization of this miracle through human effort.

The Qur'ān explains the wisdom in human beings' vicegerency and satisfies both ordinary people and the elite. The Divine Names are reflected in the whole of creation and all of them are concentrated in human beings; they are manifest in man's diverse abilities and the multiple ways in which he can utilize the creation. Also with their profound knowledge, humankind can encompass the universe with their external and inner senses, and especially with their boundless conscience.

---

[648] Qur'ān: 2: 31–33.

The mission of humankind as vicegerent on the earth is to execute God's ordinances and apply His laws. However, this task is dependent on full knowledge. In order for them to be fully capable of executing this mission, God taught them the names and prepared them for the vicegerency. God chose Adam over the angels and distinguished him by conferring on him knowledge of the names; and perceiving their impotence, the angels affirmed God's wisdom.

God fashioned Adam with a nature in which was contained the fundamental principles of all types of attainment and perfection. He created him with a disposition in which was planted the seeds of all elevated qualities. He decked him out with ten senses, and a conscience that would hold the similitudes of all beings. He prepared him by giving him three faculties that He might teach him the realities of things in all their variety. Then He taught him all the names. This verse allusively praises knowledge, and indicates its high degree for it is the pivot of the vicegerency.

Fourth example;[649]

> Say: 'I seek refuge in the Lord of the daybreak from the evil of what He has created, and from the evil of the darkness (of night) when it overspreads, and from the evil of the witches who blow on knots (to cast a spell), and from the evil of the envious one when he envies.'[650]

Said Nursi holds that this *surah* contains miraculous predictions concerning the Unseen. Commanding God's Messenger (pbuh) and his community to protect themselves from evil beings looks to all ages. Through its allusive meaning, it looks to a greater degree to our strange age, even explicitly, and calls on the Qur'ān's servants to seek refuge with God. This miraculous prediction about the Unseen is explained briefly in five signs, as follows:

All the verses of this *surah* have numerous meanings. By repeating the word "evil" four times in five sentences, the *surah* allusively explains that it is necessary to withdraw from material and immaterial evils of this age in which revolutions and clashes took place.

For example, the first verse; 'Say: 'I seek refuge in the Lord of the daybreak from the evil of what He has created,' alludes to the First and the Second World Wars which erupted due to the ambition and greed of mankind according to numeric reckoning (*abjad* and *jifr*). So, for the Muslims, the meaning of this verse is: "Do not enter these wars, but seek refuge in your Lord."

---

[649] Please see for details, Said Nursi, *Ishārāt al-I'jāz*, 113:1–5.
[650] Qur'ān 113:1–5.

This *surah* suggests the four largest evil revolutions and storms of the century. According to *jafr* (reckoning), the repetition of the phrase 'from the evil of' four times is indicative of the century of dissent which produced Genghis Khan, Hulago and the fall of the 'Abbasid dynasty which was a catastrophe for the Islamic world.

SUMMARY: COMMENTARY ON VARIOUS VERSES

1. Said Nursi did not produce a classical *tafsīr* work, he concentrated his efforts on *dirāyah* style commentaries of select verses from the Qur'ān.

2. **First example:** Nursi explains the form and eloquence of this *surah*. This short *surah* is formed of six sentences, three of which are positive and three of which are negative. Nursi's interpretation shows that the *surah* actually contains 66 *surahs*, each made up of six sentences.

3. **Second example:** Nursi's explanation of this verse is that the Qur'ān's inimitability arises from the possibilities of the disjointed letters. There are many possibilities for these letters and Nursi gives a description of the method of use.

4. They are the harbinger or something strange or different.

5. The spelling out of the letters singularly is an indication that it is alluding to the material of the art of writing, or eloquence, as though providing pen and paper for those wanting to dispute them by writing.

6. They indicate that the Qur'ān was establishing a new way and was teaching illiterate people.

7. The disjointed letters indicate the ultimate conciseness.

8. They are Divine cyphers communicated by God to His Messenger (pbuh) and show the acute intelligence of the one to whom they were revealed.

9. **Third example:** The teaching of the Names of God to Adam is a miracle that prepared humankind for the vicegerency on earth.

10. The Qur'ān offers both clear statements and evidences. It teaches humanity through signs and indications in the stories of the Prophets and their miracles. It also encourages humanity to attain similar achievements.

11. Nursi believes that the production of human thought is related to manifestation of this verse; "and He taught Adam all of the names." Man has actualized the miracles of the Prophets through human effort.

12. The Qur'ān explains the wisdom in human beings' vicegerency and satisfies both ordinary people and the elite.

13. The mission of humankind as vicegerent on the earth is to execute God's ordinances and apply His laws. But this task is dependent on full knowledge.

14. **Fourth example:** Said Nursi holds that this *surah* contains miraculous predictions concerning the Unseen.

15. This miraculous prediction about the Unseen is explained briefly in five signs.

16. All the verses of this *surah* have numerous meanings.

17. This *surah* suggests the four largest evil revolutions and storms of the century.

Fethullah Gülen and His *Tafsīr*

His Life and Education

M. Fethullah Gülen is a remarkable modern day scholar who has combined both classical and modern style interpretations in his *tafsīr* work. He is an Islamic scholar and thinker, and a prolific writer and poet. He was trained in the religious sciences by several celebrated Muslim scholars and spiritual masters.[651] Gülen is also well versed in the principles and theories of modern social and physical sciences.

Gülen was born in 1941 C.E. in the village of Korucuk in the province of Erzurum, eastern Turkey. He has a photographic memory and learnt how to read the Qur'ān from his mother at the age of four.[652] He belongs to a very pious family; his mother's love for the Qur'ān, his grandmother's deep faith in God and his father's piety had a great influence on the early formation of his character. He memorized the entire Qur'ān by the age of nine[653] and completed his education in classical Islamic disciplines at a traditional *madrasa* (religious school). During his teenage years, he was greatly influenced by the Sufi sheikh Muhammed Lütfi Efendi.[654] He was introduced to the thoughts of Said Nursi (1876–1960 C.E.)

---

[651] This introduction is cited from the book 'Essentials of the Islamic Faith,' M. Fethullah Gulen, tr; Ali Ünal, 'about the author,' The Light, New Jersey, 2005.

[652] Ali Ünal, *Fethullah Gülen: Bir Portre Denemesi* (Fethullah Gülen: A Portrait), Nil Yayinlari, Istanbul, 2002, p. 86.

[653] Latif Erdogan, *Fethullah Gülen Hocaefendi: Kucuk Dunyam* (Fethullah Gülen Hocaefendi: My Small World), Istanbul: AD Yayincilik, Istanbul, 1996, p. 34.

[654] M Hakan Yavuz, *Islamic Political identity in Turkey*, Oxford University Press, New York, 2003, p. 180.

when he met with one of his students, Muzaffer Aslan.[655] Gülen broadened his education further with a thorough study of science, eastern and western philosophy and literature.[656]

Displaying exceptional skills in focused self-study and learning, Gülen soon surpassed his peers and in 1959, he was awarded a state preacher's license. For several years, he lived in a window niche of a mosque in spiritual retreat and austerity in the city of Edirne.[657] During those years, Gülen began to form the foundations of the 'Hizmet movement' with a small group of benefactors and dedicated students. In 1966, he was promoted to a post in Izmir, Turkey's third largest province. In Edirne, Gülen used his sermons to emphasize the pressing social issues of the times, encouraging the younger generation into social activism based on core Islamic values. Through his travels and lectures in Anatolia, Gülen grew in popularity and gained the attention of the academic community, particularly the student body. In addition to religious matters, Gülen also talked about education, science, Darwinism, the economy and social justice, gaining respect amongst a wide audience. His efforts, dating from the 1960s, specifically in educational reform, have made him one of the best-known and most respected figures in Turkey. The Hizmet movement rapidly grew by entering into the media sphere, publishing various magazines and a national daily newspaper, Zaman, in 1986.[658] In 1994, it acquired a public face with the establishment of the Journalists and Writers Foundation.[659]

From 1988 to 1991, Gülen gave a series of sermons as preacher emeritus in some of the most famous mosques in the major population centers, while continuing to deliver his message in the popular conferences style throughout Turkey as well as in Western Europe.[660] Gülen was named the Foreign Policy's public intellectual of the year in 2008 and was included in Time Magazine's 2013 Top 100 list of world leaders. He received this recognition due to the progressive innovations he effected within the socio-political climate of Turkey and because

---

[655] Muhsin Canbolat, Ismail Albayrak and Kath Engebretson 'The Hizmet Educational Movement: Its Insights for Educational Leadership' in Michael T Buchanan (ed.) *Leadership and Religious Schools: International Perspectives and Challenges*, Continuum, New York, 2013, p. 186.

[656] Ergun Capan, 'Gülen's Teaching Methodology in His Private Circle,' in Islamic Albayrak (ed.), *Mastering Knowledge in Modern Times: Fethullah Gülen as an Islamic Scholar*, Blue Dome Press, New York, 2011, p. 128.

[657] Erdogan, *Kucuk Dunyam*, pp. 49–50.

[658] Muhammed Cetin, *The Gülen Movement: Civic Service without Borders*, Blue Dome Press, New York, 2009, p. 71.

[659] Alptekin, *Teacher in a Foreign Land*, p. 52.

[660] M. Fethullah Gulen, *Essentials of the Islamic Faith*, tr; Ali Ünal, 'about the author.'

of his role in the foundation and leadership of the transnational Hizmet (Service) movement; the largest and most influential religio-civic movement in Turkey and one of the largest in the Muslim world.[661]

Gülen's vision is of a twenty-first century which will witness the birth of a spiritual revolution that will revitalize long-dormant moral values; an age of tolerance, understanding, and international cooperation that will ultimately lead, through intercultural dialogue and a sharing of values, to a single, inclusive civilization.[662] He has encouraged people to establish charitable organizations in the field of education and to promote human welfare and he strongly believes that a good quality education is the key to ensuring respect for the rights of others and justice for all. With generous donations from the Turkish population, his followers have established many schools, both in Turkey and abroad. Beginning with a flagship school in the Turkic republics in Central Asia, the Hizmet Movement's schools now flourish in more than 160 countries worldwide.

Gülen believes that world peace is essential in order to promote human welfare. He asserts that this ideal can be realized through peaceful engagements that will persuade people to commit to this vision. He holds that democracy is the only viable political system and people should strive to modernize and consolidate democratic institutions in order to build a society where individual rights and freedoms are respected and protected and which upholds the principle of equal opportunities for all.[663]

His Methodology in *Tafsīr*

To date, Gülen has not yet written a conclusive *tafsīr* book including all the *surah* from the beginning to the end. However, his lectures have included interpretations of many verses and these have been collected and compiled by his students and published under the title, '*Reflections on the Qur'ān.*' This book is an exegesis on selective verses of the Qur'ān. It presents subtle points and details revealed in the verses while expounding on them in the sequential order in which they appear in the Qur'ān. The prominent Turkish scholar, Prof. Dr. Suat Yıldırım, wrote an introduction for this text, from which the majority of the quotes are extracted to aid in the examination of Gülen's *tafsīr* methodology.

---

[661] Graham E Fuller, *The New Turkish Republic: Turkey as a Pivotal State in the Muslim World*, United States Institute of Peace, Washington, 2008, p. 65.

[662] Gulen, *Essentials of the Islamic Faith*, tr; Ali Ünal, 'about the author.'

[663] Gulen, *Essentials of the Islamic Faith*, tr; Ali Ünal, 'about the author.'

Gülen's displays a comprehensive knowledge of classical commentary in addition to a cognizant contemporaneous insight within the boundaries of the science of Qur'anic exegesis.[664] The author's profound knowledge of the classical Qur'anic commentary is self-evident in his written work. Similar to all modern scholars, Gülen aspires to convey his scientific findings to the wider public without compromising the contextual material, which proves in itself a most arduous endeavor. Addressing the public while maintaining the scientific integrity of a composition is a difficult and complex issue for the exegetist and therefore the author tends to employ existing methods that will appeal to the audience. Nevertheless, he retains the technical terminology for the discussion of certain topics, whenever necessary.

Gülen aims to improve the readers' understanding of the Qur'ān by providing the intrinsic relationship between the verses within the context of the totality of the Qur'ān.[665] He holds that the Qur'ān is a source of guidance for all humanity but only the pious can benefit from it through their faith and eagerness to acknowledge the truth. The author's excellent analysis of the comparison between the general mindset of the hypocrites and the unbelievers who embraced Islam will be quoted to illustrate his comprehensive understanding;

> They are like him who kindled a fire (for light and warmth and protection). However, when the fire had just lit all around him God took away their light and left them in darkness, unseeing.[666]

He interprets this verse as follows:

> This verse vividly illustrates the inner world of the hypocrites in a simile comparing it to the state of those unappreciative of the light in the darkness of the night. The hypocrites of the early years of Islam coexisted with Muslims; thus, they could occasionally glimpse the light of faith, at least out of the corner of their eyes. Nevertheless, the dissent in their hearts and minds did not allow them to be adequately nourished from this light. These hypocrites looked but could not see the torch in the hand of the blessed Prophet (pbuh), for either their frivolous gaze undermined and dimmed the light, or deceit dulled their natural disposition and aptitudes. On the outside, they appeared to be

---

[664] M. Fethullah Gulen, *Reflections on the Qur'ān*, Foreword by Suat Yildirim, Tughra Books, New Jersey 2012, vii.

[665] Gulen, *Reflections on the Qur'ān*, Foreword.

[666] Qur'ān 2: 17.

looking, but in the face of the dazzling light of the torch, instead of intensifying their focus to see, with doubts and suspicions they neutralized the dynamism that was activated in their soul, rendering it completely inefficient. Furthermore, far from making use of the light to be able to progress on their path, they conceived of plans as to how they could start a fire out of it; the word "kindle" in the verse seems to refer to both of these interpretations. Unbelievers, on the other hand, had not been acquainted with faith and its illuminating lights. They had never experienced its enchanting and blissful atmosphere. This is why once unbelievers had felt the light of faith, they would never abandon it, and they strove to maintain a life of sincere devotion. This is because there is a black-and-white difference between disbelief and belief. For the unbelievers, it was like waking up to a new life and leaving behind another that was totally different, and they could observe Islam with all its charm. Even the comparison of the Muslims who are born and live in Muslim lands with those who embrace Islam later in life would reveal this reality.[667]

The author has comprehensive knowledge in the sciences of eloquence (*balāghah*) and grammar (*naḥw*) and utilizes such knowledge perfectly when explaining the meanings of Qur'anic verses. For example, he explains the Divine Name '*Badi*" (The Originator) from the linguistic perspective:

> The verb "*ba-da-'a*" in Arabic means creating something completely novel without imitating anything preceding it. The heavens and the earth are unique and incomparable in terms of their profundity and beauty. In other words, they are wonders of creation, before which there existed no model. In addition to the originality of their creation, nothing, no universe is more beautiful than the heavens and earth. Therefore, with their billions of beacons of light, they point to the All-Originating.[668]

He emphasizes that the stories in the Qur'ān are historic events and by narrating these events, God reveals the clues to some universal truths or laws, which will be valid until the end of time.[669] They began with Adam and will continue to happen until the end of time and, in order to benefit from the Qur'ān sufficiently, this fact should not be missed. He holds that the Qur'ān addresses all readers despite some of its verses having been revealed concerning a specific

---

[667] Gulen, *Reflections on the Qur'ān*, pp 7–8.

[668] Gulen, *Reflections on the Qur'ān*, Foreword, viii.

[669] Gulen, *Reflections on the Qur'ān*, see the interpretation of 71: 26.

occasion, specific event or a specific group of people. All who read the Qur'ān should assume that the Qur'ān is addressing them directly. He argues that the Qur'ān is issued from the All-Eternal God's Attribute of Speech and therefore it addresses everybody regardless of time and space.

His broad knowledge of Sufism influences his explanations, elements of which can be seen in the following examples: 'the locations of the stars' in Surah Wāqi'a (56:75) is explained by him as Prophet Muhammad (pbuh) for he is the star of humanity and the other Prophets. Similarly, 'the locations of the stars' are the trustworthy heart of the Archangel Gabriel, to which all the verses of the Qur'ān were entrusted. Moreover, the stars represent the verses in the Qur'ān so the places of verses in the Divine Revelation are the location of the stars and the pure hearts of the believers are their abode. Gülen concludes his interpretation by stating that it is miserable for humankind to be so cold hearted towards the final Message of God.

By utilizing modern sciences, Gülen analyses the verses that reveal the inner dimension of the hypocrites and unbelievers. He holds that hypocrisy and disbelief became an innate part of the character of the hypocrites and disbelievers, therefore when they spoke positively about the religion their aim was to deceive. If they were unable to perform evil actions against the believers, they wore a robe of hypocrisy, concealed their hate under a guise of sincerity and actively promoted democracy. However, when opportunity arose, they committed all kinds of wickedness in the name of their disbelief, advocating an oppressive ideology of might being right, and democracy as acceptable so as long as it served their interests.

A selection of Gülen's explanations of verses is provided below to further illustrate his *tafsīr* methodology.

SUMMARY: FETHULLAH GÜLEN AND HIS *TAFSĪR*

1. Gülen is a Turkish Islamic scholar, thinker, writer and poet.
2. He was born into a pious family in 1938, memorizing the entire Qur'ān by age 9 and completing his education in a madrasa.
3. He was influenced by Sufi scholar, Muhammed Lütfi Efendi, and was introduced to Said Nursi's work by Muzaffer Aslan.
4. In 1959, he was awarded a state preacher's license in Edirne and then was promoted in 1966 to Izmir.

5. In Edirne, he founded the Hizmet Movement, which is now an international socio-civic organization.

6. Through his travels and lectures in Anatolia, Gülen grew in popularity and gained the attention of the academic community, particularly the student body.

7. From 1988 to 1991, Gülen gave a series of sermons as preacher emeritus in some of the most famous mosques in the major population centers.

8. Gülen was named the Foreign Policy's public intellectual of the year in 2008 and was included in Time Magazine's 2013 Top 100 list of world leaders.

9. Gülen's vision is of a twenty-first century that will witness the birth of a spiritual revolution that will revitalize long-dormant moral values.

10. The Hizmet Movement's schools now flourish in more than 160 countries worldwide.

His *Tafsīr* Methodology

11. Gülen has not yet written a conclusive *tafsīr* book however, his lectures have included interpretations of many verses and these have been collected and compiled by his students and published under the title, 'Reflections on the Qur'ān.'

12. Gülen's displays a comprehensive knowledge of classical commentary in addition to a cognizant contemporaneous insight within the boundaries of the science of Qur'anic exegesis.

13. Gülen aims to improve the readers' understanding of the Qur'ān by providing the intrinsic relationship between the verses within the context of the totality of the Qur'ān.

14. He holds that the Qur'ān is a source of guidance for all humanity but only the pious can benefit from it through their faith and eagerness to acknowledge the truth.

15. Gülen has comprehensive knowledge in the sciences of eloquence (*balāghah*) and grammar (*naḥw*) and utilizes such knowledge perfectly when explaining the meanings of Qur'anic verses.

16. He emphasizes that the stories in the Qur'ān are historic events and by narrating these events, God reveals the clues to some universal truths or laws, which will be valid until the end of time.

17. His broad knowledge of Sufism influences his explanations.

18. Gülen utilizes modern sciences in his explanations.

Commentary Examples

As explained earlier, Gülen has not written a *tafsīr* book, but has given commentaries on many Qur'anic verses which have been collected and published by his students. Some examples are given below to illustrate his methodology in Qur'anic interpretation.

First example; *"therefore, when you are free (from one task), resume (another task)"*[670]

Gülen explains this verse with modern concepts and emphasizes the value of time.[671] He holds that this verse presents Muslims with an important philosophy on life by encouraging them to be active at all times. Believers should arrange their working hours in such a way that there should be no gaps in their lives and even when resting they should be active. For instance, when people become tired with reading and writing they can rest by lying down and sleeping, but they can also rest by changing their activity such as by reading the Qur'ān, performing prayers, doing physical exercise or engaging in beneficial conversation. The essential theme of this verse is that the believers should always be in a state of activity, so they should change their activity when they need to rest, so as to rest by working and work while resting.

After giving a theoretical explanation of this verse, Gülen elaborates further with a practical example; many wealthy people (in the Hizmet Movement) who pursue God's pleasure and desire to serve both their society and humanity at large, rent out houses that accommodate many poor and talented students. Not being content with this, they build hostels to accommodate greater numbers of students and open private schools for their education in better and more favorable conditions. In the face of the sincere demands of some "hearts" that desire to serve humanity in a much broader sphere, God has given them the opportunity to open schools and other educational institutions throughout the world. They taste the pleasure of serving lofty ideals in the highest degree yet become worried should their volunteering services become redundant, and so God Almighty opens new fields of service before them. The meaning of the verse, "When you are free (from one task), resume (another task)," manifests itself systematically in our lives, whether or not we are aware of this.

Gülen emphasizes the need for the believers to be thankful to God for the many favors He has bestowed on them; He created them as humans, gave them

---

[670] Qur'ān 94: 7.
[671] Please refer to Gulen, Reflections on the Qur'ān, 371–318.

health, showed them the way of belief and introduced them to Islam. Unfortunately, people do not appreciate the worth of the bounties and blessings of God due to their over-familiarity with them and thus fail to give proper thanks. In other countries, many people suffer indignities and deprivations such as famine, premature death and widowhood or become orphans due to merciless wars. There are also those who remain in the darkness of unbelief or in the clutches of tyrannical regimes, so it is a great blessing when Muslims are able to follow the right path and are able to fulfill their duty of worship. Therefore, they should always be active, hastening from one activity to another, fulfilling the duties that fall upon them within the framework of services rendered for God's sake and for the betterment of humanity. Gülen concludes the interpretation of this verse with a practical solution for believers; to engage in positive and virtuous activity when they are free from the previous one. To find rest in exertion and make rest the beginning of another exertion; to experience ease in hardship and make ease a propitious ground for overcoming hardships.

Second example; *"Every time they are provided with fruits there from (from Paradise), they say, "This is what we were provided before." They are given to them in resemblance (to what was given to them in the world). Furthermore, for them are spouses eternally purified; and therein they will abide."*[672]

Gülen holds that the expression, 'they are given to them in resemblance (to what was given to them in the world),' emphasizes that the bounties, blessings, and honors to be given in Paradise will be familiar in shape and color to those of this world so that they may not be unattractive because they are unknown.[673] He quotes from Said Nursi to explain this verse and states that the resemblance may be either between the blessings in this world and those to be given in Paradise or between the blessings of Paradise, which will be given to believers time and time again in recurrent forms. Every proclamation of God's greatness, every declaration of God's Oneness and Unity, every glorification of God and all praise of God is like a seed sown in the earth that will yield different fruits of Paradise.[674]

Gülen clarifies that the human intellect cannot grasp the relationship between the actions of this world and the results they will reap in the afterlife, because the human intellect considers all within the framework of cause and effect, therefore the realities of the next world cannot be grasped with this worldly intellect. He supports his argument referencing al-Ghazali who states that human beings

---

[672] Qur'ān 2: 25.
[673] Gulen, *Reflections on the Qur'ān*, 12.
[674] Gulen, ibid.

cannot even comprehend some metaphysical events in this world with the worldly mind. However, in the afterlife they will be granted the otherworldly mind where everything happens according to the principles of metaphysics and they will be able to fully understand the relationship between glorifying God and receiving a fruit of the Garden (a blessing of Paradise) in return. Similarly, they will understand clearly the connection of the bounties in the afterlife with the good deeds in this world, because the laws of physics are no longer valid in the afterlife. Gülen elaborates this statement by quoting some Prophetic traditions; the daily prescribed prayers will be a friend and companion to their performers in the grave, a person will be able to enter Paradise from its eight different gates and the Qur'ān will be embodied and intercede with God on behalf of the ones who read it in this world.[675] As a result, the believers who performed good deeds in this world will announce; "these are what we were provided with in the world or some time ago while in Paradise" whenever the bounties of Paradise are bestowed on them.[676] Therefore, there is an internal or essential similarity between worldly bounties and their counterparts in the afterlife. However, Gülen differentiates these bounties by stating that the worldly bounties are the seeds of Divine Wisdom while eternal bounties are the fruit of Divine Power. The former are temporary and blurred while the latter are permanently purified and clear. The former relate to bodily appetites while the latter represent or have the profundity of spiritual pleasure. Furthermore, God's bounties in this world are received and perceived to the degree of certainty based on knowledge while their otherworldly counterparts are favors of Mercy to be received and tasted to the degree of certainty based on experience.[677]

Third example; "(The Pharaoh said,) "Then, we will most certainly produce before you sorcery like it. So appoint a meeting between us and you, which neither we nor you will fail to keep, in an open, level place convenient (to both of us)." (Moses) said: "The meeting will be on the Day of the Festival, and let the people assemble in the forenoon."[678]

Gülen analyses the verse from a different perspective and extracts some subtle points. The first addressee of this verse was Prophet Moses (pbuh) who experienced the miraculous event of speaking to God in the Valley of Tuwa in the Sinai. He witnessed his staff miraculously change into a snake and observed his right

---

[675] Gulen, ibid.
[676] Gulen, 14.
[677] Gulen, ibid.
[678] Qur'ān 20: 58–59.

hand shine brightly. After witnessing these miracles, he had total confidence that his Lord would assist him to defeat Pharaoh's sorcerers regardless of their abilities. Gülen holds that Moses offering to meet with Egyptians on the Day of the Festival in the forenoon determines the following;[679]

- The competition, which would distinguish truth from falsehood, should not take place behind walls; rather, it should occur in an open place where people would be able to watch and witness.
- The competition should take place on a festive day so that whoever wanted to watch it could be there.
- Forenoon is the most convenient time for such an encounter, because it is a time when people are free from exhaustion and drowsiness. They feel energetic and vigorous, so it is the best time for minds to think and judge.

The people of Egypt came to watch the competition since sorcery was a popular pastime in Egypt. During this period sorcerers were the intellectual elite of the society, therefore, if Moses defeated them it would mark the beginning of a revolution in favor of belief. The sorcerers knew what Moses presented to them was not magic, and as a consequence they believed him immediately despite the Pharaoh's threats that he would hang them and cut off their hands and feet alternately.[680] The people who witnessed the submission of the elite to Moses came to believe, or at least began to doubt their own religion. Moses achieved his goal by breaking paganism and defeating Pharaoh and his claim of lordship.

Gülen draws our attention to the most significant point in this verse; the time and place that Moses chose for that important encounter. He extracts some important lessons from this event for contemporary Muslims; first, a believer should never despair due to a lack or shortage of material necessities. A Muslim should always plan to achieve numerous results with one action and search for ways to succeed in doing this. Moses expressed himself in front of all the people and was able to influence thousands with just one act. The Qur'ān teaches Muslims through the Moses narrative to utilize every opportunity in the best way. Gülen quotes a Prophetic tradition to support this message:[681]

> There lived a tyrant king who attempted to kill a young believer because he refused to return to the tyrant's faith. He was thrown down from the top of a mountain, yet he came back walking. Then he was thrown into the vicious waves of the sea, but he was saved and returned. Whatever

[679] Gulen, *Reflections on the Qur'ān*, the interpretation of 20: 58–59.
[680] Qur'ān 20: 71.
[681] Muslim, *Ṣaḥīḥ, Zuhd,* 73.

they did to try and kill that young believer, it proved useless. In the end, the young man said: "If you gather all the people together and shoot an arrow at me saying, 'In the name of the Lord of this boy,' then you will be able to kill me."

Ultimately, the king was able to kill the young believer by following his instructions however; the circumstances of the young believer's death caused more people to believe in his religion. Gülen explains that the young believer utilized his last moments in the best way and served his mission with martyrdom. Thus, believers should always think about what they can do at every moment of their life on behalf of their religion, nation, and humanity. The young man in the example planned his martyrdom in front of all the people of the land causing hundreds of people to embrace belief. Thus, he both served his cause and the conversion and eternal happiness of many others. Gülen concludes his interpretation by stating that Muslims should know the value of the religion they have been favored with and should not leave this world in return for a paltry price; rather they should serve in it by employing every opportunity, even by their death.

SUMMARY: COMMENTARY EXAMPLES

1. **First example:** Gülen explains this verse with modern concepts and emphasizes the value of time.
2. He holds that the verse presents Muslims with an important philosophy on life by encouraging them to be active at all times.
3. They should change their activity when they need to rest, so as to rest by working and work while resting.
4. After giving a theoretical explanation of this verse, Gülen elaborates further with a practical example.
5. Gülen emphasizes the need for the believers to be thankful to God for the many favors He has bestowed on them. Therefore, they should always be active, hastening from one activity to another, fulfilling the duties that fall upon them within the framework of services rendered for God's sake and for the betterment of humanity.
6. **Second example:** Gülen holds that the expression, 'they are given to them in resemblance (to what was given to them in the world),' emphasizes that the bounties, blessings, and honors to be given in Paradise will be familiar in shape and color to those of this world so that they may not be unattractive because they are unknown.
7. He references both Said Nursi and Al-Ghazali in his explanations.

8. Gülen clarifies that the human intellect cannot grasp the relationship between the actions of this world and the results they will reap in the afterlife, because the human intellect considers all within the framework of cause and effect.

9. In the afterlife, humans will be granted the otherworldly mind where everything happens according to the principles of metaphysics.

10. **Third example:** Gülen analyses the verse from a different perspective and extracts some subtle points.

11. The first addressee of this verse was Prophet Moses (pbuh) who experienced the miraculous event of speaking to God in the Valley of Tuwa in the Sinai.

12. After witnessing these miracles, he had total confidence that his Lord would assist him to defeat Pharaoh's sorcerers regardless of their abilities.

13. Gülen gives reasons for Moses offering to meet with Egyptians on the Day of the Festival in the forenoon.

14. The people who witnessed the submission of the elite to Moses came to believe, or at least began to doubt their own religion.

15. Gülen draws our attention to the most significant point in this verse; the time and place that Moses chose for that important encounter. He extracts some important lessons from this event for contemporary Muslims.

16. A believer should never despair due to a lack or shortage of material necessities.

17. A Muslim should always plan to achieve numerous results with one action and search for ways to succeed in doing this.

18. Gülen concludes his interpretation by stating that Muslims should know the value of the religion they have been favored and they should serve in it by employing every opportunity.

Bibliography

Abū Hayyan. *Tafsīr Bahr al-Muhit. 8 vols.* Riyadh, no date.

Abū Ubayda, Ibrahim ibn Muhammad. *Lughat al-Qur'ān.* Riyadh: Dar al-Watan, 1993.

Ahmed, Hasanuddin. Introducing the Qur'ān. New Delhi, India: Goodword Books, 2005.

al-A'zami, Muhammad Mustafa. *The History of The Qur'anic Text.* Selangor, Malaysia: Islamic Book Trust, 2011.

_____ *Studies in Hadith Methodology, and Literature.* Indianapolis: American Trust Publications, 1977.

Abū Dāwud. *Sunan.* Ed. M.M. 'Abdulhamid, 4 vols. 2nd imp. Cairo: 1950. English translation by Ahmad Hasan. *Sunan Abū Dāwud,* 3 vols. Lahore: 1984.

Arberry, Arthur J. *The Koran, Interpreted.* London: Oxford University Press, 1983.

Armstrong Caren. *A Western Attempt to Understand Islam.* Victor Gollanz Ltd.

Asad, Muhammad. *The message of the Qur' an translated and explained.* Gibraltar: Dar-al-Andalus, 1980.

Ali Ünal. *The Qur'ān with Annotated Interpretation in Modern English.* Feedbooks, 2007.

Baqillani. *Ijaz al Qur'ān* (The sections of poetry) A tenth century document of 'Arabic literary theory and criticism, translated and annotated by Gustane e. von Grunebaum. The University of Chicago II, 1950.

Banna, Ahmad ibn Muhammad. *Itihaaf al-Fudhala al-Bashar fi al-Qiraat alArbatha Ashar.* Beirut: Alim al-Kutub, 1987.

Burton, J. *The Collection of the Qur'ān.* UK: Cambridge University Press, 1977.

Bayhaqi. *As-Sunan al-Kubra.* 10 vols. Hyderabad: 1344–1355.

Baladhuri, Ahmad ibn Yahya. *Ansab al-Ashraf.* Ed. M. Hamidullah, Cairo: 1959.

Baqillani. *Al-Intishar al-Qur'ān.* Frankfurt: 1986 [facsimile edition]).

al-Bukhari, Muhammad ibn Ismail. *Khalq Af'al al-Ibad.* Mecca: 1970.

_____ *Kitab ad-Duafa al-Sagir.* Haleb: 1976.

_____ *Sahih with the Commentary of Ibn Hajar.* Ed. F. Abdul-Baqi, 13 vols. Cairo: al-Matba'ah as-Salafiyya, 1380. English translation by M. Muhsin Khan. *The Translation of the Meanings of Sahih al-Bukhari,* 8 vols. 2nd revised ed. Pakistan: 1973.

Cerrahoğlu, Ismail. *Tefsir Usûlu.* Ankara: Fecr Yayın Evi, 1991.

_____ *Tefsir Tarihi,* Ankara: Fecr Yayın Evi, 1988.

Curcani, S. Sharif. *At-Ta'rifaat.* Beirut: 1988.

Dani, Abū 'Amr. *Al-Ahruf al-Sab'a fi al-Qur'ān*. Ed. Adby al-Muhaymin Thah, Jeddah: Dar al-Manarah, 1997.

_____ *Al-Muhkam fi Naqt al-Masahih*. Ed. 1. Hasan, Damascus: 1960.

_____ *Al-Muqni*. Ed. M.S. Qamhawi, Cairo: no date.

_____ *Kitab an-Naqt*. Ed. M.S. Qamhawi, Cairo: no date.

Darimi. *Sunan*. Ed. Dahman. 2 vols. Damascus: 1349.

Denffer, Ahmad Von. *'ulūm Al- Qur'ān, An Introduction to the Sciences of the Qur' an*. London: Islamic Foundation, 1985.

Dhahabi, al-imam Shams ad-Din Muhammad ibn Ahmad. *Ma'rifat al-Qurra al-Kibar 'ala at-Tabaqati wal Athat*. Ed. Shu'ayb al-Arnawut, et. al. Beirut: Muassasah ar-Risalah, 1988.

_____ *SiyarA'lam an-Nubala*. Ed. Shu'ayb ai-Arnawut, et. al. Beirut: Muassasah ar-Risalah, 1996.

Diraz, Muhammad 'Abdullah. *Madkhal ilal al-Qur'ān al-Karim*. Kuwait: Dar al-Qur'ān al-Karim, 1971.

Doi, A, Rahman I. *Introduction to the Qur'ān*. Lagos: Islamic Publications Bureau, 1976.

Flogel, Gustavus. *Corani texti 'Arabicus; Concordantiae Corani 'Arabicae*. Leipzig: Brett, 1834, 1898.

Fuad, Muhammad Abdul Baqi. *Al-Mu'ajam al Mufharras Li Alfazil Qur'ān al- Kareem*. Cairo: 1988.

Ghazali, Abū Hamid. *Ihya al-'ulūm ad-Din*. Beirut: Dar al-Ma'rifah, 1980–1993.

Gülen, M. Fethullah. *Kur'ân'ın Altın İkliminde*. Izmir: Nil Yayınları, 2011.

_____ *Reflections on the Qur'ān*. tr; Ayşenur Kaplan & Harun Gültekin. New Jersey: Tughra Books, 2012.

Goldziher, Ignaz. *Die Richtungen der Islamischen Kormzauslegung*. Bril, Leiden: 1970.

Guillaume, A. *The Life of Muhammad: A Translation of Ibn Ishaq's Sirat Rasulullah*, 8th imp. Karachi: 1987.

Hamad, Ghanim Qaduri. *Rasm al-Masahif; dirasat lughawiya wa tarikhiya*. Masters diss., Cairo University: 1976.

Haythami, 'Ali ibn Abū Bakr. *Majma' az-Zawiz'id*. 10 vols. Cairo: 1352.

Haji Khalifa, Mustafa ibn 'Abdullah. *Kasha z-Zunun*. 3rd ed. Tehran: 1967.

Ḥākim, Muhammad ibn 'Abdullah, *al-Mustadrak*. Ed. M.A. 'Ata.' Beirut: 1990.

Ibn Abi Dawud. Kitab al-Masahif. Ed. A. Jeffery. Cairo: 1936, in: id., *Materials for the History of the Text of the Qur'ān*. Leiden: The Old Codices, 1937.

_____ *Kitab al-Masahif of Ibn Abi Dawud*. Ed. M. Wa'I. 2nd ed. Beirut: 2002.

Ibn Abi Shayba, 'Abd Allah ibn Muhammad. *Musannaf*. Ed. M.A. Shahin. 9 vols. Beirut: 1995.

Ibn Athir, Mubarak ibn Muhammad al-Jazari. *Al-Nihayah fi Gharib al-Hadith*. Cairo: Maktabah al-Islamiyya, 1965.

Ibn Hajar al-'Asqalani, Ahmad ibn 'Ali. *Fath al-Bari*. Ed. F. 'Abdul-Baqi. 13 vols. Cairo: 1380–1390.

_____ *Al Isaba fi Tamyiz as-Sahaba*. 4 vols. Beirut: no date [reprint of first ed. Cairo: 1328].

Ibn Hanbal, Ahmad. *Musnad*. 6 vols. Cairo: 1313. Reprinted by Ququba Press, Cairo: no date [c. 1988]) with Hadith serials in the margin.

Ibn Hazm, 'Ali ibn Sa'id. *Jamhrat al-Ansab*. Ed. E. Levi-Provencal. Cairo: 1948.

_____ *Al-Nāsikh wa al-Mansūkh fi al-Qur'ān al-Karim*, Dar al-Kutub al-Ilmiyyah, Beirut, 1986.

Ibn Hibban al-Busti, Muhammad. *Al-Majhurin*. Ed. M. Zayed. 3 vols. Halab: 1396.

Ibn Hisham. *Sirah*. Ed. M. Saqqa et al. 4 vols. 2nd ed. Cairo: 1955.

Ibn Ishaq. *As-Siyar wa al-Maghazi*. The version of Ibn Bukair. Ed. S. Zakkar. Damascus: 1978.

Ibn Khaldun. *The Muqaddima, An Introduction to History*. trans. Franz Rosenthal. 3 vols. New York: 1958. 2nd revised ed, Princeton, NJ: Princeton University Press, 1967.

Ibn Jawzī. *Tafsīr Ibn al-Jawzī (Zad al-Masir fi 'Ilm al-Tafsīr)*. 9 vols. Beirut: Al-Maktab al-Islami, 1964.

Ibn al-Jazari, Muhammad ibn Muhammad. *An-Nashr fi al-Qiraat al-'Ashru*. Beirut: Dar Kutub al-Ilmiyyah, no date.

Ibn Kathir, Ismail. *Fadail al-Qur'ān*. in vol. 7 of *Tafsīr Ibn Kathir*.

_____ *Tafsir al-Qur'ān*. 7 vols. Beirut: 1966.

_____ *Al-Bidaya wa an-Nihaya*. Cairo: 1348.

Ibn Majah, Muhammad B. Yazid. *Sunan*. Riyadh: Maktab al-Tarbiyah al-'Arābī, 1988.

Ibn Manzur, Muhammad ibn Mukarram. *Mukhtarar Tarikh Dimashq li Ibn 'Asakir*. Ed. M. al-Sagharji. 29 vols. in 15 Beirut/Damascus: 1989.

Ibn Manzur. *Lisan al-Arab*. Beirut: Dar Sadir; Dar Beirut, 1955–1956.

Ibn Mujahid. *Kitab as-Sab'a*. Ed. S. Daif. Cairo: 1972.

Ibn Qayyim al-Jawzīyyah, Muhammad ibn Abi Bakr. *I'lam al-Muwaqqi'in an Rabb al-Alamin*. Beirut: Dar al-Kutub, 1996.

Ibn Qudama, 'Abd Allah ibn Ahmed. *Al-Burhan fi Bayan al-Qur'ān*. Pt. Said: Matabah al-Huda, 1989.

_____ *Rawdat an-Nadir*. Mecca: Maktabah Dar al-Baz. 1994.

Ibn Qutaybah. *Ta'wil Mushkil al-Qur'ān*. Ed. Al-Sayyid Ahmad Saqr. Cairo: 1954; Cairo: 1973; Medina: 1981.

_____ *Al-Ma'arif*. Ed. Th. Ukasha. Cairo: 1969.

Ibn Sa'd, Muhammad. *Kitab at-Tabaqat al-Kubra*. Ed. E. Sachau et al. 9 vols. Leiden: 1905–1917.

Ibn Sayyid an-Nas. *'Uyun al-Athar*. Cairo: 1356.

Ibn Salama. *Al-Nāsikh wa al Mansūkh*. Cairo: Halabi, 1967.

Ibn Taymiya. *Muqaddima fi usual al Tafsīr*. Kuwait: 1971.

_____ *Iqtida Siratal-Mustaqim*. Ed. Dr. Nasir al-'Aql. Riyadh: Maktabah ar-Rushd, 1994.

Isfahani, Imam Raghib. *Mufarradat al Qur'ān*. Lahore: Able Hadith Academy, 1971.

Izutsu, Toshiheko. *The Structure of the Ethical terms in the Koran. A study in semantics.* Tokyo: 1950.

al-Jazari, Tahir. *At-Tibyan.* Ed. A. Abū Ghuddah. 3rd ed. Beirut: 1992.

al-Jazari, Muhammad ibn Muhammad. *Tabaqat al-Qurra.* 3 vols. Baghdad: 1932.

Jeffery, A. (ed.): *al-Mabani li Muqaddimatan fi 'Ulūm al-Qur'ān.* Cairo: 1954.

Kamali, Mohammad Hashim. *Principles of Islamic Jurisprudence.* Selangor: Pelanduk Publications, 1995.

Khalifa ibn Khayyat. *Tarikh.* Ed. S. Zakkar. 2 vols. Damascus: 1968.

Khalifa Rashad. *Qur'an: Visual Presentation of the Miracle.* Tucson, Arizona: 1982.

Malik ibn Anas. *Al-Muwatta.* Ed. M.F. 'Abdul-Baqi. Cairo: 1951.

Mawdudi, Abū'l A'la. *The Meaning of the Qur'ān.* 9 vols. Lahore: Islamic Publications, 1967–1979.

Muslim ibn Hajjaj al-Qushair. *Sahih.* Ed. F. Abdul-Baqi. 5 vols. Cairo: 1374. English translation by Abdul-Hamid Siddiqi. *Sahih Muslim.* 4 vols. Lahore: 1972.

Nadim, Muhammad ibn Ishaq al-Warraq. *Al-Fihrist.* Ed. R. Tajdud. Tehran: no date.

Nasafi, 'Abd Allah ibn Ahmad ibn Mahmud al-. *Madarik al-tanzil wa-baqa'iq al-ta'wil. Ed. Zakariyya 'Umayrat.* 2 vols. Beirut: 1995.

Peters, F.E. *A Reader on Classical Islam.* Princeton: Princeton University Press, 1994.

Saeed, Abd Allah. *Interpreting the Qur'ān.* New York: Routledge, 2006

Sabūni, Muhammad 'Ali. *At-Tibyan fi 'Ulūm al-Qur'ān.* Beirut: Dar al-Irshad, 1970.

_____ *The Recited Koran. A history of the first recorded version.* Princeton: The Darwin Press, 1975.

Salahi, 'Adil. *Recitation and Memorisation of the Qur'an.* in: *The Muslim* 3/4. 1976, 84–7.

Salih, Subhi. *Mabahith fi 'Ulūm al Qur'ān.* Beirut: Dar al-Ilm li'l-Maliyin, 1964.

Sijistani, Abū Bakr. *Tafsīr Gharib al-Qur'ān.* Cairo: Maktaba 'Alam al-Fikr, 1980.

Suyūtī, Jalal al-Din. *History of the Caliphs.* tr. by H. S. Jarrett. Calcutta: Baptist Mission Press, 1881.

_____ *Al-Itqān fi 'Ulūm al-Qur'ān.* 2 vols. Beirut: Maktab al-Thaqafiyya, 1973.

Noldeke, T. "The Koran." *Encyclopaedia Britannica,* vol. 16 (9th ed., 1891), pp. 597ff. Reprinted in Ibn Warraq (ed.). *The Origins of the Koran: Classic Essays on Islam's Holy Book.* pp. 36–63. New York: 1998.

Qadduri Ghanim. *Rasm al-Muṣḥāf Dirasatun Lughawiyyatun Tarikhiyyatun.* Baghdad: 1982.

Qadhi, Abū Ammar Yasir. *An Introduction to The Sciences of The Qur'ān.* Birmingham, UK: al-Hidaayah Publishing and Distribution, 2003.

Qattan, Manna.' *Mabahis fi 'Ulūm al-Qur'ān.* Riyadh: Dar al-Sa'udiya li-al-Nashr, 1971.

Qurtubi, Muhammad ibn Ahmad al-Ansari. *Al-Jami' li aḥkām al-Qur'ān.* 10 vols. Beirut: Dar al-Kutub al-Ilmiyyah, 1993.

Qutb, Sayyid. *Fi Zilal al-Qur'ān.* Beirut: Dar al-Shuruq, 1992.

Razi, Fakhr ad-Din. *Al-Tafsīr al-Kabir.* Beirut: Dar al-Ihya al-Turath al-'Arābī, no date.

Tabarī, Muhammad ibn Jarir. *Jarmi al Bayan- Ta'wil ayat al Qur'ān*. 30 vols. 3rd ed. Cairo: 1968.

Tahawi, Abū Ja'far Ahmad. *Sharh Mushkil al-Athar*. Ed. by Shu'ayb Arnawud. Beirut: Muassasah ar-Risalah, 1994.

Rodwell, A. *The Coran, translation with the Surahs arranged in chronological order*. London: 1876.

Tirmidhi. *Sunan*. Ed. A. Shakir et al. Cairo: 1937.

Wahidi al Nais Abūri. *Asbāb al- Nuzūl*. Cairo: 1968.

Watt, W. Montgomery Bell. *Introduction to the Qur'ān*. Edinburgh: Edinburgh University Press, l977.

Zamakhsari, Muhammad ibn 'Umar. *Al-Kashsah*. 4 volumes. Cairo: 1972.

Zarkashī, Badruddin. *Al Burhan fi 'Ulūm al-Qur'ān*. Cairo: 1958.

Zuhri. *Tanzil al-Qur'ān*. Ed. Al-Munajjid. Beirut: 1963.

al-Zurqani, Muhammad Abd al-Azim. *Manahil al-'Irfan fi 'Ulūm al-Qur'ān*. 3 vols. Beirut: Dar al-Kutub al-'Ilmiyyah, 1988.

Ubaydat, Mahmud Salim. *Dirasat fi 'Ulūm al-Qur'ān*. Jordan: Dar Ammar, 1990.